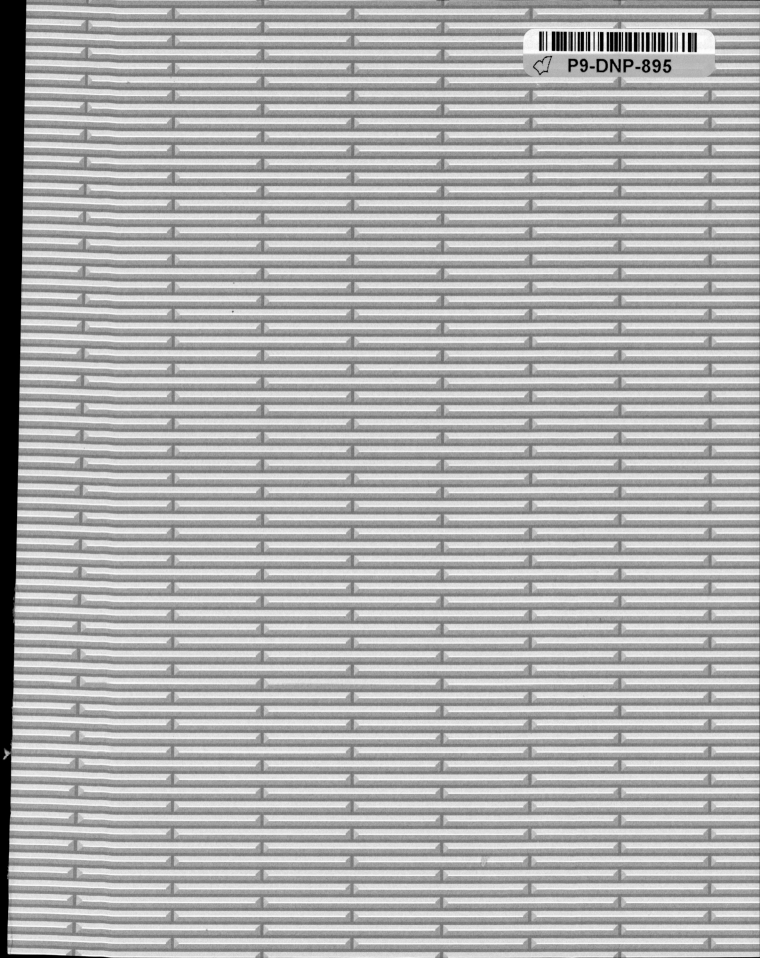

BEST OF THE BEST

FOOD&**WINE**

FOOD & WINE BEST OF THE BEST VOL. 16
EXECUTIVE EDITOR **Kate Heddings**
EDITOR **Susan Choung**
DESIGNER **Courtney Waddell Eckersley**
FEATURES EDITOR **Michael Endelman**
TEST KITCHEN SENIOR EDITOR **Kay Chun**
RECIPE TESTER **Khalil Hymore**
SENIOR WINE EDITOR **Megan Krigbaum**
COPY EDITOR **Lisa Leventer**
PRODUCTION MANAGER **Matt Carson**
DEPUTY PHOTO EDITOR **Anthony LaSala**
EDITORIAL ASSISTANT **Elyse Inamine**
TEST KITCHEN ASSISTANT **Gina Mungiovi**

FOOD & WINE MAGAZINE
SVP / EDITOR IN CHIEF **Dana Cowin**
CREATIVE DIRECTOR **Stephen Scoble**
EXECUTIVE MANAGING EDITOR **Mary Ellen Ward**
EXECUTIVE EDITOR **Pamela Kaufman**
EXECUTIVE FOOD EDITOR **Tina Ujlaki**
EXECUTIVE WINE EDITOR **Ray Isle**
EXECUTIVE DIGITAL EDITOR **Rebecca Bauer**
DEPUTY EDITOR **Christine Quinlan**
DESIGN DIRECTOR **Patricia Sanchez**

AMERICAN EXPRESS PUBLISHING CORPORATION
PRESIDENT / CHIEF EXECUTIVE OFFICER **Ed Kelly**
CHIEF MARKETING OFFICER / PRESIDENT,
  DIGITAL MEDIA **Mark V. Stanich**
SVP / CHIEF FINANCIAL OFFICER **Paul B. Francis**
VPs / GENERAL MANAGERS **Frank Bland, Keith Strohmeier**

VP, BOOKS & PRODUCTS / PUBLISHER **Marshall Corey**
DIRECTOR, BOOK PROGRAMS **Bruce Spanier**
SENIOR MARKETING MANAGER, BRANDED BOOKS **Eric Lucie**
ASSISTANT MARKETING MANAGER **Stacy Mallis**
DIRECTOR OF FULFILLMENT & PREMIUM VALUE **Philip Black**
MANAGER OF CUSTOMER EXPERIENCE
  & PRODUCT DEVELOPMENT **Betsy Wilson**
DIRECTOR OF FINANCE **Thomas Noonan**
ASSOCIATE BUSINESS MANAGER **Uma Mahabir**
OPERATIONS DIRECTOR (PREPRESS) **Rosalie Abatemarco Samat**
OPERATIONS DIRECTOR (MANUFACTURING) **Anthony White**
SENIOR MANAGER, CONTRACTS & RIGHTS **Jeniqua Moore**

FRONT & BACK COVERS
PHOTOGRAPHER **Jonny Valiant**
FOOD STYLIST **Simon Andrews**
STYLIST **Suzie Myers**

ISBN 10: 1-932624-59-7
ISBN 13: 978-1-932624-59-5
ISSN 1524-2862

Published by American Express Publishing Corporation
1120 Avenue of the Americas, New York, New York 10036

Manufactured in the United States of America

BEST OF THE BEST

the **BEST RECIPES** from the **25 BEST COOKBOOKS** of the year

FOOD&WINE
BOOKS

American Express Publishing Corporation, New York

CONTENTS

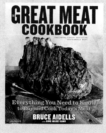

Recipe titles in **bold** are brand-new dishes appearing exclusively in *Best of the Best*.

continued on next page

CONTENTS *continued*

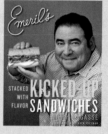

Recipe titles in **bold** are brand-new dishes appearing exclusively in *Best of the Best*.

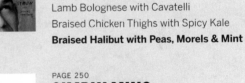

RECIPES

Braised Chicken Thighs with Spicy Kale, page 248

FOREWORD

WE'RE OFTEN ASKED how we pick the recipes for *Best of the Best*. After all, with hundreds of cookbooks published every year, it's an enormous task to find the most delicious and creative dishes. We spend a full 12 months reading, testing and retesting stacks and stacks of books to find the 25 absolute best. The work can be tedious sometimes (we made countless kale salads this year), but when we come across a discovery—something unique, tasty and easy—it's an incredible thrill.

There are a number of discoveries in this volume of *Best of the Best*. Take, for instance, chef Roberto Santibañez's dead simple *carnitas* from his book *Tacos, Tortas & Tamales*. He simmers pork shoulder in a quick mix of garlic, onion and herbs with his secret ingredient: Coca-Cola. It takes a few hours, but the end result is shredded pork that's tender and juicy, with crispy golden-brown edges. He serves it with a spicy and vibrant five-ingredient fresh green salsa.

Another example is the Creole brownie recipe from Cheryl and Griffith Day, authors of the irresistible *Back in the Day Bakery Cookbook*. How do you make a perfectly fudgy brownie even better? Start by adding cocoa nibs to the batter for an unexpected crunch, then spread a thick layer of chicory coffee–laced chocolate ganache on top. No fewer than ten editors asked for the recipe.

We hope that many of the recipes here become your new discoveries and give you the same thrill. After testing and tasting every single one, we're confident they will.

Dana Cowin
Editor in Chief
FOOD & WINE Magazine

Kate Heddings
Executive Editor
FOOD & WINE Cookbooks

THE GREAT MEAT COOKBOOK

Bruce Aidells with Anne-Marie Ramo

The Great Meat Cookbook is an epic 632-page manual jam-packed with instructions and useful tips for anyone who's ever asked: "What should I do with this piece of meat?" Meat guru Bruce Aidells, founder of Aidells Sausage Company, has updated his classic 16-year-old *Complete Meat Cookbook* for the current-day carnivore: He decodes butcher-counter jargon ("humanely raised," "grain finished," "enhanced"); teaches how to make sausages, pâtés and cured meats; and provides recipes for lesser-known (and cheaper) cuts like beef tongue, goat ribs and pork neck. Aidells even includes dishes that he calls "Meat as a Condiment" (recipes that use less than 3 ounces of meat per serving), making this book a true modern meat bible for the conscientious carnivore. PUBLISHED BY HOUGHTON MIFFLIN HARCOURT, $40

HUNGARIAN GOULASH

SERVES 6

- 2 tablespoons bacon fat, lard, or olive oil
- 3 cups chopped onions
- 2 garlic cloves, minced
- 3 tablespoons sweet Hungarian paprika
- 2 teaspoons hot Hungarian paprika (optional)
- 3 pounds boneless chuck roast (any cut), cut into 1½-inch cubes

Salt and freshly ground black pepper

- 4 cups homemade beef stock (page 21) or canned low-sodium chicken broth
- 2 teaspoons caraway seeds, ground
- 2 cups ½-inch-diced peeled Yukon Gold, red, or white boiling potatoes
- 2 cups ½-inch-diced peeled carrots
- 1 large red bell pepper, cored, seeded, and diced
- 3 medium tomatoes, peeled, seeded, and diced, or ⅔ cup drained, chopped canned tomatoes

Egg Dumplings (recipe follows)

Sour cream (optional)

- 2 tablespoons chopped fresh marjoram

AUTHOR'S NOTE

Goulash, which is traditionally served somewhat on the soupy side, is best eaten with a spoon.

EDITOR'S WINE CHOICE

Juicy, fruit-forward red: 2011 Domaine Pélaquié Côtes du Rhône

In America, any stewlike dish that contains a bit of paprika and/or tomato may be called goulash by the less-than-accurate cook. I remember being served a thick reddish concoction at Boy Scout camp that was distinguished only by being slightly more palatable than the other common camp dish, mystery meat.

Traditional goulash as made in Hungary is not thickened and doesn't contain flour; many recipes don't even have paprika. However, my recipe has both hot and sweet paprika. I always use the real stuff from Hungary—as fresh as I can find. If spicy food is not your thing, leave out the hot paprika. To make this stew a more substantial one-pot meal, I've added potatoes and carrots. You can serve the goulash over dumplings, egg noodles, or spätzle.

Garnishing goulash with a dollop of sour cream isn't traditionally Hungarian, but I love sour cream.

1. Heat the fat in a large Dutch oven over medium heat. Add the onions and garlic and cook, stirring occasionally, until softened and golden brown, about 20 minutes.

2. Add the sweet paprika and hot paprika (if using) and stir until the onions are well coated, 1 to 2 minutes. Stir in the meat, a little salt, and a few grinds of pepper. Add ½ cup of the stock, increase the heat to medium-high, and cook until the liquid is almost evaporated. Add the remaining 3½ cups stock and the caraway and bring to a boil, then reduce the heat to maintain a simmer and cook, covered, for 1 hour, or until the meat is almost tender. Skim the liquid and discard the fat.

3. Add the potatoes, carrots, bell pepper, and tomatoes. Cook for 20 minutes, or until the potatoes are tender. Degrease the surface. You can serve the goulash as is, with a souplike consistency, or you can reduce it until it just turns syrupy. To do so, strain all the solids from the soup and set aside. Bring to a boil and reduce the liquid, then add back the solids. Season the goulash to taste with salt and pepper.

continued on page 16

HUNGARIAN GOULASH
continued

SERVES 6

1 large egg, lightly beaten
1 tablespoon melted lard, bacon fat, or butter
⅓ cup water
1 teaspoon salt
1½ cups all-purpose flour

4. To serve, ladle the dumplings into warmed soup bowls and spoon in the goulash. Garnish with sour cream (if using) and a sprinkling of the marjoram.

ALTERNATIVE CUTS
Boneless short ribs, nicely marbled rump roast, beef shank removed from the bone, or brisket (beef shank and brisket will require a cooking time of 30 minutes longer or more).

EGG DUMPLINGS

1. Mix together the egg, lard, water, and salt in a medium bowl. Stir in the flour just until a soft dough forms, being careful not to overmix.

2. Drop tablespoonfuls of dough (it's okay if they're a little uneven and rustically misshapen) into a large pot of boiling salted water. The dumplings are done when they rise to the surface, about 10 minutes. Remove them with a slotted spoon and drain. If you make these ahead, add to the goulash and reheat right before serving.

SAUTÉED LAMB CHOPS
with Tomato-Eggplant Vinaigrette

SERVES 4

1   large eggplant, cut into
    1-inch dice
¼   cup plus 1 tablespoon olive oil,
    or more if needed
Salt and freshly ground black pepper
Eight   1½-inch-thick rib or T-bone lamb
        loin chops (about 2 pounds total)
2   teaspoons chopped fresh thyme

TOMATO-EGGPLANT VINAIGRETTE
¼   cup dry white wine or dry sherry
2   tablespoons good red wine
    vinegar (I use Banyuls), or more
    to taste
2   teaspoons Dijon mustard
¼   cup extra-virgin olive oil
1   cup diced (1-inch) vine-ripe
    tomatoes (I use an heirloom
    variety)
Salt and freshly ground black pepper

1   tablespoon shredded fresh
    basil leaves
2   teaspoons shredded fresh
    mint leaves

AUTHOR'S NOTE
*Instead of fresh tomatoes, you can use
1 cup frozen Oven-Roasted Tomatoes
(recipe follows) that you made during
the summer.*

EDITOR'S WINE CHOICE
*Spicy, fruit-forward Greek red:
2009 Kir-Yianni Estate*

*In northern Sonoma County, where I live, we grow many varieties of
heirloom tomatoes, which reach their peak in late summer and early
fall. Some years, when the weather is particularly mild, we have locally
grown heirlooms into November. This recipe uses tomatoes and
another late-summer vegetable, eggplant, in a light and fresh
vinaigrette to serve over sautéed lamb chops.*

1. Preheat the oven to 375°F.

2. Toss the eggplant with ¼ cup of the oil and salt and pepper to taste
in a large bowl until well coated. Spread the eggplant and any oil
remaining in the bowl on a large baking sheet and roast for 10 minutes.
Stir and, if the eggplant is dry, brush with more olive oil. Roast for 5 to
10 minutes more, or until the cubes are very soft. Set aside.

3. Season the chops to taste with salt and pepper and sprinkle with
the thyme. Heat a large skillet over medium-high heat and add the
remaining 1 tablespoon oil. Sear the chops for 2 to 3 minutes per side,
in batches if necessary, until medium-rare. The internal temperature
should be 125°F to 130°F on an instant-read thermometer. Remove and
set aside on a warm platter, covered loosely with aluminum foil, to rest
while you make the vinaigrette.

4. VINAIGRETTE Pour off the fat from the skillet. Pour the white wine
into the pan and whisk to loosen any browned bits from the bottom.
Boil to reduce by half, 2 to 3 minutes. Stir in the vinegar and cook for
30 seconds. Remove from the heat and whisk in the mustard, then
gradually whisk in the oil to form a homogenous vinaigrette. Stir in the
reserved eggplant and the tomatoes. Season to taste with salt, pepper,
and/or vinegar.

5. To serve, spoon the vinaigrette over the chops and sprinkle with the
basil and mint.

ALTERNATIVE CUTS
Lamb sirloin or shoulder chops (cook for 5 to 10 minutes longer, or
until medium) or goat chops.

continued on page 18

SAUTÉED LAMB CHOPS
continued

MAKES ABOUT 3 CUPS

2 pounds plum tomatoes, cored, peeled, and halved lengthwise

2 tablespoons olive oil

2 tablespoons finely chopped garlic

2 tablespoons chopped fresh herbs, such as basil, oregano, or thyme, or 2 teaspoons dried herbs (use one herb or a combination)

Salt and freshly ground black pepper

AUTHOR'S NOTE

You can use any variety of tomato. Juicier tomatoes will need to roast longer. Cut large tomatoes into ½-inch-thick slices before roasting.

OVEN-ROASTED TOMATOES

Once roasted, the tomatoes can be packed into ½-pint freezer containers and frozen to be used throughout the year for a simple and delicious tomato sauce.

1. Preheat the oven to 250°F.

2. Arrange the tomatoes, cut sides up, on a baking sheet or in a roasting pan. Drizzle with the oil and sprinkle with the garlic, herbs, and salt and pepper to taste. Roast until the juices given off by the tomatoes have begun to thicken, 1 to 2 hours. Using a spatula, scrape the tomatoes and all the juices into nonreactive containers. *(Use at once, or cool, cover, and refrigerate for up to 1 week or freeze for up to 1 year.)*

Bone-in chops
give this dish
the best
lamb flavor.

PORK CHOPS WITH LEEKS IN MUSTARD SAUCE

SERVES 4

Four 1½- to 2-inch-thick bone-in pork
rib chops (2½ to 3 pounds total)

FRESH THYME AND ROSEMARY RUB
2 teaspoons salt
1 teaspoon freshly ground
   black pepper
2 teaspoons chopped fresh thyme
1 teaspoon chopped fresh rosemary

2 slices thick-cut bacon, cut
   crosswise into ¼-inch-wide strips
4 cups thinly sliced leeks
   (white and pale green parts;
   see Author's Note)
2 teaspoons chopped garlic
¼ cup brandy
1 cup homemade pork stock
   (recipe follows) or canned low-
   sodium chicken broth
2 teaspoons chopped fresh sage
2 tablespoons Dijon mustard
⅓ cup crème fraîche or sour cream
Salt and freshly ground black pepper

AUTHOR'S NOTE
*You can substitute thinly sliced yellow
or red onions or a mixture of onions
and shallots for the leeks.*

EDITOR'S WINE CHOICE
*Lively, medium-bodied red: 2011
Avignonesi Rosso di Montepulciano*

You can brine these chops or season them, wrap them in plastic wrap, and refrigerate for up to 24 hours; the salt in the seasoning will help make the chops juicy.

1. Pat the chops dry with paper towels.

2. RUB Combine all the ingredients and sprinkle generously over both sides of the chops. *(For more flavor and juiciness, wrap the chops in plastic wrap and refrigerate overnight.)* Let the chops stand at room temperature for 1 hour.

3. Heat a large heavy skillet over medium heat. Add the bacon and cook, stirring, until lightly crisp. Remove the bacon and set aside. Increase the heat to medium-high, add the chops, and sear until nicely browned on the first side, 3 to 4 minutes. Flip and brown the other side, 3 to 4 minutes more. Remove the chops and set aside.

4. Pour off all but 2 to 3 tablespoons of the fat from the pan, add the leeks, and cook, stirring, until softened, about 7 minutes. Stir in the garlic and cook for 1 minute more. Add the brandy and stock and scrape up any browned bits from the bottom of the pan.

5. Add the bacon and sage, then bury the chops in the leeks and add any accumulated juices. Reduce the heat to a simmer, cover, and cook for 3 to 5 minutes. Turn over the chops, cover, and cook for 3 to 5 minutes more, or until the internal temperature reaches 135°F to 140°F on an instant-read thermometer. Transfer the chops to a warm platter and set aside while you finish the pan sauce.

6. Skim off any surface fat and, if there is still liquid in the pan, reduce until it is just about evaporated. Whisk in the mustard until well incorporated with the leeks. Stir in the crème fraîche and simmer for 2 to 3 minutes, or until lightly thickened. Season to taste with salt and pepper. Spoon the sauce over the chops and serve.

ALTERNATIVE CUTS
Pork T-bone loin chops, boneless loin chops, tenderloin medallions, sirloin chops, or blade-end loin chops, all cut 1½ to 2 inches thick.

BASIC MEAT STOCK

You can use this recipe to make beef, veal, bison, pork, or lamb stock. Simply use any meaty bones available to you, making sure they're in 3- to 4-inch pieces. "Meaty" means there is meat attached to the bones; don't use naked bones.

1. Preheat the oven to 475°F.

2. Put the bones in a large roasting pan and sprinkle lightly with salt and pepper. Roast until golden brown, about 45 minutes, turning the bones once or twice so that they brown evenly.

3. Transfer the bones to a large pot and cover with water by about 2 inches. Remove and discard the fat from the roasting pan. Add the 1 cup water to the roasting pan and bring to a boil over medium heat, scraping up the browned bits from the bottom of the pan. Pour this deglazing liquid into the pot and bring to a boil, then reduce the heat to a simmer. Skim and discard the fat and scum accumulated on the surface. Add the onion, celery, carrots, bay leaf, and thyme and simmer, uncovered, skimming often, for 2 hours, adding water as necessary to keep the bones covered.

4. Strain the stock through a fine-mesh sieve into a storage container; discard the solids. Set aside to cool completely. (*The stock can be covered and refrigerated for up to 5 days or frozen for up to 3 months. Freeze it in smaller containers so you always have some at the ready.*)

MAKES ABOUT 6 CUPS

- 4 pounds beef, veal, bison, pork, or lamb shanks, necks, and/or other meaty bones, cut into 3- to 4-inch pieces

Salt and freshly ground black pepper

- 1 cup water
- 1 large onion, not peeled, quartered
- 2 celery stalks, cut into 2-inch pieces
- 2 large carrots, peeled and cut into 2-inch pieces
- 1 bay leaf
- 2 fresh thyme sprigs

PAN-GRILLED VEAL CHOPS
with Tomato–Blue Cheese Butter & Cherry Tomato Salad

SERVES 4

TOMATO–BLUE CHEESE BUTTER

- 3½ ounces blue cheese (see headnote), diced
- 4 tablespoons (½ stick) butter, softened
- 1 tablespoon minced shallot
- 2 teaspoons coarsely ground black pepper
- 1 tablespoon tomato paste
- 1 teaspoon Aleppo pepper or ½ teaspoon cayenne pepper
- ½ teaspoon vodka (optional; see Author's Notes on page 24)

- Four 1¼- to 1½-inch-thick veal rib or T-bone loin chops (2 to 2½ pounds total)
- 1 large garlic clove, cut in half

Salt and freshly ground black pepper

CHERRY TOMATO SALAD

- 1 cup halved cherry tomatoes or diced vine-ripened tomatoes
- 1 tablespoon finely chopped shallot or scallion
- 1 tablespoon extra-virgin olive oil
- 2 teaspoons sherry vinegar
- 6 fresh basil leaves, cut crosswise into thin shreds

Salt and freshly ground black pepper

- 1 tablespoon olive oil

EDITOR'S WINE CHOICE
Fresh, light-bodied Beaujolais: 2011 Jean Paul Brun Terres Dorées L'Ancien

Certain flavors have an affinity for each other: tomato and blue cheese, basil and tomato, blue cheese butter and grilled meat. With these combinations in mind, I came up with a couple of simple condiments that enhance veal chops, which can be somewhat bland. The tomato–blue cheese butter is ideal with grass-fed veal, but also goes well with the lighter formula-fed veal.

There are many types of blue cheeses, from milder Danish blues to the full-flavored and pungent Roquefort, and trying different varieties is a great way to experiment with this recipe. I like the blue cheese from Rogue Creamery in Oregon and often use a younger, milder one called Oregon Blue, but you may enjoy the stronger Rogue River Blue with veal as well. I also like making this butter with Stilton and Gorgonzola.

Cherry tomatoes remain sweet and flavorful long after other tomatoes have gone out of season, but if it's the middle of winter and you can find only tasteless ones, skip the salad. In the summer, substitute ripe heirloom tomatoes, cut into ½-inch dice, for the cherry tomatoes.

1. BUTTER Pulse the blue cheese in a food processor until it has the texture of coarse meal. Add the remaining ingredients and process to form a homogenous paste. Spread a 12-by-8-inch sheet of plastic wrap on a work surface and scrape the butter onto the plastic wrap. Shape and roll the mixture into a log about 2 inches in diameter; seal the butter in the wrap. Refrigerate until firm, at least 1 hour, or until ready to use. (*You can make the butter up to a day ahead and refrigerate it. You can also freeze the butter for up to 2 months.*)

2. Rub the chops on both sides with the cut sides of the garlic. Discard the garlic. Season the chops with about ¼ teaspoon salt and ⅛ teaspoon pepper per side. Set aside.

3. No more than 30 minutes before you are ready to cook the veal chops, make the tomato salad (if made too far in advance, it will become watery): Toss the tomatoes, shallot, oil, vinegar, and basil together in a small bowl. Season to taste with salt and pepper. Set aside.

continued on page 24

PAN-GRILLED VEAL CHOPS
continued

4. Heat a large cast-iron skillet or ridged grill pan over high heat. Brush the chops with the oil and add to the pan, making sure not to overcrowd the chops; if necessary, cook them in 2 batches. Sear for 2 to 3 minutes, or until nicely browned on the first side. Flip and sear the other side for 2 minutes. Reduce the heat to medium-high and cook for 3 minutes more per side, or until the internal temperature registers 125°F to 130°F on an instant-read thermometer for medium-rare or 130°F to 135°F for medium. Remove the chops to a warm platter and top each with a ¼-inch-thick pat of Tomato–Blue Cheese Butter. Let rest for 5 minutes, loosely covered with aluminum foil.

5. Smear the mostly melted butter over the chops, divide the tomato salad among the plates, and serve.

ALTERNATIVE CUTS

Veal sirloin chops, boneless veal loin chops, or veal blade chops (blade chops should be cooked to medium doneness so that they are not chewy).

BEEF KEBABS
with Maple-Horseradish Glaze

4 SERVINGS
ACTIVE: 30 MIN; TOTAL: 1 HR

GLAZE

- ⅓ cup pure maple syrup
- 3 tablespoons prepared horseradish, drained
- 1 tablespoon fresh orange juice
- 2 teaspoons fresh lemon juice
- 2 teaspoons soy sauce
- 1 teaspoon chopped thyme
- ½ teaspoon chopped sage
- ½ teaspoon Worcestershire sauce

RUB

- 2 teaspoons salt
- 2 teaspoons chopped thyme
- 2 teaspoons chopped sage
- 1 teaspoon freshly ground black pepper
- 1 teaspoon finely chopped garlic
- 2 pounds boneless rib eye steaks, cut into 1½-inch cubes

Olive oil, for brushing

EDITOR'S WINE CHOICE
Spiced, black cherry–scented Syrah: 2009 Bonny Doon DEWN Bien Nacido

BRUCE AIDELLS ONLINE

🅕 *Bruce Aidells, America's Meat Guru*

These kebabs develop a terrific char from the maple syrup in the glaze. Aidells likes using juicy, flavorful rib eye steaks. For a less-expensive option, try flatiron, tri-tip or chuck-eye Delmonico steaks.

1. MAKE THE GLAZE In a medium bowl, combine all of the glaze ingredients.

2. MAKE THE RUB In another medium bowl, combine the salt, thyme, sage, pepper and garlic. Add the cubed beef and toss to coat. Let stand at room temperature for at least 30 minutes or up to 1 hour.

3. Light a grill. Thread the meat onto skewers and brush with olive oil. Grill the skewers over moderately high heat for 8 to 10 minutes for medium-rare meat, brushing on the glaze and turning the skewers every 2 minutes. Let the skewers rest for 5 minutes. Brush once more with the glaze and serve.

NOTE This glaze is also excellent on grilled pork chops and steaks. To make sure the glaze does not burn, keep a close eye on the meat, which will need to cook longer than the kebabs. For best results, turn the chops or steaks frequently.

IN MY KITCHEN

Ted Allen with Barry Rice

Ted Allen knows all too well that hurried cooking can lead to bad food. As host of Food Network's *Chopped,* he sees what happens when frenzied contestants toss together meals under strict time limits. In his second cookbook, Allen encourages home cooks to relax and celebrate the act of preparing meals. It's an enticing proposition, and Allen cheerfully talks you through dishes that take a bit of time (Chinese-style pork buns) and many that don't, like his three-step chicken with pancetta and sage (page 30). The recipes are entertaining-friendly and designed to impress. For instance, shrimp scampi are baked on skewers, then served on a lattice of fresh zucchini ribbons (page 28). It looks complicated but is actually quite simple, and can be prepped in advance—one of the many tips, tricks and epiphanies that come with each recipe. PUBLISHED BY CLARKSON POTTER, $35

SCAMPI SKEWERS WITH LEMON ZUCCHINI

SERVES 4 AS AN APPETIZER OR LIGHT LUNCH

ZUCCHINI

2	medium zucchini
3	tablespoons extra-virgin olive oil

Grated zest of 1 lemon

1	tablespoon fresh lemon juice
¼	teaspoon sugar
¼	teaspoon fine sea salt

Pinch of freshly ground black pepper

SHRIMP

½	cup panko or dried coarse baguette bread crumbs
8	tablespoons (1 stick) unsalted butter, at room temperature
1	large egg yolk
2	garlic cloves, minced
1	teaspoon grated lemon zest
1½	tablespoons fresh lemon juice
1½	tablespoons dry white wine
1	tablespoon finely chopped basil leaves
1	tablespoon finely chopped flat-leaf parsley leaves
¾	teaspoon kosher salt
1	pound medium shrimp, peeled and deveined, tails on

AUTHOR'S NOTES

Both the zucchini base and the skewers are great for prepping a couple of hours before company comes; cover them and keep them chilled.

This dish is equally good when the shrimp are replaced by seared scallops, a fillet of mild fish, or any number of other things.

EDITOR'S WINE CHOICE

Vibrant, medium-bodied Greek white: 2012 Skouras Moscofilero

Garlic, butter, and lemon are, of course, a holy trinity for shrimp—everybody loves the combination. But my favorite thing about this dish is its use of the humble zucchini: uncooked, cut paper-thin, wilted slightly by a short bath in lemon vinaigrette, then beautifully arranged beneath a skewer full of shrimp.

1. PREPARE THE ZUCCHINI Trim the ends from the zucchini so that the zucchini fit the plates you intend to use. Using a mandoline or vegetable peeler, cut the zucchini into paper-thin slices and stack them flat (don't pile them in curls in a bowl, or they'll stay curly). Arrange 6 to 9 slices on each of 4 plates in rows or a basket weave pattern. Reserve leftover zucchini for another use (or do what I do: hit them with salt and pop them in your mouth).

2. Whisk together the olive oil, lemon zest, lemon juice, sugar, salt, and pepper. Drizzle the vinaigrette over the zucchini, and set aside for at least 15 minutes to soften and flavor the zucchini.

3. MEANWHILE, PREPARE THE SHRIMP Preheat the oven to 425°F.

4. In a small bowl, combine the panko, butter, egg, garlic, lemon zest, lemon juice, wine, basil, parsley, and salt.

5. Place 2 shrimp on a cutting board, nestled tail to body, forming a yin-yang design, and thread onto a skewer. Repeat with two more pairs of shrimp, 6 shrimp per skewer. Trim the skewers with scissors if necessary to fit on the serving plates.

6. Put the shrimp in a baking dish. Cover with the butter mixture, dotting it on top. Bake until the shrimp are pink and just cooked through, 10 to 12 minutes.

7. Place one shrimp skewer atop each plate of zucchini salad, and serve.

CHICKEN PAILLARDS WITH PANCETTA & SAGE

SERVES 4

4   boneless, skinless chicken
      breast halves
Kosher salt and freshly ground
      black pepper
1   large egg, beaten
12   sage leaves (8 whole, 4 chopped)
6   thin slices of pancetta
2   tablespoons extra-virgin olive oil
1   tablespoon unsalted butter
1   shallot, minced
1   tablespoon all-purpose flour
½   teaspoon thyme leaves
¼   cup dry white wine
1   cup chicken stock, preferably
      homemade, or low-sodium
      store-bought

EDITOR'S WINE CHOICE
*Ripe, lively Beaujolais: 2011 Louis Claude
Desvignes Morgon Côte du Py*

Here's my simple, chicken-y take on saltimbocca. With just a paper-thin piece of pancetta, or a similar cured meat such as prosciutto, you can easily transform a chicken breast. The sage is both a flavorful and decorative touch.

1. Pound the chicken breasts to an even thickness of ¼ inch. Sprinkle with salt and pepper, and flip. Brush lightly with the egg. Press 2 sage leaves onto each piece of egged chicken, then cover with pancetta (about 1½ slices per breast), and press again. Refrigerate for 15 minutes.

2. Heat a large sauté pan over medium-high heat for about 5 minutes. When the pan is hot, add the olive oil and the chicken, pancetta side down. Cook until golden brown, about 3 minutes. Flip the chicken, and cook until cooked through, 2 to 3 minutes. Transfer to a warm plate and cover with foil.

3. Add the butter to the pan, reduce the heat to medium, and cook the shallot until soft, 3 minutes. Add the flour, stir, and cook for another 2 minutes. Add the thyme and wine, and deglaze, scraping up the brown bits; simmer for 3 minutes. Add the stock and chopped sage, and simmer until thickened, a few minutes. Serve the chicken on a pool of the sauce.

THREE CHICKEN BREAST ENHANCEMENTS
Here are three techniques for getting flavor into white meat chicken: barding [wrapping] the breast with pancetta (cured, but not smoked, Italian bacon), marinating it in a fiery vinaigrette and cooking over charcoal, and baking it with a Parmesan crust.

Serve with bread for the buttery wine and sage sauce.

HARICOTS VERTS & BABY GREENS
with Fingerlings & Pesto Vinaigrette

SERVES 4

PESTO VINAIGRETTE

1	tablespoon pine nuts, toasted
1	teaspoon coarsely chopped garlic
1	teaspoon coarsely chopped shallot
½	cup packed basil leaves
1	tablespoon freshly grated Parmesan cheese
1½	tablespoons Champagne or other white wine vinegar
⅓	cup extra-virgin olive oil

Kosher salt and freshly ground black pepper

SALAD

½	small red onion, sliced paper-thin
Four	½-inch slices baguette

Extra-virgin olive oil, for brushing

1	garlic clove, peeled and sliced in half

Kosher salt

½	pound fingerling potatoes, cut into ½-inch pieces
½	pound haricots verts, cut into 2-inch lengths
2	good handfuls of baby greens

EDITOR'S WINE CHOICE
Zesty northern Italian white: 2012 Scarpetta Friulano

As much as I like pesto, incorporating it into a vinaigrette laid bare a shortcoming: it lacks acidity. A little tang from white wine vinegar makes it even yummier. It also makes an excellent dressing for French green beans and creamy, golden fingerling potatoes, which just seem to need to be together.

You could bang out the pesto in a food processor, but grinding it the old-school way into a paste (hence "pesto," of course) in a mortar and pestle is fast and fun; it also seems to inform your dish with a history, a soulfulness from everything you ever mashed in that battered, fragrant bowl. I use a Mexican molcajete, carved from volcanic stone.

1. MAKE THE PESTO Combine the pine nuts, garlic, and shallot in a mortar and grind into a paste. Add the basil leaves, and grind them into the mix. Stir in the Parmesan, vinegar, and olive oil, and season with salt and pepper, and set aside.

2. MAKE THE SALAD In a small bowl, soak the onion in ice water to reduce the sharpness.

3. Heat a grill pan or skillet over medium-high heat. Brush the baguette slices with olive oil and toast on both sides until golden brown, 1 to 2 minutes per side. Rub each on one side with the garlic clove, sprinkle with salt, and cut into 1-inch croutons.

4. In a large bowl, prepare an ice bath, and place a colander in the sink. In a medium saucepan filled halfway with water, bring the water to a boil and season well with salt. Add the potatoes and cook for 6 minutes. Add the beans to the potatoes, and continue cooking until both the beans and potatoes are tender but not too soft, 3 to 4 minutes. Drain in the colander, then plunge the colander into the ice bath to stop the cooking.

5. To serve, toss the greens with some of the vinaigrette, then divide among 4 plates. Toss the beans and potatoes with vinaigrette, and divide over the greens. Drain the onion, pat dry with paper towels, and sprinkle over the salads along with the croutons. Serve at once.

FRESH BREADSTICKS

with an Endless Variety of Flavors

MAKES 16 BREADSTICKS
ACTIVE: 10 MIN; TOTAL: 50 MIN

1 pound pizza dough, thawed if frozen (see Author's Note)

SUGGESTED TOPPINGS
Maldon sea salt and freshly ground black pepper
Sea salt and crushed red pepper
Sea salt and fennel seeds
Spicy smoked paprika
Finely grated Parmesan, cheddar or Gruyère cheese
Toasted sesame oil and sesame seeds

AUTHOR'S NOTE
You can make your own dough from scratch or buy frozen pizza dough—just try to find a brand that's low in sodium and preservatives. I use Brooklyn Pizza Dough brand, which has almost no weird ingredients and thaws on the countertop in about 3 hours.

Allen serves these breadsticks as a cocktail snack or as an accompaniment to soups or salads. He puts them in the oven just as his guests arrive. "The smell," he says, "is at least half of the fun."

1. Preheat the oven to 425°F. Line 2 baking sheets with parchment paper.

2. On a lightly floured work surface, using a lightly floured rolling pin, roll out the dough to a 12-by-16-inch rectangle. Using a pizza cutter or sharp knife, cut the dough into sixteen 1-inch-wide strips and transfer them to the prepared baking sheets. Sprinkle with toppings and let rest in a warm place for 30 minutes.

3. Bake the breadsticks for about 10 minutes, until light golden and cooked through. Serve warm.

TED ALLEN ONLINE
tedallen.net
Ted Allen
@ChopTedAllen

THE MILE END COOKBOOK

Noah & Rae Bernamoff with Michael Stokes & Richard Maggi

Noah Bernamoff was an unhappy law-school student and his wife, Rae, had recently lost her job at the Metropolitan Museum of Art when they founded Mile End Delicatessen, a tribute to Montreal Jewish delis, in 2010. A few years later their tiny Brooklyn restaurant is a phenomenon, the couple has a sandwich outpost in Manhattan and they've released their first cookbook: a guide to creating their homey yet refined Jewish dishes in your kitchen. Though the book includes a 13-day recipe for making smoked brisket, this isn't just deli food—it's modern Jewish comfort food executed with an ambitious, seasonal and artisanal slant. The Bernamoffs' chopped liver (page 40) neatly sums up their food philosophy. It's made smooth with schmaltz—rendered chicken fat, a remnant of Old World cooking that also happens to fit today's nose-to-tail cooking trend—and then spiced with *quatre-épices,* a blend of white pepper, ginger, cloves and cinnamon that gives the spread a slightly exotic aroma. PUBLISHED BY CLARKSON POTTER, $27.50

BORSCHT

SERVES 6

FOR THE BEET STOCK

  6 cups water
  1 large onion, chopped
  1 pound beets (about 2 medium beets), peeled and grated
  1 medium carrot, peeled and grated
  4 stalks of celery, trimmed and chopped
  2 Beefsteak or Jersey tomatoes, chopped
  3 whole allspice berries
  2 teaspoons dill seeds
  1 fresh bay leaf
2 or 3 sprigs of parsley
2 or 3 sprigs of dill
  1 sprig of thyme

FOR THE SOUP

  1 tablespoon canola oil
  1 bunch Tuscan kale or chard, thick stems removed, cut into ribbons
  1 carrot, grated
  ¼ head of green cabbage, trimmed and thinly sliced
Diamond Crystal kosher salt and freshly ground black pepper
Lemon juice, for serving
Crème fraîche, for serving

RAE: *What I love about our updated version of this peasant soup is that it's based on an actual beet broth—not beef stock, as in a lot of Russian borschts, and not even vegetable stock to which beets have been added. This is a really beet-y, and surprisingly hearty, borscht. And it's completely vegetarian.*

MAKE THE BEET STOCK Combine all the stock ingredients in a large pot and bring to a boil; reduce the heat and simmer, covered, for 1½ to 2 hours. When the stock is cool enough to handle, strain it through a fine mesh sieve, pressing down on the mixture to extract all the liquid. Discard the solids and set the stock aside; it can be stored in the refrigerator for up to a week.

MAKE THE SOUP Pour the oil into a large pot; place it over medium heat and add the kale, carrot, and cabbage. Cook, stirring frequently, until the kale and cabbage are al dente. Pour the reserved stock into the pot and stir. Season with salt and pepper to taste. Serve the borscht hot; finish each bowl with a squeeze of lemon juice and a little crème fraîche.

Beet broth
makes
this borscht
vegetarian.

POTATO SALAD

MAKES ABOUT 10 CUPS

FOR THE DRESSING

- 2   large egg yolks
- 2   tablespoons spicy brown mustard, such as Gulden's

Juice of 1 lemon

- 2   tablespoons white wine vinegar
- 1¼ teaspoons Diamond Crystal kosher salt
- 3   garlic cloves, peeled
- 1¾ cups canola oil

FOR THE SALAD

- 3   pounds small red potatoes

Diamond Crystal kosher salt

- 2   tablespoons extra-virgin olive oil
- 6   scallions, roots trimmed off
- ⅔   cup chopped fresh flat-leaf parsley leaves and stems
- 1   cup thinly sliced red onion

Freshly ground black pepper

NOAH: *This is the Zelig of potato salads—it can turn up anywhere and fit in just fine. It's as good on the dinner table served with schnitzel as it is at a picnic. The dressing is tart and super-savory, sparkling with lemon juice and spicy brown mustard, which mingle so beautifully with the flavors of scallions, red onion, and parsley.*

MAKE THE DRESSING Combine all the dressing ingredients except the oil in the bowl of a food processor. Process until smooth and roughly tripled in volume, about 3 minutes. Then, with the processor running, add the oil in a slow, steady stream through the hole in the top; continue processing until the oil is fully emulsified. Set the dressing aside.

MAKE THE SALAD Place the potatoes in a large pot and add enough water to cover them by 2 inches; add about ½ cup of salt and bring to a boil. Lower the heat and simmer until a knife inserted into one of the potatoes meets no resistance, 15 to 20 minutes. Drain the potatoes and, when they're cool enough to handle, quarter them; then let them cool completely.

Heat the oil in a pan or skillet over high heat. Cut the scallions in half crosswise and add them to the pan with a generous pinch of salt. Cook the scallions, turning them once or twice, until they're lightly charred, 3 to 4 minutes. Transfer the scallions to a cutting board and chop them into 1-inch pieces.

Combine the scallions, potatoes, parsley, and red onion in a large bowl. Add about 2 cups of the dressing to the bowl and mix vigorously with a wooden spoon until the dressing has been thoroughly incorporated and the potatoes have broken up a bit. Season with salt and pepper to taste. The potato salad will keep in the refrigerator for up to 3 days.

CHOPPED LIVER

SERVES 8 AS AN APPETIZER

- ½ cup schmaltz (see Editor's Note)
- 3 cups chopped onion
- 1 pound chicken livers
- 1 fresh bay leaf
- 1 sprig of thyme
- 4 large eggs, boiled, peeled, and coarsely chopped
- 1 teaspoon quatre-épices (equal parts white pepper, ginger, cloves, and cinnamon)

Diamond Crystal kosher salt and freshly ground black pepper
- 3 scallions, sliced into thin rings

FOR SERVING

Sieved egg (a peeled hard-boiled egg pressed through the coarse holes of a box grater)
Pickled red onions
Gribenes (see Editor's Note)
Pletzel (see Editor's Note)

EDITOR'S NOTE
The Bernamoffs make their own gribenes (chicken skin cracklings), pletzel (a traditional Jewish bread) and schmaltz (chicken fat, rendered from the gribenes) and include those recipes in The Mile End Cookbook. Schmaltz is available in the refrigerated section of most supermarkets. Alternatively, you can use melted butter.

EDITOR'S WINE CHOICE
Focused, full-bodied Chardonnay: 2011 Wyatt

RAE: *This version of the classic Jewish comfort food has converted more than a few nonbelievers; it even worked for me, someone who never liked chopped liver growing up. It's got a luscious flavor and texture, and the crunchy, salty garnishes put it over the top. We swap pickled onions for the traditional fried topping for a needed brightness, and our pletzel makes for the perfect vehicle. I recommend using a meat grinder, but if you don't have one, pulsing the ingredients in a food processor works too.*

Heat the schmaltz in a large sauté pan over medium-high heat. Add the onion and fry until the edges start to brown. Add the chicken livers, bay leaf, and thyme. Lower the heat slightly and cook, stirring often, until the livers are just barely cooked through, about 10 minutes. Set the liver-and-onion mixture aside and let it cool to room temperature. Remove the bay leaf and thyme sprig and add the eggs and quatre-épices. Season with salt and pepper to taste. Pass the mixture through the small die of a meat grinder, or pulse in a food processor until coarsely chopped. Fold in the scallions and adjust the salt and pepper to taste. Garnish with the sieved egg, pickled red onions, and gribenes; serve with pletzel.

MONTREAL-SEASONED HANGER STEAK

2 SERVINGS
TOTAL: 40 MIN

- 2 tablespoons smoked paprika
- 2 tablespoons coarsely ground black pepper
- 2 tablespoons coriander seeds, crushed
- 1 tablespoon garlic powder
- One 1-pound hanger steak, trimmed
- Kosher salt
- 3 tablespoons olive oil or rendered beef fat
- 1 thyme sprig
- 1 garlic clove, crushed
- 1 tablespoon finely chopped lamb bacon or pork bacon (see Note)
- 1 tablespoon finely chopped beef salami (see Note)
- 6 tablespoons chicken stock or low-sodium broth
- 2 tablespoons Chinese black vinegar or balsamic vinegar
- 2 teaspoons Champagne vinegar
- 1 tablespoon veal demiglace
- Maldon sea salt
- 3 chives, cut into 1-inch lengths, for garnish

EDITOR'S WINE CHOICE
Dark, concentrated Napa Cabernet Sauvignon: 2011 Oberon

NOAH & RAE BERNAMOFF

mileenddeli.com

 Mile End

 @mileenddeli

When the Bernamoffs set out to add steak to their menu at Mile End, they reached into their smoked- and cured-meat pantry and came up with this recipe, which calls for lamb bacon and beef salami in the sauce. The dish, they feel, is "culturally consistent with Montreal's storied history of producing excellent smoked meat."

1. In a small bowl, combine the paprika, pepper, coriander seeds and garlic powder and mix well.

2. Preheat the oven to 450°F. Pat the steak dry and season liberally all over with kosher salt. Rub ¼ cup of the steak seasoning all over the steak; reserve the remaining seasoning for another use.

3. In a large cast-iron skillet, heat 1 tablespoon of the olive oil. Sear the steak over high heat until nicely browned on the bottom, about 4 minutes. Turn the steak over, add the remaining 2 tablespoons olive oil to the skillet along with the thyme and garlic and cook for 3 minutes, basting the steak with oil. Place the skillet in the oven and roast the steak for 2 minutes for medium-rare meat. Let the steak rest for 8 minutes.

4. Meanwhile, in a small saucepan, cook the bacon and salami over moderate heat until crispy, about 2 minutes. Add the chicken stock, black vinegar and Champagne vinegar and simmer until reduced by half, about 5 minutes. Stir in the veal demiglace and simmer for 2 minutes. Season the sauce with kosher salt.

5. Slice the steak across the grain and transfer to a platter. Drizzle with the sauce and season with Maldon salt. Garnish with the chives and serve.

NOTE At the restaurant, the Bernamoffs make the steak sauce with their own lamb bacon and beef salami, but they say you can use any bits of charcuterie you might have on hand.

A GIRL & HER PIG

April Bloomfield with JJ Goode

The waits are legendarily long at April Bloomfield's no-reservations New York City restaurants (The Breslin, the Spotted Pig and the John Dory), so this book is a godsend for those who want a taste of her bold English-meets-Italian food. Bloomfield describes herself as a "very particular cook" and a "bit of a control freak." Her recipes aren't complicated, but, she admits, they can be a bit fussy, as in the roasted "pointer-finger-sized" young carrots (not peeled) that she matches with cool (not room temperature) avocados in a tart and aromatic salad (page 44). The instructions for croutons in her roast chicken with tomato-and-bread salad (page 50) are extremely detailed so that the panzanella gets an "elusive texture . . . soggy and crispy at once." Though you don't have to follow every single direction, doing so will not only lead to more delicious results, but will make you a better cook. PUBLISHED BY ECCO, $30

CARROT, AVOCADO & ORANGE SALAD

SERVES 4

- 4 medium garlic cloves, smashed and peeled

Maldon or another flaky sea salt

- 1½ teaspoons cumin seeds, toasted and ground (see Note on Spices, page 46)
- 1½ teaspoons coriander seeds, toasted and ground (see Note on Spices, page 46)
- 1 to 1½ teaspoons crumbled dried pequin chilies or red pepper flakes (see Editor's Note)
- ¼ cup plus 2 tablespoons extra-virgin olive oil
- 30 or so similarly sized (each about the size of your pointer finger) young carrots, not peeled, ½ inch of the green tops left on
- 3 tennis-ball-sized oranges
- 3 ripe Hass avocados, chilled
- 2 tablespoons freshly squeezed lemon juice

A handful of small, delicate cilantro sprigs

EDITOR'S NOTE

Fiery pequin (or piquin) peppers are grown in Mexico. When dried, they develop a smoky, nutty, citrusy flavor. Look for them at Latin markets or online at melissas.com.

EDITOR'S WINE CHOICE

Orange-scented Argentinean white: 2011 Finca Domingo Torrontes

This is my Six Degrees of Kevin Bacon salad. The two main ingredients—carrot and avocado—might not seem compatible or connected, but your first bite will convince you otherwise. The carrots are roasted with cumin and paired with orange, both classic pairings for the vegetable. The citrus goes great with cilantro, and both are a fine match for avocado. Before you know it, you have this fresh, vibrant salad. I love the carrots roasted to the same creamy softness of avocado. The contrast comes not from the texture but from the fact that one's warm from the oven and the other's cool from the fridge.

Sorry if I got your hopes up, but despite the salad's nickname, there's no bacon.

Preheat the oven to 400°F.

Pound the garlic with a healthy pinch of salt in a mortar until you have a wet, fairly smooth paste. (You can also do this on a cutting board, chopping and mashing and chopping and mashing until you're satisfied.) Put the paste in a large mixing bowl. Add the cumin, coriander, chilies, and ¼ cup of the olive oil and stir well, then add the carrots and toss well so they're coated with the oil and spices. Sprinkle on 3 healthy pinches of salt, crushing the grains with your fingers as you add them, and toss again.

Put the carrots in a large shallow baking dish in one layer. Scrape out the extra garlic, spices, and oil from the bowl and spread evenly on top of the carrots. Pour ¼ cup water into an empty spot in the casserole (you don't want to wash off the tasty oily stuff) and tilt the dish so the water spreads across the bottom.

Cover the dish tightly with foil and put it in the oven. Cook the carrots for 25 minutes. Take off the foil and keep cooking until the carrots are lightly browned, and about as tender and creamy as avocado flesh, but not so soft that they threaten to fall apart, about 35 minutes more.

While the carrots are roasting, segment the orange. Squeeze the membranes into a small bowl to release the juice. Set it aside.

When the carrots are done, take the dish out of the oven and let it sit until the carrots have cooled a bit but are still warm.

continued on page 46

These young,
slender
carrots
require no
peeling.

CARROT, AVOCADO & ORANGE SALAD
continued

Meanwhile, take the avocados from the fridge. Halve them lengthwise, remove the pits, and peel the halves. Cut the flesh lengthwise into slices about the same size as the carrots—the slices should be sturdy enough that they don't break up when you toss them.

Put the avocado slices in a large mixing bowl and add the reserved orange juice, the lemon juice, the remaining 2 tablespoons olive oil, and a healthy pinch or two of salt. Toss gently and well with your hands. Push the avocado to one side of the bowl. Add the carrots a handful at a time, scraping and tossing them in the beautiful green liquid in the bowl before adding the next handful. Make sure to scrape out and add all the garlicky spices left in the baking dish. Toss it all together gently, being careful not to break the avocado slices.

Stack the carrots, avocado, and orange segments on a platter or in a serving bowl so they're facing this way and that. Top with the cilantro and serve right away.

NOTE ON SPICES There's nothing like buying whole spices and toasting and grinding them yourself. These simple steps amplify their flavor and fragrance. Here's how to do it: Put the spices in a small pan and set it over medium-high heat. (If there's more than one spice in a recipe that requires toasting, I like to do them separately.) Toast, shaking the pan frequently, until the spices smell really sweet and inviting, anywhere from 2 to 4 minutes. Remember that it's less about precise timing than it is about feel—rather than toasting them for 1 minute and 33 seconds, keep a close eye on the spices and take a whiff every now and then. After they're toasted, use your mortar and pestle or spice grinder to reduce them to a powder.

ROASTED PEANUTS WITH ROSEMARY & GARLIC

- ¼ cup extra-virgin olive oil
- 12 skin-on garlic cloves
- ½ cup lightly packed rosemary leaves
- 3 cups salted skin-on roasted peanuts, preferably small Spanish peanuts
- 1 tablespoon Maldon or another flaky sea salt, or more to taste
- 5 or so dried pequin chilies or pinches of red pepper flakes

EDITOR'S NOTE

These peanuts are best while still hot. Serving them in a warmed ceramic dish retains their heat.

EDITOR'S BEER CHOICE

Classic, refreshing English bitter ale: Fuller's ESB

At The Breslin, we serve snacks like scrumpets, which are breaded and deep-fried shreds of fatty lamb, and boiled peanuts fried in pork fat. But at The John Dory, I wanted the bar snacks to be a bit lighter, more appropriate as preludes to platters of oysters and bowls of razor clam ceviche. So I came up with these salty, roasty peanuts tumbled with slightly crispy rosemary and sweet, soft cloves of garlic, rustic in their papery skins. It's a nice thing to set out at a party or to nibble on while watching a movie.

Heat the olive oil in a wide pan with high sides over medium-high heat until it just begins to smoke. Add the garlic cloves, adjust the heat if necessary to cook them at a steady sizzle, and cook, tipping the pan occasionally so the oil pools and almost covers the cloves, until the garlic has some golden brown spots and the skins begin to split and blister, about 5 minutes.

Push the garlic to one side of the pan, put the rosemary in the oil next to the garlic, and add the peanuts to the space remaining in the pan. Turn the heat down to medium and let the rosemary sizzle in the oil for a minute, stirring it a little, then stir it together with the peanuts and garlic. Let them all quietly and steadily sizzle together—you're infusing the flavors of the garlic and rosemary into the peanuts, cooking the garlic more so it'll be soft and creamy, and reinvigorating the roasted peanuts— stirring and tossing the peanuts often, so they all get to spend some time against the bottom of the pan, about 5 minutes. About a minute before that, sprinkle on the salt, crumble in the chilies, and stir well.

Take the pan off the heat and let the peanuts carry on cooking gently in the hot pan, stirring now and then, until they've cooled a bit. Have a taste, and stir in a little more salt or crumbled chilies if you fancy it. Serve warm or at room temperature.

Roasted Peanuts with Rosemary
& Garlic, page 47

Roast Chicken with Tomato & Bread Salad, page 50

ROAST CHICKEN WITH TOMATO & BREAD SALAD

SERVES 4

FOR THE BREAD SALAD

2¼ pounds firm but ripe summer tomatoes, blanched, peeled, and cored (see Note on Tomatoes)

1 large garlic clove, peeled

Maldon or another flaky sea salt

4 whole salt-packed anchovies, rinsed, soaked, and filleted

A very small handful of basil leaves, plus a few leaves for garnish

¼ cup extra-virgin olive oil, plus a generous drizzle

2 tablespoons red wine vinegar

Freshly ground black pepper

Croutons (see Note on Croutons), still slightly warm

FOR THE CHICKEN

One 4-pound chicken, patted dry

Kosher salt

2 tablespoons extra-virgin olive oil

EDITOR'S WINE CHOICE

Earthy, focused red Burgundy: 2010 Domaine Mongeard-Mugneret Bourgogne Pinot Noir

---

I do occasionally like a more elaborate roast chicken—perhaps some basil butter tucked underneath the skin—but here it's better simple, because you're serving it with a lovely salad.

A really nice panzanella, which is what this salad is, is all about getting the bread soggy and crispy at once. That makes it really nice to eat. To achieve this elusive texture, you must use stale bread and then toast it. That way, the croutons will be able to absorb some of the dressing without going all mushy. This is a classic panzanella, fantastic for showcasing summer tomatoes, preferably in an assortment of colors and sizes, whether you decide to follow my instructions and blanch and peel them (I like the ragged look and fleshy texture that gives them) or not.

MARINATE THE TOMATOES Cut the tomatoes into very large chunks and trim off any hard or pale bits (if using cherry or grape tomatoes, leave them whole). Use your fingers to push out the seeds and juice from the tomato chunks into a small container, and reserve for another purpose. It's fine if you need to tear up the tomatoes a bit to get out the juices. Put the tomatoes in a large bowl.

Combine the garlic and a healthy pinch of salt in a mortar and pound it to a smooth paste. Add the anchovies and basil and pound again until you have a fairly smooth paste. (If you don't have a mortar, chop and mash the ingredients on a cutting board with a chef's knife.)

Combine the garlic-anchovy paste in a small bowl with the ¼ cup olive oil, the red wine vinegar, and a few twists of black pepper. Have a thorough stir, and pour the mixture over the tomatoes. Gently toss them around a bit so the dressing gets into every nook and crevice. Set them aside for at least 30 minutes. (You can refrigerate them, covered, for up to a day. Let them come to room temperature before you use them.)

COOK THE CHICKEN Preheat the oven to 450°F. Let the chicken sit at room temperature for 15 minutes or so. Generously salt the chicken all over, including inside the cavity, and let it sit for another 15 minutes. Put the chicken in a roasting pan or baking dish, drizzle it with the olive oil, and pop it into the oven. Roast for 30 minutes, then reduce the heat to 400°F and continue to cook just until the skin is light golden brown and the juices run clear when you pierce the thickest part of the thigh, about 20 minutes more. Transfer the chicken to a cutting board and let it rest for 15 minutes.

Carve the chicken into pieces—drums, thighs, and breast slices.

ASSEMBLE THE SALAD Put the croutons in a bowl, drizzle half the tomato marinating liquid over them, and toss well. Arrange the bread and tomatoes on a platter so the rustic salad looks elegant, and drizzle on some or all of the remaining marinating liquid. Finish with a generous drizzle of olive oil and a sprinkling of basil leaves, and serve right away alongside the chicken.

NOTE ON TOMATOES In several recipes, I call for fresh tomatoes to be blanched and peeled. Here's how to do it: Bring a large pot of water to a boil. Use a knife to make a shallow X through the skin in the bottom of each tomato. Working in batches of tomatoes of similar size, carefully plunge them into the boiling water and blanch for 20 seconds for larger tomatoes, about 10 seconds for small ones. Transfer them to a big bowl of ice-cold water. Drain them and pull the skin off the tomatoes. You can gently scrape them with a knife to loosen any stubborn skin. Cut out the tough core, unless you're working with cherry or grape tomatoes.

NOTE ON CROUTONS I make croutons from stale rustic Italian bread, the crust removed, with a light, hole-riddle crumb. For the bread salad, I tear the crumb of a large loaf into long strips of different lengths. It's nice for them to be about the same width (about 1 inch), so they toast evenly.

To make the croutons: Spread the bread pieces on a tray in one layer and bake them in a 400°F oven, shaking the pan and tossing the pieces now and then, until they're golden brown and crunchy all the way through, 10 to 15 minutes; they shouldn't give at all when you squeeze them. Keep a close eye on them to be sure they don't get too dark.

SAUSAGE-STUFFED ONIONS

SERVES 4

4   medium red onions (about 8 ounces each), peeled, stem ends trimmed, root ends trimmed but left intact

About 3 tablespoons extra-virgin olive oil

Maldon or another flaky sea salt

1   head garlic

A small handful of small thyme sprigs, plus 1 teaspoon leaves

½   cup Italian sausage, homemade (recipe follows) or store-bought (removed from casing if necessary)

1   cup heavy cream

EDITOR'S WINE CHOICE

Medium-bodied, red berry–scented Sangiovese: 2009 La Maialina Chianti Classico

Each year that I worked at The River Café, Ruth [Rogers] and Rose [Gray] took some of the staff on a trip to a different region of Italy. One of the trips was to Piemonte, where we spent a few days in Bra, the city where the Slow Food movement was born. The food was wonderful, of course, but it began to feel like every dish we ate contained the same local sausage. By the end of the trip, we were a bit sausaged out. At our last dinner in Bra, the waiter brought out a big roasted onion standing on a plate, and we all started nudging each other, joking that even this would be stuffed with sausage. In heavily accented English, our waiter described the dish. We giggled like kids when he told us what was inside. Good thing, then, that it was really tasty.

Preheat the oven to 400°F.

Put the onions in a medium Dutch oven or other ovenproof pot with a lid. Drizzle some olive oil into your hand and rub it onto the onions. You'll probably end up using about 2 tablespoons. Grab some salt and crush it between your fingers as you sprinkle it all over each onion, turning the onions to make sure the salt adheres to all sides.

Tear off the outermost layers of peel from the garlic head so the cloves are exposed. Put it in the middle of the onions and drizzle on a little olive oil. Scatter the thyme sprigs over the onions, and pour ⅓ cup water around the onions and garlic.

Cover the pot and put it in the oven. Cook just until the onions are lightly browned and soft enough that you can insert a knife into the center with barely any resistance, 50 minutes to 1 hour, depending on the size of your onions. Let them sit, covered, on the top of the stove until they're cool enough to handle, so they get even softer. (Leave the oven on.)

Carefully transfer the onions to a plate or cutting board, leaving the liquid behind in the pot. Use a small spoon to scoop out a few layers of the insides of each onion, and stuff each one with about 2 tablespoons of the sausage. Add the scooped-out onion bits to a 12-inch ovenproof pan or small baking dish. (When you add the cream and water, the liquid should come a little less than halfway up the sides of the onions.) Squeeze the soft flesh of the garlic cloves into the pan, and add the thyme leaves, cream, 1 cup of water, and 1 teaspoon salt.

continued on page 54

SAUSAGE-STUFFED ONIONS
continued

Bring the mixture to a full boil, add the stuffed onions, sausage side up, and baste them with the liquid for a minute or so.

Pop the pan into the oven, uncovered, and cook, basting the onions every 10 minutes or so, until the sauce is thick but not gloopy, about 40 minutes. Taste the sauce and add a little more salt, if you'd like. Bring the pan to the table, spoon a little of the sauce over the top of each onion, and dig in.

SIMPLE SAUSAGE

I love stuffing sausage into casings and forming little links, and you can do the same, if you'd like. But to keep things simple, I've given you a loose sausage mix, which you can form into patties (for a lovely breakfast sausage, just leave out the fennel and chilies) and brown in a pan. Or try tossing browned chunks with orecchiette and broccoli rabe, or use it to make Sausage-Stuffed Onions.

MAKES 2½ POUNDS

SPECIAL EQUIPMENT: MEAT GRINDER OR MEAT GRINDER ATTACHMENT OF A STAND MIXER

- 1½ pounds boneless pork shoulder, cut into 1-inch pieces
- 1 pound pork fatback, cut into 1-inch pieces
- 2 tablespoons kosher salt
- ½ nutmeg, grated
- 2 teaspoons fennel seeds, ground
- 10 dried pequin chilies, crumbled, or pinches of red pepper flakes

Combine the shoulder and fatback in a large mixing bowl and toss well. Cover the bowl with plastic wrap and pop it in the freezer until the edges of the meat get crunchy, about 1 hour.

Use a meat grinder (or the grinder attachment of a stand mixer) to grind the mixture through a large die into a bowl.

Add the salt, nutmeg, fennel, and chilies, then mix with your hands, folding over and pushing down on the mixture, for a minute or two. You're trying to get the fat and meat and seasoning evenly distributed, but you're also mixing it so it gets a bit sticky. This will help the sausage stay firm and hold together.

If you'd like, make a little patty and fry it up to test the seasoning. You can add a bit more fennel, nutmeg, chili, and/or salt, if you'd like. Use it straightaway, or cover with plastic wrap and keep it in the fridge for 2 to 3 days or the freezer for up to a month.

MERLOT-BRAISED SMOKED PORK BELLY WITH APPLES

8 SERVINGS
ACTIVE: 30 MIN; TOTAL: 4 HR

2   tablespoons olive oil
One 2¼-pound piece of skinless
     meaty slab bacon
1   tablespoon unsalted butter
1   large Spanish onion,
     peeled and cut into eighths
9   garlic cloves
2   large sweet-tart apples, such as
     Fuji, peeled and coarsely chopped
     into various sizes
3   cups Merlot
1   cup apple juice
Flaky sea salt, preferably Maldon

EDITOR'S WINE CHOICE
Inky, Merlot-based Bordeaux: 2010 Saint Glinglin Saint-Émilion Grand Cru

In this hearty dish, smoked pork belly (often called slab bacon) braises slowly in a luscious mix of red wine and apples until it's super-tender. Bloomfield cuts the apples into pieces of various size so that some cook down into the sauce while others stay whole.

1. Preheat the oven to 300°F. In a large enameled cast-iron casserole, heat the olive oil. Add the bacon, fat side down, and cook over moderately high heat until lightly browned, about 5 minutes. Add the butter, onion wedges and garlic, but don't stir. Cover the casserole and cook over moderately low heat for 3 minutes. Stir the onion and garlic, then cover and cook, stirring occasionally, until the onion is lightly golden, about 10 minutes.

2. Stir in the apples, wine and apple juice and bring to a boil. Cover the casserole and braise the bacon in the oven for 3 to 3½ hours, until the meat is very tender; stir the apples and onions every 45 minutes, piling them on top of the bacon and smushing them a little with a spoon. Season with salt.

3. Transfer the bacon to a platter, spoon the sauce and apples around the meat and serve.

SERVE WITH Mashed potatoes.

APRIL BLOOMFIELD ONLINE
aprilbloomfield.com
@AprilBloomfield

Creole Brownies, page 66

THE BACK IN THE DAY BAKERY COOKBOOK

Cheryl & Griffith Day with Amy Paige Condon

Since opening their Savannah, Georgia, bakery in 2002, Cheryl Day and her husband, Griffith, have become famous for their neo-retro aesthetic, or, as they say, being "both comfortably old-fashioned and hip." Their first cookbook is dedicated to the classics of the Southern baking repertoire, with a handful of kitschy sweets thrown in, like Pinkies Chocolate Lunch-Box Treats, a delicious version of Hostess Sno Balls. But even when they're making something very traditional, like a sour cream coffee cake (page 62), the Days can't help but add something new—in this case, a dose of aromatic cardamom. Even their brownies aren't just brownies; they are Creole-inspired bars glazed with a thick and gooey chicory coffee–chocolate ganache (pictured at left). PUBLISHED BY ARTISAN, $25

SUNNY LEMON BARS

Sweet, Brilliant Flavor

MAKES 12 LARGE OR 24 SMALL BARS

FOR THE CRUST

- ½ pound (2 sticks) unsalted butter, melted
- ½ cup granulated sugar
- 1½ teaspoons pure vanilla extract
- 1½ teaspoons fine sea salt
- 2 cups unbleached all-purpose flour

FOR THE FILLING

- 2¼ cups granulated sugar
- 6 tablespoons unbleached all-purpose flour
- 6 large eggs
- 1 cup fresh lemon juice

Confectioners' sugar for dusting

EDITOR'S NOTE

The thick, buttery base on these bars creates an ideal crust-to-filling ratio.

The buttery shortbread crust has a nice crisp texture that is balanced by the tart and creamy lemon curd topping. Serve the bars with a light dusting of confectioners' sugar on top.

Position a rack in the middle of the oven and preheat the oven to 350°F. Grease a 9-by-13-by-2-inch baking pan and line with parchment, allowing the ends of the paper to hang over two opposite edges of the pan.

TO MAKE THE CRUST In a medium bowl, stir the butter, granulated sugar, vanilla, and salt until well blended. Add the flour all at once and stir until it is just incorporated.

Press the mixture evenly into the bottom of the prepared pan. Bake for 15 to 18 minutes, until the crust is lightly golden.

WHILE THE CRUST IS BAKING, MAKE THE FILLING In a medium mixing bowl, whisk the granulated sugar and the flour together until thoroughly combined. Add the eggs and lemon juice and whisk until well mixed.

When the crust is done, carefully remove it from the oven, set the pan on a heatproof surface, and pour in the lemon filling. Turn the oven temperature down to 300°F, return the pan to the oven, and bake for 20 to 25 minutes, until the filling looks puffy on top and the center no longer jiggles. Let cool to room temperature, then refrigerate for at least 3 hours.

Cut into bars and sprinkle the tops with confectioners' sugar. Serve chilled. The bars will keep in an airtight container in the refrigerator for up to 3 days.

BLACKBERRY COBBLER
Yum! Is All We Can Say

SERVES 8 TO 10

FOR THE TOPPING

- 2 cups unbleached all-purpose flour
- 1 tablespoon baking powder, preferably aluminum-free
- 3 tablespoons granulated sugar
- ½ teaspoon fine sea salt
- ¼ teaspoon ground cardamom
- 6 tablespoons cold unsalted butter, cut into ½-inch cubes
- ¾ cup heavy cream

FOR THE FILLING

- 6 cups fresh blackberries
- ½ cup sugar
- 1 tablespoon cornstarch
- 1 tablespoon grated lemon zest (from about 2 lemons)

Heavy cream for brushing
- 2 tablespoons flavored sugar (see Sweet Note: Sugar and Spice) or granulated sugar

Ice cream for serving (optional)

One of Griff's fondest memories is picking wild berries around his family's cabin in Wisconsin. The deep-purple blackberries were his favorite. His dad would make fresh vanilla bean ice cream in one of those big old rock-salt ice cream makers. When the ice cream was frozen, they would top it with a mixed-berry compote. This cobbler is an ode to Griff's cabin memories.

Position a rack in the lower third of the oven and preheat the oven to 350°F. Butter a 9-inch deep-dish pie plate.

TO MAKE THE TOPPING Whisk together the flour, baking powder, sugar, salt, and cardamom in a large bowl. Drop in the butter and, working quickly, cut it in with a pastry blender. You should have various-sized pieces of butter, from sandy patches to pea-sized chunks, and some larger bits as well.

Pour the cream over the flour mixture and toss together with a rubber spatula or your hands until you have a very soft dough. If there are still a few bits of flour in the bottom of the bowl, gently knead the dough until it is fully incorporated. Be sure not to overwork the dough; it is better to have a few dry patches than a tough dough. The dough will be soft and sticky.

Turn the dough out onto a sheet of plastic wrap or wax paper and cover with another sheet. Using a rolling pin, gently roll the dough into a 9-inch round. Place the dough on a baking sheet, still covered with plastic wrap, and refrigerate while you make the filling. (You can make the dough up to 6 hours before baking the cobbler.)

TO MAKE THE FILLING Combine the berries, sugar, cornstarch, and lemon zest in a large mixing bowl, tossing together to mix. Pour the filling into the prepared pie plate.

Remove the chilled dough from the refrigerator and cut a hole in the middle with a 2-inch-wide cookie cutter, in any shape you like, to create a steam vent. Gently place the dough on top of the filling. Brush it lightly with cream and sprinkle with the flavored sugar.

Bake for 60 to 75 minutes, until the top is golden and puffed and the fruit is bubbling with juices. Transfer to a wire rack to cool for at least 30 minutes before serving.

Serve the cobbler warm or at room temperature, with your favorite ice cream, if desired. The cobbler is best served the same day, but it can be covered with plastic wrap and refrigerated for up to 3 days.

SWEET NOTE: SUGAR AND SPICE

Flavored sugars add another dimension of taste and texture to scones, muffins, pies, and cobblers—and even to your morning tea or coffee. They are easy to make at home.

Fill a 1-quart Mason jar with granulated sugar and add your choice of the following flavors:

➤ **FOR VANILLA SUGAR,** split 2 vanilla beans in half and scrape the seeds into the sugar. Add the bean pods and seal tightly with the lid. The flavor will be more pronounced if you wait 2 weeks before using. You can keep this sugar almost indefinitely in the airtight jar; just replenish with more sugar after each use. The vanilla beans should stay fragrant for up to 1 year.

➤ **FOR CINNAMON SUGAR,** add 3 tablespoons ground cinnamon and 2 to 3 cinnamon sticks to the sugar and seal tightly. Store for up to 1 year.

➤ **FOR CARDAMOM SUGAR,** add ½ cup whole green cardamom pods to the sugar. Seal the jar and store for up to 1 year.

CINNAMON–SOUR CREAM COFFEE CAKE

A Cinch to Make

SERVES 8 TO 10

FOR THE STREUSEL

- ¼ cup packed light brown sugar
- ½ cup unbleached all-purpose flour
- 1½ teaspoons ground cinnamon
- ¼ teaspoon fine sea salt
- ¾ cup chopped pecans (optional)
- 3 tablespoons cold unsalted butter, cut into cubes

FOR THE CAKE

- 2½ cups cake flour (not self-rising)
- 2 teaspoons baking powder, preferably aluminum-free
- ½ teaspoon baking soda
- ½ teaspoon fine sea salt
- ¼ teaspoon ground cardamom
- 12 tablespoons (1½ sticks) unsalted butter, at room temperature
- 1½ cups granulated sugar
- 3 large eggs, at room temperature
- 1½ teaspoons pure vanilla extract
- 1¼ cups sour cream

FOR THE GLAZE

- ¾ cup confectioners' sugar
- 3 tablespoons honey

This recipe makes the quintessential coffee cake, the kind you find in an old-fashioned coffee shop or diner, served with a steaming cup of joe. The addition of cardamom gives it a flavorful and unexpected zing. With a honey drizzle on the crumb topping, it's fancy enough for an afternoon gathering of friends or a Sunday brunch.

Position a rack in the lower third of the oven and preheat the oven to 350°F. Spray a 10-inch tube pan with vegetable oil spray and line the bottom with a ring of parchment.

TO MAKE THE STREUSEL In a small bowl, combine the brown sugar, flour, cinnamon, salt, and pecans, if using. Cut in the butter with a pastry blender until the crumbs are the size of peas. Put the topping in a covered container and set in the freezer while you mix the cake batter.

TO MAKE THE CAKE Sift together the flour, baking powder, baking soda, salt, and cardamom; set aside.

In the bowl of a stand mixer fitted with the paddle attachment (or in a large mixing bowl, using a handheld mixer), cream the butter and granulated sugar for 4 to 5 minutes, until light and fluffy. Add the eggs one at a time, mixing well after each addition. Add the vanilla and sour cream and mix just until blended.

With the mixer on low, add the flour mixture in thirds to the butter mixture, mixing until just combined and no streaks of flour are visible; scrape down the sides of the bowl as necessary.

Scrape half the batter into the prepared tube pan and spread it evenly with a spatula. Sprinkle with ¾ cup of the streusel. Spoon the rest of the batter into the pan, spreading it evenly, and top with the remaining streusel. Bake for 50 to 60 minutes, until a cake tester inserted in the center of the cake comes out clean. Let the cake cool in the pan on a wire rack for 30 minutes.

WHILE THE CAKE COOLS, MAKE THE GLAZE Mix the confectioners' sugar, honey, and 2 tablespoons water together in a small bowl. Set aside.

Turn the cake out of the pan, then invert onto a serving plate, with the streusel side up. Use a fork to drizzle the glaze over the top of the cake. Wrapped in plastic wrap, the cake will keep at room temperature for 2 to 3 days.

CHOCOLATE BREAD
Buttery, Rich, Dark Chocolate

MAKES ONE 10-INCH LOAF

- 2½ cups unbleached all-purpose flour
- ¼ cup Dutch-processed cocoa powder, such as Valrhona (see Authors' Note)
- ⅓ cup granulated sugar
- 1¼ teaspoons instant yeast
- 6 tablespoons unsalted butter, cubed, at room temperature
- 1 teaspoon fine sea salt
- 1 cup bittersweet chocolate chips
- ¼ cup turbinado sugar
- 2 tablespoons heavy cream

AUTHORS' NOTE

Valrhona cocoa powder is one of the darkest, most intensely flavored Dutch-processed cocoa powders available. Unlike other cocoa powders, Valrhona adds a deep chocolate color to the chocolate bread.

The bits of bittersweet chocolate scattered throughout accentuate the sweetness and soft crumb of our Chocolate Bread. Our friend Kelly Yambor, executive chef of Savannah's famed Elizabeth on 37th, orders multiple loaves for parties and wine tastings. You can serve chocolate bread a number of ways: with a sharp white cheddar; toasted, with a spread of Nutella; or as French toast, with strawberries and whipped cream.

In the bowl of a stand mixer fitted with the dough hook, combine the flour, cocoa, granulated sugar, and yeast and mix on low speed. Add 1 cup water and mix for 3 minutes. Let the dough rest in the mixer bowl for 20 minutes.

After it has rested, add the cubed butter and salt to the dough and mix on medium speed until the dough comes together and the sides of the bowl are clean, about 5 minutes. The dough will develop a satiny sheen. Turn the speed to low, add the bittersweet chocolate chips, and mix until incorporated, 1 to 2 minutes.

Transfer the dough to a lightly floured surface and shape it gently into a round loaf. Put the dough seam side down in a bowl that has been lightly coated with vegetable oil spray. Cover with plastic wrap and let the dough rise in a warm, draft-free place for 2 hours, or until it doubles in size.

Sprinkle 2 tablespoons of the turbinado sugar over the bottom of a 10-by-5-inch loaf pan. Turn the dough out onto a lightly floured surface and gently form it into an 8-by-6-inch rectangle. With a long side facing you, gently roll the dough up into a log. Place seam side down in the pan. Cover the pan loosely with plastic wrap and let the dough rise again until doubled, about 1½ hours.

Position a rack in the middle of the oven and preheat the oven to 350°F. When the dough has risen, gently brush it with the heavy cream. Sprinkle the top with the remaining 2 tablespoons turbinado sugar. Bake for 30 to 45 minutes, until the sugar on top is caramelized. Let the loaf cool for 30 minutes, then remove it from the pan and let it cool completely on a wire rack. Wrapped in plastic wrap, the bread will keep at room temperature for up to 2 days.

Sprinkling turbinado sugar on top adds a great crunch.

CREOLE BROWNIES
Complex, Fudgy & Decadent

MAKES 12 LARGE OR 24 SMALL BROWNIES

FOR THE BROWNIES

½	pound (2 sticks) unsalted butter, cut into cubes
8	ounces unsweetened chocolate, coarsely chopped
2½	cups sugar
½	teaspoon fine sea salt
2	teaspoons pure vanilla extract
4	large eggs
1	cup unbleached all-purpose flour
¼	cup cocoa nibs (see Authors' Note)

FOR THE GANACHE

1	cup heavy cream
8	tablespoons (1 stick) unsalted butter, cut into cubes
⅓	cup sugar
¼	teaspoon fine sea salt
16	ounces bittersweet chocolate, finely chopped
¼	cup hot freshly brewed New Orleans–style chicory coffee or strong regular coffee
1	teaspoon pure vanilla extract

Fleur de sel for sprinkling (optional)

AUTHORS' NOTE
Cocoa nibs are seeds of the cocoa plant that are fermented, roasted, and then cracked and separated from the husks, leaving a crunchy texture and a subtle chocolate flavor. They make a great substitute for roasted nuts or chocolate chips in baked goods.

For the people who fall into the "fudgy" camp when it comes to brownie devotion, this one leads that category with a serious ganache topping infused with chicory coffee. The cocoa nibs give the brownie a crunchy yet tender texture.

Position a rack in the middle of the oven and preheat the oven to 350°F. Lightly grease a 9-by-13-by-2-inch baking pan and line with parchment, allowing the ends of the paper to hang over two opposite edges of the pan.

TO MAKE THE BROWNIES Set a large heatproof bowl over a saucepan of barely simmering water (do not let the bottom of the bowl touch the water), add the butter and chocolate, and stir frequently until melted and smooth.

Remove the bowl from the heat, add the sugar, salt, and vanilla and stir until completely combined. Add the eggs one at a time, mixing well after each addition. Add the flour and stir until the batter is smooth, 2 to 3 minutes. Stir in the cocoa nibs.

Pour the batter into the prepared baking pan and bake for 20 to 22 minutes. When the brownies are done, a slight crack will have formed around the edges. Remove the pan from the oven and let the brownies cool completely on a wire rack.

TO MAKE THE GANACHE Combine the cream, butter, sugar, and salt in a large heatproof bowl, set it over a saucepan of barely simmering water (do not let the bottom of the bowl touch the water), and stir until the butter is melted. Add the chocolate and stir until the chocolate has melted and the mixture is completely smooth.

Remove the bowl from the heat, add the coffee and vanilla, and stir until smooth. The ganache will thicken as it cools.

TO FINISH THE BROWNIES Invert the brownies onto a baking sheet and remove the parchment. Pour the thickened ganache over the brownies, spreading it evenly with a spatula or a butter knife into a thick layer on top. Let the brownies stand until the ganache is completely set and sprinkle with fleur de sel if desired.

Cut into squares. The brownies will keep in an airtight container at room temperature for up to 1 week.

DAYDREAM COOKIES

MAKES 32 COOKIES
TOTAL: 40 MIN

- 2 cups all-purpose flour
- 1 teaspoon baking soda
- 1½ sticks unsalted butter,
   at room temperature
- 1¼ cups sugar
- 2 teaspoons pure vanilla extract
- 3 tablespoons vegetable oil

The Days say that these popular sugar cookies are the "best of the best." They love how the cookies "poof up while they're baking and collapse and crackle as they cool."

1. Preheat the oven to 350°F and set the racks in the middle and lower thirds of the oven. Line 2 baking sheets with parchment paper.

2. In a medium bowl, sift together the flour and baking soda. In another medium bowl, using an electric mixer, beat the butter, sugar and vanilla at medium speed until light and fluffy, about 3 minutes. At low speed, drizzle in the oil until incorporated. Add the dry ingredients in 3 additions, beating just until combined.

3. Using a small ice cream scoop or tablespoon, scoop out the dough and roll it into balls. Arrange the balls about 1 inch apart on the prepared baking sheets. Flatten each cookie with the tines of a fork in a crisscross pattern.

4. Bake the cookies for about 15 minutes, shifting the pans halfway through baking, until they are light golden around the edges. Transfer the cookies to a rack to cool.

MAKE AHEAD The cookies can be stored at room temperature for up to 3 days.

CHERYL & GRIFFITH DAY ONLINE

backinthedaybakery.com

f *Back in the Day Bakery*

t *@BacknthDayBakry*

Kachin Chicken Curry, page 70

BURMA

RIVERS OF FLAVOR

Naomi Duguid

Very few Americans are familiar with the food of Burma, but this beautiful cookbook makes an excellent case that we should be. Now more open to foreigners than it has been for decades, Burma (also known as Myanmar) has a beguiling cuisine that shares elements with its neighbors India, Thailand and China: hearty noodle dishes, fiery curries, tart salads and colorful stir-fries. Intrepid culinary adventurer Naomi Duguid, who has written six pioneering books on Asian food, is the perfect guide to this little-known cuisine. Some of her dishes require a cache of special ingredients, like dried shrimp powder or fermented tea leaves, but many of them use common seasonings sold at any good grocer. For instance, the juicy Kachin Chicken Curry (pictured at left) gets intense flavor from a simple paste of garlic, ginger, coriander, turmeric and chiles. PUBLISHED BY ARTISAN, $35

KACHIN CHICKEN CURRY

SERVES 4

About 1½ pounds chicken parts, chopped into about 15 pieces (see A Note on Chopped Chicken)
1 tablespoon minced garlic
1 tablespoon minced ginger
1 teaspoon salt
2 to 4 dried red chiles, seeded and minced (see Editor's Note)
Scant 1 teaspoon ground coriander seed
¼ teaspoon turmeric
1 tablespoon water, or as needed
1 tablespoon peanut oil or vegetable oil, if slow-cooking
2 tablespoons minced scallion greens or chopped cilantro (optional)

EDITOR'S NOTE
Duguid prefers dried red Thai chiles, which are available at amazon.com *and most Asian markets.*

EDITOR'S WINE CHOICE
Full-bodied, pear-inflected Oregon Pinot Gris: 2011 Willamette Valley Vineyards

This dish can be cooked in a bowl set in a steamer or in a tightly covered pot. The chicken is chopped into small pieces, on the bone. It cooks more quickly than it would in large pieces, and more surface area is exposed to the flavor paste and the broth.

The chicken is rubbed with a flavor paste of garlic, ginger, ground coriander, turmeric, and dried red chiles. It steams in its own juices, emerging tender and succulent.

Rinse the chicken pieces, remove most of the skin, and set aside. Place the chicken in a wide bowl.

Pound together the garlic, ginger, salt, chiles, coriander, and turmeric in a mortar to make a paste. Alternatively, mash the garlic and ginger with the side of a knife. Place in a small bowl, add the salt, chiles, coriander, and turmeric, and use the back of a spoon to blend them.

Stir the water into the paste, and add it to the chicken. Turn and mix the chicken and paste until the pieces are well coated. Set aside while you organize your cooking method.

IF STEAMING THE CHICKEN You need a shallow bowl that will fit into your steamer basket when the lid is on and that is large enough to hold all the chicken. You also need a pot that is just about the same diameter as your steamer, so that no steam escapes.

Pour about 3 inches water into the pot and set the steamer basket in the pot. Transfer the chicken and flavorings and the reserved skin to the wide shallow bowl and place in the steamer. Put on the steamer lid, then heat the water over high heat. When it comes to a strong boil, turn the heat down slightly. Steam the chicken until cooked through, 1¼ to 1½ hours. Check on it after 45 minutes: be careful as you lift off the lid not to burn yourself on the steam, then stir the chicken so that pieces that are underneath will be exposed to the hot steam. Cover again and resume steaming.

Check one of the largest pieces of chicken for doneness after an hour or so. Also check that the pot has enough water and is not running dry. When all the chicken is cooked through, remove the steamer from the pot, again taking care not to burn yourself on the steam.

IF SLOW-COOKING THE CHICKEN Add 2 tablespoons more water and the oil to the chicken. Place in a wide heavy pot with a tight-fitting lid, add the reserved skin, and stir to mix well. Place over medium-low heat, with the lid on, and bring to a simmer. Reduce the heat to low and cook for 1 hour, or until all the chicken is cooked through. The chicken will be bathed in a light sauce and will be tender and succulent.

TO SERVE Remove the skin and discard. Serve hot or at room temperature, topped, if you like, with a sprinkling of scallion greens or cilantro.

A NOTE ON CHOPPED CHICKEN I prefer that the chicken be chopped into small pieces, about 10 pieces to the pound. That translates into the following: Chop each drumstick into 2 pieces, the thighs into 3; split the breasts and cut each half-breast into 4 pieces; and chop the wings into 2 pieces. If you are lucky enough to have a good butcher, ask him or her to chop a whole chicken into small pieces; otherwise, use kitchen shears or a sharp cleaver to cut it up. Rinse off the chopped chicken thoroughly to get rid of stray shards of bone, then pat dry.

TO DOUBLE THE RECIPE Double all the amounts and cook in two bowls set in stacked steamers; if using the sealed-pot method, use a 10- to 12-inch heavy pot, so the chicken is not stacked too deep. The cooking time will be a little longer.

SHRIMP CURRY

SERVES 4

Generous 1 pound shrimp, peeled
     and deveined
  ¼ cup minced shallots
  ½ teaspoon minced garlic
  3 tablespoons peanut oil
  ⅛ teaspoon turmeric
1½ cups chopped ripe tomatoes or
     canned crushed tomatoes
  ¾ cup water
  2 teaspoons fish sauce
  2 green cayenne chiles,
     seeded and minced, or to taste
     (see Editor's Note)
  ½ teaspoon salt, or to taste
About ¼ cup cilantro leaves (optional)
  1 lime, cut into wedges (optional)

EDITOR'S NOTE
*Long, wrinkly and thin-skinned, green
cayenne chiles have a pungent heat.
If they're not available, you can substitute
any fresh green chile you like, such as
serrano or jalapeño.*

EDITOR'S WINE CHOICE
*Vibrant, floral Provençal rosé: 2012
La Mascaronne Quat'saisons*

*Tomato is a classic foil for shrimp. Here the combination makes an
appealing curry with plenty of sauce for drizzling on rice. Pair it with
Smoky Napa Stir-Fry (page 76) or a salad of cooked greens.*

*If you find yourself with leftovers, add a little water, taste, and adjust
the seasoning, then chill to serve as a delicious cold soup.*

Rinse the shrimp and set aside. If you have a mortar, pound the minced
shallots and garlic to a paste.

Heat the oil in a wok or a wide heavy skillet over medium-high heat.
Add the turmeric and stir, then toss in the shallots and garlic, lower the
heat to medium, and cook, stirring frequently, until softened and
translucent, about 2 minutes. Add the tomatoes and cook for several
minutes at a medium boil, stirring occasionally, until the tomatoes are
well softened and the oil has risen to the surface.

Add the water and fish sauce, bring to a medium boil, and add the
shrimp. Cook for several minutes, or until the shrimp start to turn pink,
then toss in the minced chiles and salt, stir briefly, and remove from
the heat. Taste and adjust the seasoning if necessary.

Turn out into a bowl, top with the cilantro leaves, if using, and put out
lime wedges, if you wish. Serve hot or at room temperature.

CRAYFISH CURRY
For a crayfish version of this curry, use 1½ pounds crayfish in their shells
and increase the fish sauce to 1 tablespoon and the green chiles to 4.

Brothy, light and fresh-tasting, this curry is also low in fat.

FLUFFY LEMONGRASS FISH

SERVES 3 AS A MAIN COURSE,
5 AS AN APPETIZER

One 1¾- to 2-pound whole snapper or other firm-textured fish, such as lake perch or trout, cleaned, scaled, and head cut off, or 1½ pounds halibut steaks
¼ teaspoon turmeric
½ teaspoon salt, or to taste
2 tablespoons minced shallots
1 teaspoon minced garlic
2 teaspoons minced ginger
2 stalks lemongrass, trimmed and minced
¼ cup peanut oil
2 teaspoons fish sauce
1 to 2 tablespoons Fried Shallots (recipe follows)
1 tablespoon fresh lime juice, or to taste
1 or 2 limes, cut into wedges

EDITOR'S WINE CHOICE
Grapefruit-scented, medium-bodied Chablis: 2011 Joseph Drouhin Premier Cru Vaillons

This dish is ideal for those who don't like dealing with fish bones. It comes to the table aromatic with lemongrass and ginger. Be sure not to taste for seasoning until after you have added the lime juice; it brings all the flavors together. Serve as a main course, with a salad or a vegetable side, or as an appetizer.

Rinse the fish. Put about ¾ inch water in a 10- to 12-inch heavy skillet and place over medium-high heat. Add ⅛ teaspoon of the turmeric and ½ teaspoon salt and slide the fish into the water. Bring to a boil, then lower the heat to maintain a gentle boil. Turn the fish over after 3 minutes (2 minutes if using steaks) and cook for another 1 to 2 minutes, or until it is just barely cooked through. Flake with a fork to test for doneness; the flesh should be opaque.

Remove the fish to a platter and let cool for a few minutes. (Set the broth aside for another purpose.) Lift the flesh off the bones and pull it into smaller flakes or pieces; discard the skin and bones.

If you have a mortar, pound the shallots, garlic, ginger, and lemongrass to a paste; set aside. Alternatively, put them in a miniprocessor and process.

Place a wide heavy skillet or a wok over medium heat. Add the oil, then stir in the remaining ⅛ teaspoon turmeric. Add the shallots, garlic, ginger, and lemongrass and cook, stirring frequently, until softened, about 5 minutes. Add the fish and stir to break it into smaller pieces and to combine it with the oil and flavorings, then add the fish sauce and stir. Cook for several minutes, until the fish is lightly touched with gold.

Transfer to a shallow serving bowl, add the fried shallots, and toss. Add the lime juice and toss again, then taste; add a little salt if you wish. Put out the lime wedges so guests can squeeze on extra lime juice.

FRIED SHALLOTS & SHALLOT OIL

MAKES A GENEROUS ¾ CUP FLAVORED OIL
AND ABOUT 1¼ CUPS FRIED SHALLOTS

1   cup peanut oil
2   cups (about ½ pound) thinly
    sliced Asian or European shallots

Here you get two pantry staples in one: crispy fried shallots and delicious shallot oil. Drizzle shallot oil on salads or freshly cooked greens, or onto soups to finish them. You can fry up shallots each time you need them, but I prefer to make a large batch so they're around when I need a handful to flavor a salad.

The trick with fried shallots is to cook them slowly, so they give off their moisture and get an even golden brown without any scorched or blackened patches. Once they're removed from the oil and left to cool, they crisp up.

Place a wide heavy skillet or a large stable wok over medium-high heat and add the oil. Toss in a slice of shallot. As the oil heats, it will rise to the surface, sizzling lightly. When it's reached the surface, add the rest of the shallots, carefully, so you don't splash yourself with the oil, and lower the heat to medium. (The shallots may seem crowded, but they'll shrink as they cook.) Stir gently and frequently with a long-handled wooden spoon or a spider. The shallots will bubble as they give off their moisture. If they start to brown early, in the first 5 minutes, lower the heat a little more. After about 10 minutes, they should start to color. Continue to cook, stirring occasionally to prevent them from sticking to the pan or to each other, until they have turned a golden brown, another 3 minutes or so.

Line a plate with paper towels. Use tongs or a spider to lift a clump of fried shallots out of the oil, pausing for a moment to shake off excess oil into the pan, then place on the paper towel. Turn off the heat, transfer the remaining shallots to the plate, and blot gently with another paper towel. Separate any clumps and toss them a little, then let them air-dry 5 to 10 minutes, so they crisp up and cool. (If your kitchen is very hot and humid, they may not crisp up; don't worry, the flavor will still be there.)

Transfer the shallots to a clean, dry, widemouthed glass jar. Once they have cooled completely, seal tightly. Transfer the oil to another clean dry jar, using all but the very last of it, which will have some stray pieces of shallot debris. (You can set that oil aside for stir-frying.) Once the oil has cooled completely, cover tightly and store in a cool dark place.

SMOKY NAPA STIR-FRY

SERVES 4

About ¾ pound Napa cabbage
½ cup hot water
1 scant tablespoon oyster sauce
2 tablespoons peanut oil
⅛ teaspoon turmeric
2 dried red chiles (see Editor's Note on page 70)
1 medium shallot, minced
1 teaspoon minced ginger
¼ teaspoon salt, or to taste

EDITOR'S NOTE

Try swapping in other types of cabbage or even bok choy for the Napa cabbage.

Another light take on green vegetables. The oyster sauce, available in Asian grocery stores and well-stocked groceries, gives a smoky undernote to the dish. Try to find fresh young Napa cabbage for extra crispness.

Cut the cabbage crosswise into ¼-inch slices, then slice them crosswise to make bite-sized pieces (you should have 4 loosely packed cups). Place in a bowl of cold water to wash thoroughly, then lift out, drain, and set aside.

Pour the hot water into a small bowl, add the oyster sauce, and stir well. Set aside.

Place a medium or large wok or large deep skillet over high heat. Add the oil, then lower the heat to medium-high and stir in the turmeric. Add the chiles, shallot, and ginger and stir-fry for about 30 seconds, until the shallot starts to soften.

Raise the heat to high, toss in the chopped greens and salt, and stir-fry, tossing and pressing the greens against the hot sides of the pan. When they have wilted and softened, 2 to 3 minutes, add the oyster sauce mixture. Bring to a boil, turn and stir for another 15 seconds or so to distribute flavors and finish cooking the greens, and turn out into a wide shallow bowl.

Serve hot or at room temperature.

EVANGELINE'S CRANBERRY GALETTE

6 SERVINGS
ACTIVE: 20 MIN; TOTAL: 1 HR 30 MIN PLUS
30 MIN COOLING

PASTRY

- 1½ cups all-purpose flour, plus more for dusting
- 2 tablespoons sugar

Pinch of kosher salt

- ⅓ cup vegetable shortening or lard
- 3 tablespoons cold unsalted butter, grated on the large holes of a box grater
- 5 tablespoons ice water

FILLING

- 8 ounces frozen cranberries
- 1 cup sugar
- 1 large egg, beaten

Unsweetened whipped cream, for serving

This Christmas dessert is based on a recipe passed on to Duguid by a family friend, Evangeline Bellefontain. In Duguid's version, she sets the pastry in a pie plate, piles on the sweet-tart cranberry filling, then simply folds in the edges of the dough with her hands, creating a beautiful rustic galette.

1. MAKE THE PASTRY In a medium bowl, combine the 1½ cups of flour with the sugar and salt. Add the shortening and blend it in with your fingers. Add the grated butter and blend with your fingers until the mixture resembles coarse meal. Drizzle in the ice water and mix with a wooden spoon just until the pastry comes together. Pat the pastry into a 1-inch-thick disk and wrap it tightly in plastic wrap. Refrigerate for at least 30 minutes or up to 3 days.

2. MAKE THE FILLING Preheat the oven to 425°F. In a medium bowl, toss the cranberries with the sugar.

3. On a lightly floured sheet of parchment paper, using a lightly floured rolling pin, roll out the pastry to a 12-inch round. Invert the pastry onto an 8-inch pie plate. Mound the cranberry filling in the center and fold the pastry over the filling, leaving a 3-inch opening in the center of the galette. Brush the pastry with the beaten egg.

4. Bake the galette for about 40 minutes, until the cranberries are bubbling and the pastry is golden. Transfer the galette to a rack to cool for at least 30 minutes. Serve with whipped cream.

MAKE AHEAD The galette can be kept at room temperature for up to 6 hours.

NAOMI DUGUID ONLINE

naomiduguid.com

f *Naomi Duguid*

t *@naomiduguid*

THE RIVER COTTAGE FISH BOOK

Hugh Fearnley-Whittingstall & Nick Fisher

In his eighth River Cottage title, British celebrity chef Hugh Fearnley-Whittingstall takes on a towering subject: sourcing and cooking sustainable fish and shellfish. The cookbook tackles the subject with Fearnley-Whittingstall's typical mix of do-gooder enthusiasm, empowering instruction and immediately appealing, Eurocentric cooking. For the eager student, there are well-written sections on the biology and ecology of fish, knife-skills tutorials, diagrams showing how to build your own smoker and more. If you just want incredible seafood-focused meals, there are 135 great, mostly quick recipes, like a wonderfully detailed take on *salade niçoise* (page 80). It's hard to read this book and not learn something; the light, fragrant sea bass with thyme and lemon (page 84), for example, uses a unique "steam-braising" technique that can be adapted to almost any kind of fish. PUBLISHED BY TEN SPEED PRESS, $45

SALADE NIÇOISE

SERVES 4

- 7 ounces (200 grams) small new potatoes
- 7 ounces (200 grams) green beans, topped, tailed, and halved
- 4 eggs, at room temperature
- Two 4-ounce (120-gram) cans of sustainably caught tuna in oil
- 2 butterhead lettuces, floppier outer leaves discarded
- A handful of small black and/or green olives
- 8 to 12 anchovy fillets in oil, cut in half lengthwise if large

FOR THE DRESSING
- 1½ tablespoons olive oil
- 1½ tablespoons sunflower oil (ideally from the tuna can)
- 1 tablespoon white wine vinegar
- ½ teaspoon Dijon mustard
- A pinch of sugar
- Salt and freshly ground black pepper

EDITOR'S WINE CHOICE
*Fresh, elegant Provençal rosé: 2012
Commanderie de la Bargemone*

At its best, this classic dish is a sheer delight. But in the wrong hands it can become a bit of a mess. Anyone who's eaten a few different salades niçoises will have come across an ingredient that has no business being there—fennel, cucumber, green peppers, capers, pine nuts? We wouldn't be so arrogant as to claim ours as the ultimate version, and there's no accounting for taste, but we reckon we're in the zone here, both in terms of authenticity and flavor. In our view, canned tuna is better and more authentic than fresh. (And, on that basis, this recipe would be equally at home in the chapter on Fish thrift and standbys.) Choose a brand that's line-caught sustainably.

As with any simple dish, it's important to get every ingredient absolutely right. The tuna must be canned in oil, not brine, while the lettuce should be a butterhead type, not romaine or, God forbid, iceberg—and only the crisper, inner leaves at that. The eggs should be boiled until the yolk is set but still just soft in the middle, the green beans must be really young and fresh, and the olives should be baby niçoise ones, if you can get them. Once you have gathered these beautiful ingredients, putting the salad together is a simple matter.

Cook the potatoes in boiling salted water until tender, adding the French beans to the pan about 5 minutes before the potatoes are done. Drain and leave to cool.

Meanwhile, bring a small pan of water to a boil, add the eggs, and simmer for 5 to 7 minutes (5 minutes for small eggs, 7 minutes for large). Drain and rinse under cold running water to stop them cooking further. Peel and halve the eggs.

Drain the tuna (reserving a little of the oil for the dressing) and break it into chunks. Make the dressing by whisking all the ingredients together. Rather than tossing everything together with the dressing, which can result in all the fish falling to the bottom of the dish, it's best to build up the salad in layers. Begin by arranging the lettuce leaves over a large, shallow serving dish (or use individual dishes, if you prefer), then distribute the potatoes over them. Strew the beans on next, and trickle some dressing over the whole lot. Next come the eggs and the olives, with a little more dressing, and finally the tuna and the anchovies, with a spoonful of dressing to finish it all off. Eat right away, preferably in the sunshine, with a well-chilled rosé.

A little oil from the tuna can makes a briny vinaigrette.

SPAGHETTI WITH COCKLES

SERVES 2

- 4 tablespoons good olive oil
- 2 tablespoons white wine
- 1 pound (500 grams) cockles, scrubbed (and purged if you think they may be very gritty; see Note on Purging)
- 2 garlic cloves, sliced into paper-thin slivers
- One 14-ounce (400-gram) can of chopped tomatoes, or 1 pound (500 grams) fresh tomatoes, skinned and chopped

A pinch of sugar

- 1 bay leaf
- 7 ounces (200 grams) spaghetti or linguine
- 2 tablespoons (25 grams) unsalted butter and a trickle of olive oil
- 1 tablespoon chopped fresh flat-leaf parsley (optional)

Salt and freshly ground black pepper

EDITOR'S WINE CHOICE
Bright, lemony Sicilian white: 2011 Terre Nere Etna Bianco

This is our take on spaghetti alle vongole—vongole *being the Italian name for various species of clam. Cockles, which are very similar bivalves, work just as well in this classic seafood pasta dish.*

Set a large saucepan over medium heat and add 1 tablespoon of olive oil and the white wine. Throw in the cockles, cover the pan, and give it a shake, then cook for 2 to 3 minutes, until all the cockles are open (discard any that steadfastly refuse to do so).

Tip the contents of the pan into a colander set over a bowl to collect the juices. Strain the juices through a fine sieve, or even a cloth, to get rid of any grit or shell fragments. Pick two-thirds of the cockles out of their shells, then set all the cockles, shell on and shell off, aside.

Heat the remaining olive oil in a large frying pan, add the garlic, and fry until it's just beginning to color. Quickly throw in the tomatoes, followed by the cockle cooking liquid, the sugar, bay leaf, and some salt and pepper. Cook over gentle heat, stirring from time to time, for 25 to 30 minutes, until you have a thick, pulpy sauce.

When the sauce is nearly done, bring a large pan of water to the boil. Salt it generously, then add the spaghetti or linguine and cook until al dente.

Add all the cockles to the tomato sauce with a tablespoon of butter and the parsley, if using, and toss over medium heat for a minute, until they are piping hot. Drain the pasta and toss with the second tablespoon of butter and a trickle of olive oil. Divide between two warmed dishes and ladle the cockle and tomato sauce over the top. Serve right away—without Parmesan!

ALSO WORKS WITH
➤ Palourdes and other small clams

NOTE ON PURGING Cockles live a couple of inches beneath the muddy sand. Rinse them off in a bucket of clean seawater as you find them. They should then be purged in a fresh bucket of seawater (or salted cold tap water) to which you've added a handful of rolled oats or bread crumbs, and left for at least a few hours, or overnight. After that, all they will need is a quick scrub under the cold tap and they're ready for cooking.

STEAM-BRAISED SEA BASS WITH THYME & LEMON

SERVES 4

- 1 tablespoon olive oil
- 1 tablespoon unsalted butter
- 1 tablespoon white wine
- A squeeze of lemon juice
- 2 strips of finely pared lemon zest
- A couple of sprigs of thyme
- 2 or 3 bay leaves
- ½ teaspoon fennel seeds (optional)
- 1 small garlic clove, finely sliced (optional)
- 1½ to 2¼ pounds (750 grams to 1 kg) thick black sea bass, pollock, or cod fillet, cut into ¾- to 1¼-inch-thick (2- to 3-cm-thick) medallions
- Salt and freshly ground black pepper

EDITOR'S WINE CHOICE
Zesty, herb-scented Sauvignon Blanc: 2011 Michel Bailly & Fils Les Loges Pouilly-Fumé

Here's a recipe that demonstrates the simplicity and effectiveness of a technique we've dubbed "steam-braising," of which we are extremely fond. Cook this and you'll see how easy and adaptable it is. The fish sits in just a little bit of simmering, aromatic liquid in a covered pan and is half-poached, half-steamed, while being infused with lovely flavors. It'll be perfectly cooked in less than 10 minutes and will have created its own delicious little sauce. This particular recipe includes quite a few aromatic flavorings, but it also works with just a bay leaf and a scrap of garlic.

Put the olive oil, butter, and white wine in a large, wide saucepan or a deep frying pan along with a tablespoon of water, the lemon juice, zest, thyme, and bay—and the fennel seeds and garlic, if you're using them. Bring to a simmer. Season the fish medallions lightly with salt and pepper, then arrange them in the pan in a single layer. Cover and cook for 4 to 6 minutes, depending on the thickness of the fish, turning them once, very carefully, so they don't break up. That's it.

All you need do now is transfer the fish to warmed plates and spoon over the juices. Boiled spuds or mashed potatoes and something fresh and green—broccoli, perhaps, or spring greens—are the only accompaniments you need.

ALSO WORKS WITH
- Ling
- Brill and most other white fish
- Grey mullet cutlets
- Small whole flatfish

> "We make bold sandwiches using classic techniques. We didn't invent any of them, but we know their powers and how to use them well."
> —CAROLINE FIDANZA

SALTIE

Caroline Fidanza with Anna Dunn, Rebecca Collerton & Elizabeth Schula

Not far from a gritty expressway, Saltie is an unassuming 500-square-foot sandwich shop in Brooklyn. But these aren't just any sandwiches, they are "complete little meals on bread," as the shop's debut cookbook says. "Culinary microcosms. Staged experiences. Dioramas." (Saltie also makes fantastic soups and baked goods.) Beautifully composed and carefully considered, the creations from Caroline Fidanza and her Saltie cohorts use top-notch ingredients and are often stuffed so full that tackling them requires a knife and fork. The garlicky Italian-American (page 90) layers fried zucchini with pesto, mozzarella and tomato on fluffy homemade focaccia (page 92). The same bread is the starting point for the Iberian-leaning Town Ho, a devastatingly simple construction of fried egg, sea salt and smoked paprika aioli (page 94)—just a few examples of the big flavors to come out of a very small kitchen. PUBLISHED BY CHRONICLE BOOKS, $25

BEEF SHIN & FARRO SOUP

MAKES 2 SERVINGS

- 1 meaty, 3- to 4-inch crosscut beef shank
- Sea salt and freshly ground black pepper
- 3 tablespoons extra-virgin olive oil, plus more for drizzling
- 3 carrots
- 2 leeks
- ¼ cup fresh parsley leaves, stems reserved
- 1 cup farro
- 4 red radishes, thinly sliced
- 4 scallions, thinly sliced

EDITOR'S WINE CHOICE
*Light-bodied, berry-rich Dolcetto: 2010
San Fereolo Valdibà*

I started cooking with other cuts of meat like this when we opened Marlow & Daughters butcher shop in an effort to become more knowledgeable about how to use them at home. These cuts of meat are really exceptional; they may take a little coaxing but have great flavor and nutritional value and provide the opportunity to taste beef in a way that isn't just about a steak or a hamburger. I like serving meat in this way, as a small flavor-building element rather than a big hunk on a plate. It's also economical—a little goes a long way. Beef shin in particular gives a great beefy essence to this soup. Be patient and leave yourself plenty of time to make this soup—the beef shank will take many hours to cook.

Season the beef shank well with salt and pepper and let it sit for at least 1 hour at room temperature or up to overnight, covered in the refrigerator, if you have the time and foresight.

In a heavy-bottomed soup pot over medium-high heat, heat the 3 tablespoons olive oil. Add the beef shank and sear until nicely browned on all sides, about 15 minutes total. Remove it from the pot, discard the oil, and return the shank to the pot. Add enough water to reach about two-thirds of the way up the sides of the shank. Cut 1 carrot and 1 whole leek in half lengthwise and add to the pot, along with the stems from the parsley. Cover the pot, bring to a simmer, and cook the beef shank until tender, about 4 hours. Check on it periodically, adding water as necessary if it gets too low. Once the beef shank is cooked, you can hold it in the refrigerator and make the soup the next day.

Otherwise, toward the end of the cooking time, bring a saucepan three-quarters full of well-salted water to a boil. Add the farro and cook until tender, about 10 minutes. Drain the farro and toss with a little olive oil. Set aside. Slice the remaining 2 carrots and 1 leek thinly on the diagonal (bias).

When the meat is tender, remove from the heat and let cool slightly, then remove the meat from the bone and pull or slice it into bite-size pieces. Put the meat back in the broth and add the sliced carrots, leeks, and radishes. Place over medium-low heat and simmer until the vegetables are cooked through, about 10 minutes. Taste and season the broth with salt. Add the farro and scallions and cook just to warm through. Ladle the soup into bowls and garnish with the parsley leaves and a grind of black pepper. Serve hot.

This light,
soothing soup
has just a
few ingredients.

ITALIAN-AMERICAN
Fried zucchini, tomato, mozzarella, pesto, mayonnaise

MAKES 2 SANDWICHES

- 2 large eggs
- ½ cup all-purpose flour
- ½ cup cornmeal
- Kosher salt
- 1 large zucchini, cut on the diagonal into slices about ¼ inch thick
- Olive oil for frying
- 2 sandwich-size pieces of Focaccia (recipe follows)
- 4 tablespoons mayonnaise, preferably homemade (recipe follows)
- 1 ball fresh mozzarella, thinly sliced
- 1 large tomato, sliced
- 2 tablespoons basil pesto, preferably homemade (recipe follows)

EDITOR'S WINE CHOICE

Bright, strawberry-scented sparkling rosé: NV Scharffenberger Brut Rosé

Here's a sandwich that proves how consistently good fried vegetables and mayonnaise are together. And in this case, fried vegetables, mayonnaise, and mozzarella. At first I thought that the combination of mayonnaise and mozzarella might go against a principle instilled in me by Anne Fidanza—that these two ingredients are not friends. Contrary to what she might think, they most certainly are.

Also, this sandwich is best eaten when the zucchini is first fried, but you can reheat the zucchini in a 350°F oven.

Break the eggs into a shallow bowl and whisk to blend. Put the flour and cornmeal in two separate shallow bowls. Add a pinch of salt to both the flour and cornmeal and stir to combine.

Dredge each slice of zucchini first in the flour, then the beaten egg, then the cornmeal. Set the breaded zucchini aside on a platter or baking sheet.

Heat a large cast-iron skillet over medium-high heat and pour in enough olive oil to cover the bottom of the pan evenly. When the oil is hot, add some of the breaded zucchini in a single layer. Do not crowd the pan. Cook, turning once, until golden brown on both sides, about 2 minutes per side. When the zucchini are done, transfer to a plate lined with paper towels and sprinkle with salt while they are still hot. Repeat to cook all of the zucchini.

Cut the focaccia in half horizontally and put on a plate, cut-sides up. Spread both cut sides with the mayonnaise. Place 2 or 3 pieces of zucchini on each bottom half of the bread, followed by 2 slices of mozzarella and 2 slices of tomato. Spread the pesto on top of the tomato. Replace the tops of the bread and press lightly to help the sandwich hold together. Serve right away.

continued on page 92

The focaccia
for this
sandwich is
airy, chewy
and crisp.

ITALIAN-AMERICAN
continued

MAKES ENOUGH FOR 8 TO 10 SANDWICHES

6¼	cups all-purpose flour
2	tablespoons kosher salt
1	teaspoon active dry yeast
3½	cups warm water
¼	cup extra-virgin olive oil, plus more for greasing and drizzling

Coarse sea salt

AUTHOR'S NOTES

This easy recipe calls for a large plastic food-storage container, about a 6-quart capacity, with a tight-fitting lid. Otherwise, you can use a large mixing bowl and cover the dough with plastic wrap.

Unfortunately, focaccia suffers a rapid and significant deterioration in quality after the first day. It is also impossible to make bread crumbs with focaccia. Ideally, bake and eat focaccia on the same day. If there is some left over, wrap it tightly in plastic and store at room temperature for one day more. Day-old focaccia is delicious in soup.

FOCACCIA

Focaccia is the bread that we use for most of the sandwiches at Saltie. The reasons for choosing this soft-but-chewy Italian yeast bread were equally pragmatic and delicious. We considered what we could reasonably produce and decided a bread that we could make on a baking sheet would be much more economical in terms of time and space than one that required more individual attention. As has been the case with many of our choices at Saltie, landing on focaccia at first may have seemed the solution to how to do something in the best and most efficient way, but it quickly became the fact-of-the-matter only possible choice that it is today. Now I can't imagine life without focaccia. Its fluffy, oily welcome greets me daily.

In a large bowl, whisk together the flour, salt, and yeast. Add the warm water to the flour mixture and stir with a wooden spoon until all the flour is incorporated and a sticky dough forms (no kneading required). Pour the ¼ cup olive oil into a 6-quart plastic food container with a tight-fitting lid (see Author's Notes). Transfer the focaccia dough to the plastic container, turn to coat, and cover tightly. Place in the refrigerator to rise for at least 8 hours or for up to 2 days.

When you're ready to bake, oil an 18-by-13-inch baking sheet. Remove the focaccia dough from the refrigerator and transfer to the prepared pan. Using your hands, spread the dough out on the prepared pan as much as possible, adding oil to the dough as needed to keep it from sticking. Place the dough in a warm place and let rise until about doubled in bulk. The rising time will vary considerably depending on the season. (In the summer, it may take only 20 minutes for the dough to warm up and rise; in the winter it can take an hour or more.) When the dough is ready, it should be room temperature, spread out on the sheet, and fluffy feeling.

Preheat the oven to 450°F.

Pat down the focaccia to an even thickness of about 1 inch on the baking sheet tray and begin to make indentations in the dough with your fingertips. Dimple the entire dough and then drizzle the whole thing again with olive oil. Sprinkle the entire surface of the focaccia evenly with sea salt.

Bake, rotating once front to back, until the top is uniformly golden brown, about 15 minutes. Transfer to a wire rack to cool, then slide out of the pan. Use the same day.

MAYONNAISE

MAKES ABOUT 2 CUPS

- 2 egg yolks
- 1 teaspoon white wine vinegar
- 1 teaspoon Dijon mustard
- 1½ teaspoons kosher salt, plus more for seasoning
- 2 cups pure olive oil
- 4 tablespoons water, or as needed

Juice of ½ lemon (optional)

Combine the egg yolks, vinegar, mustard, and 1½ teaspoons salt in a food processor and pulse to mix. With the machine running, begin to add the olive oil in a slow, steady stream. After adding about one-third of the oil, the mixture will start to come together. You will be able to hear this as well as see it. Initially you will hear the whoosh of the ingredients in the machine deepen, and then it will quiet as the mayonnaise starts to thicken. At this point add 2 tablespoons of the water to thin the mayonnaise and prevent it from breaking.

Continue to add the oil. As the mixture thickens up again, add the remaining 2 tablespoons water, a little at a time, just as needed to correct the consistency. Once all of the oil has been added, turn off the machine and taste the mayonnaise. Add more salt as necessary. Also taste for acidity; if the mayonnaise seems a little flat, add the lemon juice to brighten it.

PESTO

MAKES ABOUT 1 CUP

- 8 garlic cloves
- ½ cup pine nuts

Sea salt

Leaves of 1 large bunch fresh basil

- ¼ cup extra-virgin olive oil
- 1 cup grated Parmigiano-Reggiano or *pecorino toscano*

Freshly ground black pepper

Put the garlic, pine nuts, and a pinch of salt in a food processor, blender, or mortar and process or pound with a pestle to a coarse purée. Add the basil leaves and drizzle in the olive oil to loosen the mixture as you continue to process or pound. Mix until the pesto is well blended but not perfectly smooth. Transfer to a clean bowl, stir in the cheese, and season with pepper and additional salt, if needed.

The pesto can also be made with a chef's knife on a cutting board—just chop the garlic and pine nuts together finely and fairly uniformly and then start incorporating the basil and olive oil, a little at a time. It will be a bit rougher but just fine.

Cover with plastic wrap, pressing it against the surface of the pesto, and refrigerate for up to 3 days.

THE TOWN HO

Pimentón aioli, fried egg

MAKES 1 SANDWICH

- 1 sandwich-size piece of Focaccia (page 92)
- 3 tablespoons Pimentón Aioli (recipe follows)
- 1 large egg

Sea salt

This sandwich began as Rebecca [Collerton]'s snack. And every time she made it for herself, I would sulk—both because she didn't offer to make me one and because I probably just had thoughtlessly eaten something unremarkable so I wouldn't be hungry anymore. I would enviously watch her eat it with a knife and fork, so pleased with herself for finally remembering that she deserved something good.

Cut the focaccia in half horizontally and put on a plate, cut-sides up. Spread both cut sides with the aioli. Set aside.

Heat a nonstick skillet and fry the egg (see Sunny Eggs Three Ways, page 96). When the egg is cooked, sprinkle it with sea salt and shimmy it onto the bottom piece of aioli-dressed bread. Replace the top and serve right away.

PIMENTÓN AIOLI

MAKES ABOUT 2 CUPS

- 2 large garlic cloves
- 1 teaspoon sea salt
- 2 egg yolks
- 1½ teaspoons *pimentón*
- 1 tablespoon plus 1 teaspoon sherry vinegar
- 2 cups pure olive oil
- 4 tablespoons water, or as needed

Kosher salt

We make this aioli at Saltie with garlic and pimentón, *a smoked paprika from Spain that is a particular favorite of Rebecca's—it's like her magic powder. Pimentón is one of those things that seems like a cheat, because it comes out of a cute little tin yet imparts a depth of flavor that is hard to put your finger on. Smoky? Yes, but bright and aromatic, easy and balanced. It seems to make everything taste better.*

Aioli is simply garlic mayonnaise and can be variously seasoned with herbs, citrus, or spices. It can also be used without any flavor other than the assertive garlic.

Put the garlic in a mortar with the sea salt and pound into a paste with a pestle. The sea salt will act as an abrasive and assist in breaking down the garlic. If you don't have a mortar and pestle, mince the garlic on a cutting board, sprinkle with the sea salt, and continue to mince until the salt is well incorporated and starts to break down the garlic. Make a paste by spreading the mixture on the board with the flat side of your knife blade. Continue along, alternating between chopping and spreading until you have achieved a smooth paste.

Transfer the garlic paste to a food processor. Add the egg yolks, *pimentón,* and vinegar and pulse to mix. With the machine running, begin to add the olive oil in a slow, steady stream. After adding about

EDITOR'S WINE CHOICE

*Green apple–inflected sparkling wine:
NV Castellroig Cava Brut*

one-third of the oil, the mixture will start to come together. Add 2 tablespoons of the water to thin the aioli and prevent it from breaking. Continue to add the oil. As the mixture thickens up again, add the remaining 2 tablespoons water, a little at a time, just as needed to correct the consistency. Once all of the oil has been added, turn off the machine and taste the aioli. If additional seasoning is needed, add a pinch of kosher salt, which will dissolve more easily at this point. The aioli will keep, covered tightly in the refrigerator, for up to 1 week.

continued on page 96

THE TOWN HO
continued

MAKES 1 SERVING

1 to 2 tablespoons extra-virgin
          olive oil
    2 large eggs

SUNNY EGGS THREE WAYS

Cooking eggs sunny-side up can be an elusive art. The technique holds the allure of a perfect, unmangled egg with a virtually guaranteed nice runny yolk.

For this challenge, I like to make sure my attention is entirely on cooking the egg; there is a perfect moment that I am devoted to finding each time. It's a task that takes only minutes to perform, but it is totally engaging.

There are three approaches to the fried egg that I have come to rely on. The most foolproof method I know for creating a perfect sunny-side-up egg is to place it in a warm pan with olive oil briefly, then transfer it to a hot oven until the white sets. For the classic skillet method, I alternate between the methods detailed below.

I fry my eggs in extra-virgin olive oil, but you can certainly use butter.

For an oven-fried sunny egg, preheat the oven to 400°F. Heat the olive oil in an ovenproof skillet over medium heat. When the oil is warm but not hot, crack the eggs gently into the pan and cook without disturbing just until the white starts to set, about 1 minute. Transfer to the oven and bake just until the white sets completely, about 3 minutes longer.

For a quick-fried sunny egg, coat a skillet with the olive oil, place over medium heat, and carefully crack the eggs into the pan. When you start to hear the eggs sputtering, turn the heat down to low until you don't hear it anymore. If you hear sputtering again, reduce the heat a little more. Cook until set, about 5 minutes.

For a slow-fried sunny egg, put the pan over low heat with the olive oil and eggs, and just wait patiently for the eggs to heat and cook through, about 8 minutes. I like to tilt the pan to shimmy the egg into the curve at the edge and then tip it up again, so the egg coddles in the oil and cooks evenly. I also like to use a spoon to baste the whites for the same purpose.

Whichever way you like to cook them, serve your sunny eggs right away.

CITRUS SALAD
with Ricotta & Focaccia

4 SERVINGS
ACTIVE: 20 MIN; TOTAL: 50 MIN

- 2 medium shallots, thinly sliced
- 2 teaspoons thyme leaves
- 1 tablespoon fresh lemon juice
- ¼ cup extra-virgin olive oil

Sea salt

- 4 citrus fruits, preferably a mix of sweet and tart
- ½ pound fresh ricotta cheese
- 4 slices of focaccia, homemade (page 92) or store-bought, for serving

Fidanza's juicy citrus salad is especially beautiful made with different-colored fruits. You can try it with white or pink grapefruit, Meyer lemon, tangelos and a variety of oranges such as navel, red-fleshed Cara Cara and blood oranges.

1. In a medium bowl, combine the shallots, thyme and lemon juice with 3 tablespoons of the olive oil and a pinch of sea salt. Let the shallots macerate at room temperature for 30 minutes.

2. Using a sharp knife, carefully peel the citrus fruits, removing all of the bitter white pith. Working over a medium bowl to catch the juices, cut in between the membranes and release the sections into the bowl. Squeeze the juice from the membranes into the bowl; discard the membranes.

3. Drizzle the citrus with the remaining 1 tablespoon of olive oil and season with sea salt. Arrange the shallots on top. Smear the ricotta on the focaccia and top with the citrus salad.

SALTIE ONLINE

saltieny.com

f *Saltie*

t *@Saltieny*

Overstuffed Nutters, page 100

BAKING OUT LOUD

Hedy Goldsmith with Abigail Johnson Dodge

For years, diners at Michael's Genuine in Miami have fallen in love with Hedy Goldsmith's homemade Oreos, red velvet Twinkies and other playful desserts. Now the pastry chef and TV personality shares those recipes in her first book. Raised on junk food but later converted to real baking by studying Maida Heatter's cookbooks, Goldsmith is a master at upgrading nostalgic supermarket favorites. Her Childhood Treats chapter, she says, is an "homage to the fast, fatty, calorie-driven, chemically enhanced goodies" she grew up eating. Goldsmith, however, swaps out the processed ingredients and captures the essence of the original. Her Overstuffed Nutters (pictured at left), for example, are coaster-size riffs on Nutter Butters, packed with fluffy filling. Likewise, her tangerine pots de crème are a sophisticated take on an Orange Julius, reimagined as rich, creamy, tangy puddings (page 104). PUBLISHED BY CLARKSON POTTER, $27.50

OVERSTUFFED NUTTERS

MAKES 18 SANDWICH COOKIES

FOR THE COOKIES

1	cup all-purpose flour
½	teaspoon baking soda
1	cup quick-cooking oatmeal
¼	cup chopped salted peanuts (preferably Virginia)
½	cup (1 stick) unsalted butter, at room temperature
½	cup (packed) dark brown sugar
½	cup granulated sugar
½	teaspoon kosher salt
½	cup creamy peanut butter (preferably organic), at room temperature
1	extra-large egg, at room temperature
1	teaspoon vanilla bean paste or pure vanilla extract

FOR THE FILLING

3	cups confectioners' sugar
10	tablespoons (1¼ sticks) unsalted butter, at room temperature
¾	cup creamy peanut butter (preferably organic), at room temperature
1¼	teaspoons vanilla bean paste or pure vanilla extract
½	teaspoon kosher salt

EDITOR'S NOTE

These cookies would be fabulous for making ice cream sandwiches. To do so, bake larger cookies and replace the filling with ice cream.

My fascination with retro desserts began with my mom's love for the original peanut-shaped cookie of my childhood. She would have gladly passed up a meal for a cup of coffee and a plate of Nutter Butters.

I didn't mess with the recipe too much. I just combined two great recipes into one fantastic dessert: oatmeal raisin cookies (minus the raisins) and my favorite peanut butter cookie recipe. It's the same as the original, only better. You may call me cocky or foolish to think that I could improve on a classic, but you should try my cookies before you decide. I know my mom would think they're awesome.

1. To make the cookies, position racks in the upper middle and lower middle of the oven, and preheat the oven to 375°F (350°F if using a convection oven). Line 2 baking sheets with parchment paper or nonstick liners.

2. In a large bowl, sift together the flour and baking soda. Add the oatmeal and peanuts and stir until well blended.

3. Using an electric mixer fitted with the paddle attachment, beat the butter on medium speed for about 3 minutes, until soft and smooth. Add the brown sugar, granulated sugar, and salt and beat on medium-high speed for 5 minutes, until light and fluffy. Scrape down the sides of the bowl. Add the peanut butter and beat for 30 seconds or until combined. Add the egg and vanilla and beat until just combined. Add the flour mixture, and beat on low speed until just combined. Do not overmix.

4. Using a 1-tablespoon ice cream scoop, shape the dough into balls and arrange them about 2 inches apart on the prepared baking sheets. Using the palm of your hand, flatten each mound slightly.

5. Bake for 11 to 13 minutes (10 to 12 minutes if using a convection oven), switching the baking sheets' positions halfway through baking, until golden brown around the edges.

6. Transfer the baking sheets to wire racks and let cool completely. Store in an airtight container until ready to fill, or for up to 5 days.

7. To make the filling, using an electric mixer fitted with the paddle attachment, beat the confectioners' sugar, butter, peanut butter, vanilla, and salt on medium speed for about 3 minutes, until soft and smooth.

8. Scrape the filling onto a work surface and shape it into an 18-inch-long log. Cut the log into 1-inch pieces. Arrange half the cooled cookies bottom side up on a work surface. Put one piece of filling in the center of each cookie. Don't be afraid to overstuff these—the more filling the better. Top with the remaining cookies, top side up, and press gently to push the filling to the edge.

9. Store in an airtight container until ready to serve, or for up to 2 to 3 days.

OLD-SCHOOL RASPBERRY BARS

MAKES 24 BARS

- 3 cups all-purpose flour
- 1½ teaspoons baking powder
- 1½ teaspoons kosher salt
- 1½ cups (3 sticks) unsalted butter, at room temperature
- 1½ cups granulated sugar
- 2 teaspoons vanilla bean paste or pure vanilla extract
- 2 teaspoons finely grated lemon zest
- 3 extra-large egg yolks, at room temperature
- 1⅓ cups raspberry jam (see Editor's Note)
- ⅓ cup confectioners' sugar, for dusting

AUTHOR'S NOTE

Using a box grater to shred this dough is a great workout for your forearms. That said, if you're not into the workout, you can shred the dough in a food processor—just be sure to shape the dough into a long log that will fit into your processor's feeding tube. Also, be sure to work only with very frozen dough.

EDITOR'S NOTE

Goldsmith makes her own raspberry jam for these bars and includes the recipe in Baking Out Loud.

These guys are so unpretentious and easy to make, I hope they don't get overlooked by the experienced baker. Years ago, an assistant of mine shared with me her grandmother's technique of using a box grater to evenly distribute the dough. Unique, yes. Grating the dough gives these bars a light and airy texture. Careful with your knuckles, though!

1. To make the crust, sift together the flour, baking powder, and salt.

2. Using an electric mixer fitted with the paddle attachment, beat the butter on medium speed for about 3 minutes, until soft and smooth. Add the granulated sugar, vanilla, and lemon zest and beat on medium-high speed for about 2 minutes, until well blended. Add the egg yolks, one at a time, and beat for 1 minute or until well blended. Add the flour mixture and beat on medium speed until just blended.

3. Scrape the dough and any remaining floury bits onto a work surface and knead 3 to 4 times, until it all comes together into a smooth dough.

4. Divide the dough in half (weigh the halves if you have a scale), shape into logs, and wrap in plastic wrap. Freeze the logs for 2 hours, or until very firm.

5. Position a rack in the center of the oven, and preheat the oven to 350°F (325°F if using a convection oven). Line the bottom and sides of a 9-inch square baking pan with parchment paper or foil and grease it lightly (preferably with Pam).

6. Put a large box grater on a plate, and using the large holes, shred one of the logs (keep the other one frozen). Scatter the dough pieces evenly in the prepared baking pan, being careful to not press on the pieces. (You want the layers to be nice and fluffy.) Using a small offset spatula, spread the jam evenly over the dough without pressing down on the dough. Shred the remaining log and scatter the pieces evenly over the jam. The pan will be very full.

7. Bake for 54 to 56 minutes (40 to 45 minutes if using a convection oven), until the top is slightly puffed and evenly browned. Transfer the baking pan to a wire rack and let cool completely.

8. To serve, use the foil or parchment liner to lift the cookie from the pan and onto a cutting board. Peel away the foil or paper, and using a large knife, cut the cookie into 4 strips. Cut each strip into 6 equal pieces and dust with the confectioners' sugar. Store in an airtight container for up to 1 week.

For an easy shortcut, use good-quality jarred jam for the bars.

TANGERINE CREAMSICLE POTS DE CRÈME

SERVES 6

1½ cups heavy cream
1 vanilla bean, split
1 tablespoon finely grated tangerine zest
Pinch of kosher salt
6 extra-large egg yolks
½ cup sugar
½ cup fresh tangerine juice

AUTHOR'S NOTE

I like to make pots de crème with other citrus fruits, like Meyer lemons, grapefruit, or key limes. Feel free to substitute any of those here, adding up to 1 tablespoon of additional sugar to the recipe.

The Orange Julius was a hit at the 1964 New York World's Fair. Who knew that orange juice, milk, and vanilla would be so delicious? It blew my mind as a kid, and I've been thinking of the perfect vehicle for the flavors ever since. This recipe is my homage to that amazing combo.

1. Pour the heavy cream into a medium saucepan. Scrape all the seeds from the vanilla bean, and add them to the saucepan along with the bean, the tangerine zest, and salt. Cook over medium heat until very warm but not boiling, about 4 minutes.

2. Remove the pan from the heat, cover, and set aside for at least 30 minutes.

3. Position a rack in the center of the oven, and preheat the oven to 300°F (275°F if using a convection oven).

4. Arrange six 6-ounce ramekins in a baking pan that has 2-inch-high sides.

5. In a medium bowl, whisk the egg yolks and sugar until blended.

6. Over medium heat, bring the cream mixture back to barely a simmer. While whisking constantly, slowly pour the warm cream mixture into the yolk mixture until blended. Stir in the tangerine juice.

7. Pour the custard through a fine-mesh strainer into a clean bowl. Fish out the vanilla bean, scraping any remaining custard and seeds back into the mixture. Discard the zest.

8. Pour the strained custard into the prepared ramekins. Put the baking dish into the oven, carefully fill the baking pan with very hot water to come halfway up the sides of the ramekins, and tightly cover the pan with foil.

9. Bake for 35 to 45 minutes (20 to 30 minutes if using a convection oven), or until the center of the custard jiggles slightly when a ramekin is gently shaken.

10. Transfer the baking pan to a wire rack, uncover, and let the pots de crème cool completely.

11. Remove the ramekins from the water bath and cover them with plastic wrap. Refrigerate for at least 8 hours, or up to 2 days. Serve chilled.

MILK CHOCOLATE JELLIES WITH SMOKED SUGAR

MAKES 32 JELLIES
TOTAL: 30 MIN PLUS 2 HR CHILLING

- 1 tablespoon powdered unflavored gelatin
- 6 ounces brewed espresso or strong brewed coffee, cooled
- 19½ ounces milk chocolate, finely chopped
- 8 ounces smoked granulated sugar (see Note) or granulated sugar (1 cup)

Goldsmith's adorable little chocolate candies are creamy, like chocolate pudding, with a nice crunchy sugar coating. They can be sprinkled with regular sugar, but smoked sugar makes them even more spectacular.

1. Line an 8-inch square baking dish with plastic wrap. In a small bowl, sprinkle the gelatin over the espresso. Let stand for 5 minutes.

2. Meanwhile, put the chocolate in a large heatproof bowl. Bring a saucepan of water to a boil. Remove the saucepan from the heat and place the bowl of chocolate over the saucepan, making sure that the bottom of the bowl does not touch the water. Stir until the chocolate is melted, then whisk in the espresso mixture until smooth.

3. Pour the chocolate mixture into the prepared baking dish. Cover and refrigerate until firm, about 2 hours.

4. Invert the jelly onto a cutting board and cut into 1-inch squares. Coat the jellies in the sugar and serve chilled.

NOTE Smoked sugar is available at specialty stores and online at *rareteacellar.com*.

MAKE AHEAD The jellies can be wrapped in plastic and refrigerated for up to 3 days.

HEDY GOLDSMITH ONLINE

hedygoldsmith.com

f *Hedy Goldsmith*

t *@hedygoldsmith*

JAPANESE FARM FOOD

Nancy Singleton Hachisu

It sounds like a plot from a fish-out-of-water romantic comedy: A young California girl comes to Japan for the food and ends up marrying an organic egg farmer. But that's exactly what happened to Nancy Singleton Hachisu, who moved to the country 25 years ago and now lives there with her family in the northern Saitama prefecture. The uniqueness of her cross-cultural life is clear from the book's pictures as well as her recipes: no-frills dishes that match super-fresh ingredients with just a few Japanese pantry staples. "Our food is bold, clear and direct," she says. Her salt-massaged cucumber salad gets rich depth from miso and smashed sesame seeds (page 110). The melting texture and salty-sweet flavors of her stir-fried eggplant are astonishing, especially since the dish is made with so few ingredients (page 114). These wonderfully simple recipes are an eye-opening lesson in how to cook with balance and restraint while creating deep, authentic flavors. PUBLISHED BY ANDREWS MCMEEL, $35

CHOPPED SUMMER SALAD WITH MISO

Miso-Aji Natsu Yasai Sarada

SERVES 6

1 medium red or orange
   tomato, cored
1 Japanese cucumber, unpeeled
4 small green peppers,
   cored and seeded
2½ ounces (75 grams) "cotton" or
   silk tofu (see Editor's Note below)
1 tablespoon organic miso
1 tablespoon organic rice vinegar
2 tablespoons organic rapeseed oil
6 shiso leaves, cut into fine threads
   (see Editor's Note on page 110)

EDITOR'S NOTE

*Japanese "cotton" tofu (momen-dofu),
so named because after the tofu is
pressed its rough surface resembles
cotton, is smoother than American
soft tofu. You can make your own tofu
using Hachisu's recipe in* Japanese
Farm Food *or purchase silken tofu.*

*When you cook a lot, you end up with little odds and ends of
vegetables or sauces. I love creating new dishes from the bits and
pieces and also being able to incorporate those serendipitous little
leftovers into a new menu. This salad is the result of one of those
days. I was making lunch at the school and had only a few of each
kind of vegetable. A bit of tofu left over from lunch the day before
sparked the inspiration of strewing some diced tofu on top of the
chopped salad before dressing. The cold, custard texture played off
well with the miso vinaigrette and bright summer vegetables.*

Chop the tomato, cucumber, and green peppers into ¼-inch (6-mm)
uniform dice and scrape each one into the same medium-sized bowl.
Do not toss. Cut the tofu carefully into ½-inch (12-mm) squares.

Muddle the miso with the vinegar and whisk in the oil. Right before
serving, toss the vegetables, then spoon onto individual plates (or onto
a larger dinner plate that you will use to serve the rest of your meal).
Drizzle with the miso dressing, drop a few cubes of tofu on top, and
strew with the shiso threads. Serve immediately.

NOTE ON MISO Selecting miso can be bewildering. I would stick with one semimild, pleasant-flavored miso before you start experimenting with others. After all, unless you are preparing Japanese food on a daily basis, it may take you a while to make it through one container of miso. Here again, we buy miso from our local producer, Yamaki, who ferments the soybeans and grain with a natural mold (*koji*) for more than a year. And again the Yamaki miso is available in the U.S. under the Ohsawa label. I use brown rice miso, but barley miso is an excellent (though a bit darker-flavored) alternative. I have also noticed local miso in the Portland, Oregon, area, but have not tried it. Steer clear of miso with unusual flavors, such as dandelion-leek (at least for Japanese food).

NOTE ON RAPESEED OIL More commonly known as canola oil, rapeseed oil is extracted from rape blossoms (similar to rapini) and is the oil used by generations of Japanese farm families. My first taste of organic small-scale–produced rapeseed oil was eye opening. The oil had a clarity and brightness that I had heretofore not tasted in other so-called flavorless oils. I buy two varieties in 16.5-kg drums (big). One oil is made from organic Australian rapeseed, the other from Japanese. Both are excellent, but the Japanese oil is lighter, more elegant, and cleaner for deep-frying (but about 50 percent more expensive). I strongly urge you to discover your own "eye-opening" oil; be sure to pour out a little in a spoon and taste. The oil should be pleasant and fresh tasting, not flat, heavy, or flavorless.

SALT-MASSAGED CUCUMBER WITH MISO & SESAME

Kyuri Momi

SERVES 6

- 1¾ pounds (800 grams) Japanese cucumbers (7 or 8 small)
- ½ tablespoon fine sea salt
- 4 tablespoons unhulled sesame seeds
- 3 tablespoons brown rice miso
- 2 tablespoons rice vinegar
- 6 shiso leaves (see Editor's Note)

EDITOR'S NOTE

Shiso is a Japanese herb with spiky leaves and an aromatic, mint-like flavor. It is available at Japanese markets and some Asian grocers.

Kyuri momi along with abura miso *are, hands down, the quintessential summer dishes of any farm family. My husband calls them his soul food. In the middle of summer we can't even give away the slender cucumbers and eggplants. Everyone grows them, so summer means eating eggplant and cucumbers in a myriad of ways. They're said in the same breath: nasu/kyuri.*

Before my mother-in-law lived under the same roof, I would stop her at our door when she tried to drop off big bags of each. Somehow I thought of the field as my own private vegetable shop. I could saunter over and pluck a bit of this or that for any meal. I didn't know that you have to pick the whole row every two days, otherwise the plants stop producing. We wait all year long to eat cucumbers and eggplant and revel in them when we have them in abundance, eating them at every meal.

Slice the cucumbers into paper-thin rounds and toss with the salt in a medium-sized bowl. Let sit 10 minutes.

Toast the sesame seeds over medium-high heat in a dry frying pan until they are fragrant and start to pop. Grind the sesame seeds with a *suribachi* (Japanese grinding bowl) or mortar until most of the seeds have broken down and are almost pastelike. Add the miso and rice vinegar and blend until creamy.

Squeeze the cucumbers by handfuls to express the water, then add to the sesame-miso mixture.

Stack the shiso leaves, roll into a cigar shape, and slice into fine tendrils; toss gently but well with the cucumbers.

RATIO sesame : miso : vinegar—4 : 3 : 2

VARIATIONS If you can find them, use young *sansho* leaves sliced from the stem instead of shiso. Or add finely slivered ginger to the cucumbers or ginger juice (grate ginger and squeeze out the juice in your fist) to the dressing.

CHICKEN SALAD WITH SESAME-MISO VINAIGRETTE

Toriniku Sarada Goma-Miso Vineguretto

SERVES 6

- 2 skinless, boneless chicken breasts (about 9 ounces/250 grams each)
- 2 tablespoons sake
- 2 teaspoons grated ginger
- 1 teaspoon sea salt
- 2 small heads of butter lettuce

Sesame-Miso Vinaigrette (recipe follows)

EDITOR'S NOTE

The sesame-miso vinaigrette would also be fantastic on a simple mix of greens. It's worth making extra.

EDITOR'S WINE CHOICE

Juicy, full-bodied white: 2010 Foxglove Chardonnay

When Tadaaki asked me, "How would you like to be a Japanese farmer's wife?" I told him I'd have to think about it. I didn't know if I could stay in Japan forever, and having grown up in the San Francisco Bay Area, I wasn't sure I could become as "organic" as this guy was. Tadaaki's ideal life was a life without electricity. I couldn't live without a washer and dryer. I wondered what kind of life we would have together. Though I did decide to make the plunge, I experienced periodic bouts of uncertainty at the irrevocable path upon which I had embarked. So my older sister Pam came to Japan to help give me some perspective.

Tadaaki invited us for lunch at his parents' to introduce them to Pam. We took the train and Tadaaki met us at the station wearing geeky dress-up clothes with sleeves too short. Where were the jeans? But for lunch he made a Chinese chicken salad from his own chickens with a sesame-miso vinaigrette. Who was this guy? Pam immediately saw through the clothes and gave her seal of approval. And over the next few years, she often admonished me to "be nice to Tadaaki," as if she thought I might lose such a paragon. And that's how I became a Japanese farmer's wife.

Fill a deep frying pan or wok halfway with water and bring to a simmer over high heat. The pan should be large enough to be able to set a steamer over but not in the simmering water.

Sprinkle each chicken breast with 1 tablespoon sake, then smear each piece with 1 teaspoon grated ginger and ½ teaspoon salt. Wrap in foil. Set the foil-wrapped chicken in the steamer and cook for 20 minutes over medium-high heat. Remove the steamer from the heat and allow the chicken pieces to cool in their juices.

Tear off any outer discolored leaves of the lettuce and cut off the stem end with a sharp knife about 1 inch (2.5 cm) from the bottom (this helps remove unwanted dirt). If possible, don't wash the lettuce—just wipe any clinging dirt with a damp towel. Leave the lettuce leaves whole if they are not too big, otherwise cut crosswise into 3-inch (7.5-cm) wide pieces.

Make the sesame-miso vinaigrette—but reserve a teaspoon or so of the ground sesame seeds to sprinkle on the salad after dressing. Whisk again right before serving.

When the chicken is cool, remove it from the foil packets but do not discard the liquid. Shred the chicken by hand into ¼-inch (6-mm) thick pieces and moisten with a tiny bit of the steaming liquid if the meat seems slightly dry.

When ready to serve, mound the lettuce attractively on a large platter or individual plates. Strew the chicken pieces over the top, drizzle sparingly with some sesame-miso vinaigrette, and sprinkle with reserved roughly ground sesame seeds.

SESAME-MISO VINAIGRETTE
GOMA MISO VINEGURETTO

Miso and sesame are sort of a match made in heaven, especially if you add a little vinegar to cut their richness. Good on poached chicken salad.

Measure the sesame seeds into a small frying pan and roast over medium-high heat while lifting and shaking the pan to avoid burning the seeds. (They burn easily!) When the seeds start to pop, remove from the heat.

Slide the seeds into a Japanese grinding bowl (*suribachi*) or mortar and grind roughly (reserve a teaspoon or so of the smashed seeds to sprinkle on the salad after dressing). Mash in the miso to form a thick paste and add the vinegar to lighten (and brighten) the miso-sesame mixture. Whisk in the rapeseed oil slowly until emulsified. (Be sure to whisk again right before dressing your salad.)

RATIO sesame : miso : rice vinegar : rapeseed oil—2 : 1 : 2 : 4

MAKES ENOUGH FOR 1 MAIN-DISH SALAD

2 tablespoons unhulled sesame seeds
1 tablespoon brown rice miso
2 tablespoons rice vinegar
4 tablespoons rapeseed oil

STIR-FRIED EGGPLANT & GINGER WITH MISO

Nasu No Abura Miso

SERVES 6

- 2 tablespoons best-quality miso (see Editor's Note)
- 1½ tablespoons sake
- 1 pound (450 grams) Japanese eggplants (4 or 5 small)
- 6 tablespoons rapeseed or cold-pressed sesame oil
- 2 whole dried red peppers, torn in half
- 1 tablespoon slivered ginger
- 1 tablespoon finely sliced shiso leaves (see Editor's Note on page 110)

EDITOR'S NOTE

Feel free to use any type of miso here. Light yellow shiro miso has a mild flavor; red aka miso will make the dish more intense.

EDITOR'S WINE CHOICE

Minerally, light-bodied red: 2011 Descendientes de J. Palacios Pétalos Mencía

I used to say I don't like brown food, an unfortunate attitude given that most Japanese country food is flavored with miso or soy sauce and therefore cast with a brownish hue. But one night Christopher urged me to try the abura miso Tadaaki had just finished tossing together in his wok. I yielded to pressure and picked up a few slices with my chopsticks. They were hot, creamy, and subtly salty. In this archetypal summer dish, the miso's haunting salty/sweet character combines well with the melting eggplant, and the sake serves to give balance. No sugar is necessary because the vegetables are flavorful and naturally sweet. And as Christopher predicted, I couldn't stop scooping up more and more mouthfuls.

Muddle the miso with the sake in a small bowl. Slice the eggplant down the middle lengthwise, then diagonally crosswise into slightly less than ½-inch (1-cm) slices.

Heat the oil with the dried red peppers in a large wok or skillet over medium heat until the peppers turn bright red. Throw in the ginger and eggplant pieces and toss gently for several minutes, until the eggplant slices are shiny and soft. Add the miso-sake mixture, and stir gingerly to evenly coat the slices without smashing or breaking them. Sprinkle in the shiso leaves, toss once, and serve while still blisteringly hot.

RATIO oil : miso : sake—6 : 2 : 1.5

COUNTRY MISO SOUP

Inaka No Miso Shiru

4 SERVINGS
ACTIVE: 20 MIN; TOTAL: 45 MIN

Two 6-inch pieces of kombu
    (see Note)
1 cup (about ⅓ ounce) bonito
    flakes (see Note)
1½ tablespoons organic *inaka miso*
    (see Note)
1 medium carrot, halved lengthwise
    and sliced into ⅛-inch-thick
    half-moons
¼ medium daikon, quartered
    lengthwise and sliced
    ⅛ inch thick
1 large spring onion or 4 scallions,
    light green and white parts only,
    cut into 1-inch lengths
Julienned yuzu or lemon zest and
    chopped scallions, for garnish

Hachisu flavors this soup with just a hint of inaka miso, *a coarsely ground farmhouse variety. "The soup's very lightness compels you to pick up the bowl and slurp the broth in between bites of softened vegetables," she says.*

1. In a medium saucepan, cover the kombu with 4 cups of cold water and bring just to a boil; you will see small bubbles form on the edge of the kombu. Remove and discard the kombu. Add the bonito flakes to the saucepan and simmer for 8 minutes. Remove the saucepan from the heat and let stand for 8 minutes. Strain the dashi (broth) through a fine sieve into a large measuring cup. You should have about 2⅔ to 3 cups of dashi; if not, add enough water to make at least 2⅔ cups.

2. Place the miso in a small bowl. In a clean saucepan, bring the dashi to a simmer. Add the carrot and cook over moderate heat for 3 minutes. Add the daikon and spring onion and cook for 3 minutes longer. Whisk ¼ cup of the dashi into the miso until smooth, then add the miso mixture to the soup.

3. Ladle the soup into bowls, garnish with the yuzu zest and scallion and serve.

SERVE WITH Steamed rice.

NOTE Kombu is a type of dried kelp. Bonito flakes are made from smoked and dried tuna. *Inaka miso* is a coarse miso made from rice or barley. These ingredients are available at Japanese markets and *amazon.com.*

NANCY SINGLETON HACHISU ONLINE

nancysingletonhachisu.com

 Nancy Singleton Hachisu

 @nancyhachisu

MIKE ISABELLA'S

CRAZY GOOD ITALIAN

Mike Isabella with Carol Blymire

Mike Isabella, the Washington, DC, chef and love-him-or-hate-him *Top Chef* contestant, creates delicious modern Italian American food that draws from his big New Jersey–based family, his restaurant background and his two seasons on TV. (Thankfully, his cookbook includes the recipe for those incredible gnocchi from the Ellis Island episode of *Top Chef: All-Stars*.) Isabella's not an Italian-food purist, but he likes to do things right. In one chapter he urges you to make fresh agnolotti from scratch, a daunting four-page recipe; in the next he's got a recipe for totally inauthentic but incredibly tasty fish tacos with a crunchy fennel slaw and basil aioli (page 120). *Crazy Good Italian* is unpretentious and fun, taking you to a place somewhere between the Jersey Shore and the Amalfi Coast. PUBLISHED BY DA CAPO PRESS, $35

EGG NOODLES WITH SPINACH, OVEN-DRIED TOMATO & LEMON

SERVES 4 AS A SMALL PLATE
ACTIVE TIME: 1 HOUR
INACTIVE TIME: 2 HOURS

- ¾ pound grape tomatoes, halved
- 2 teaspoons plus 1 tablespoon extra-virgin olive oil
- 1½ teaspoons kosher salt (divided)
- 1 teaspoon dried oregano
- 1 cup small-diced onion
- 1 tablespoon minced garlic
- 5 ounces fresh baby spinach
- ¼ pound dried fettuccine egg noodles
- 2 large eggs
- ½ cup ricotta cheese
- ½ cup whole milk
- ¼ cup mascarpone, at room temperature
- Zest of ½ lemon
- 1 cup plus ½ cup shredded provolone cheese

EDITOR'S WINE CHOICE
Citrusy, full-bodied Italian white: 2011 Bibi Graetz Casamatta Toscana

The oven-dried tomatoes are what make this dish. You'll want those plump, warm tomatoes in every bite.

1. Preheat the oven to 225°F.

2. In a mixing bowl, toss the tomatoes with 2 teaspoons olive oil, ¼ teaspoon salt, and oregano until evenly coated.

3. Place a baking rack on a baking sheet and arrange the tomatoes flesh side up on the rack. Roast for 1½ to 1¾ hours. The tomatoes will shrivel but remain slightly plump in the center. Let cool at room temperature.

4. Raise the oven temperature to 375°F and bring a pot of salted water to a boil for the pasta. A good rule of thumb is to use 1 tablespoon of kosher salt per quart of water in your pot.

5. Heat the remaining 1 tablespoon olive oil in a large sauté pan over medium heat. Add the onions to the pan and sweat them for 5 to 6 minutes or until soft and translucent. Add the garlic and sauté for 2 minutes longer.

6. Add the spinach and ¼ teaspoon salt to the pan, tossing gently to wilt the spinach. Remove from heat, transfer to a large mixing bowl, and let cool to room temperature. Stir in the roasted tomatoes.

7. Add the egg noodles to the boiling water for 3 to 5 minutes, or until al dente. Drain, then toss noodles with the spinach mixture and let cool.

8. In a blender, purée the eggs, ricotta, milk, mascarpone, lemon zest, and remaining 1 teaspoon salt for 30 to 45 seconds or until smooth. Stir the purée into the spinach and noodle mixture along with 1 cup shredded provolone.

9. Transfer the mixture to a greased 8-by-8-inch baking dish and top with the remaining ½ cup shredded provolone.

10. Place the baking dish on a baking sheet in the oven for 35 to 40 minutes, or until the dish is heated through and the cheese is melted and bubbling. Remove from oven and let rest for 5 minutes before serving.

Ricotta and
provolone
make this
dish cheesy
and luscious.

ITALIAN FISH TACOS
with Fennel Slaw & Basil Aioli

SERVES 4 PEOPLE AS A SMALL PLATE;
MAKES 8 SMALL TACOS

ACTIVE TIME: 30 MINUTES

INACTIVE TIME: 20 MINUTES

1	cup water
½	cup champagne vinegar
½	cup sugar
½	cup shaved fennel bulb
¼	cup thinly sliced red onion
¼	cup thinly sliced red bell pepper, seeds and ribs removed
¼	cup shredded carrot
1	tablespoon extra-virgin olive oil
2	teaspoons fennel fronds
¼	teaspoon plus ½ teaspoon kosher salt
¾	pound cleaned bluefish fillet, skin removed, cut into 8 equal pieces (1.5 ounces each)
1	tablespoon canola oil
8	small (5-inch) flour tortillas
½	cup Basil Aioli (recipe follows)

I love tacos, and fish tacos are one of my favorite things to make. Fennel slaw and basil aioli give these fish tacos a Mediterranean feel. Flour tortillas are preferable to corn for the tacos in this recipe because they are softer and more pliable. If you can't find bluefish for this recipe, you could use tilapia or striped bass.

1. Heat an indoor grill pan or an outdoor grill to medium-high. In a medium saucepan, bring the water, champagne vinegar, and sugar to a boil over high heat, stirring to dissolve the sugar.

2. Combine the fennel, onion, pepper, and carrot in a large heatproof mixing bowl. When the liquid comes to a boil, remove from heat and pour it over the vegetables. Let the vegetables marinate at room temperature until cooled, about 15 to 20 minutes. Strain and discard the liquid. Toss olive oil, fennel fronds, and ¼ teaspoon salt with the vegetables.

3. Evenly brush the bluefish fillets on all sides with canola oil and season with remaining ½ teaspoon salt. Grill the bluefish for 2 to 3 minutes on each side, or until just cooked. While the fish is cooking, warm the tortillas on the grill.

4. To assemble, spoon Basil Aioli into the tortillas and top with bluefish and fennel slaw. Serve immediately.

NOTE Use a mandoline to slice the vegetables as thin as you can.

BASIL AIOLI

MAKES APPROXIMATELY ¾ CUP

ACTIVE TIME: 15 MINUTES

16	large basil leaves
2	cloves roasted garlic
2	large egg yolks
1	tablespoon lemon juice
½	teaspoon kosher salt
½	cup canola oil

1. Bring a medium saucepan of water to a boil. Set a bowl of ice water to the side. Blanch the basil leaves for 30 seconds and shock in ice water. Squeeze all the water from the leaves and rough chop.

2. In a food processor or blender, blend the basil, garlic, egg yolks, lemon juice, and salt for 10 seconds on medium speed.

3. With the food processor on, slowly add the canola oil. Blend for 15 seconds, or until a thick emulsion forms.

NOTE The aioli is best consumed the same day it's made. It will turn brown if refrigerated longer than 8 hours.

EDITOR'S WINE CHOICE
Ripe Sicilian white: 2011 Donnafugata Anthilia

MARINATED LAMB KABOB
with Yogurt & Dill Pesto

SERVES 4 AS A SMALL PLATE
ACTIVE TIME: 35 TO 40 MINUTES
INACTIVE TIME: 4 HOURS

- 2 teaspoons cumin seeds
- ½ cup plain Greek yogurt
- 1 tablespoon extra-virgin olive oil
- 2 teaspoons lemon juice
- ¼ teaspoon plus 1¾ teaspoons kosher salt
- 1 pound top round lamb, cut into 1-by-½-inch pieces
- 4 bamboo skewers, soaked in water
- ½ cup Dill Pesto (recipe follows)

I use top round lamb in this recipe because it's the best piece of the lamb leg for making kabobs. It's a small cut—usually 1 or 2 pounds—and it's incredibly tender with great flavor.

1. Toast the cumin seeds in a dry sauté pan over medium heat for 5 minutes, shaking the pan often to prevent burning. Transfer to a spice grinder and grind into a powder.

2. In a mixing bowl, combine the ground cumin, yogurt, olive oil, lemon juice, and ¼ teaspoon salt.

3. Put the lamb in a glass baking dish, pour the yogurt marinade over the meat, and toss to coat. Cover and refrigerate for at least 4 hours or overnight.

4. Remove the lamb from the refrigerator 15 minutes before you're ready to cook. Spear the lamb onto skewers, blotting any excess yogurt with a paper towel.

5. Heat an outdoor grill (or indoor grill pan) to medium-high. Season lamb with the remaining salt. Grill the lamb for 2 minutes, turn over, and grill for 1 minute longer. Serve with Dill Pesto on the side.

DILL PESTO

MAKES APPROXIMATELY ½ CUP
ACTIVE TIME: 15 TO 20 MINUTES

- 2 tablespoons walnuts
- 2 cups dill, tightly packed
- ¼ cup grated kefalograviera cheese (Greek cheese similar to Parmigiano-Reggiano)
- 1 teaspoon minced garlic
- ½ teaspoon kosher salt
- ⅓ cup extra-virgin olive oil

1. Toast the walnuts in a dry sauté pan for 5 minutes over medium heat, shaking the pan often to prevent burning.

2. In a food processor, combine the toasted walnuts, dill, kefalograviera cheese, garlic, and salt. Process while slowly adding the olive oil until a paste forms, approximately 30 to 45 seconds. You may need to stop and scrape down the sides of your food processor to incorporate all the ingredients.

NOTE Pesto can be refrigerated for up to 3 days. This pesto is meant to be a little "broken" in that it will separate slightly. Just whisk it for a few seconds to bring it back together before serving.

EDITOR'S WINE CHOICE
Earthy, cherry-rich Chianti Classico: 2010 Volpaia

SPARERIBS WITH ITALIAN PLUM GLAZE

SERVES 4 AS A SMALL PLATE
ACTIVE TIME: 1 HOUR, 30 MINUTES
INACTIVE TIME: 2 HOURS

- 2 tablespoons canola oil
- 3 pounds spareribs, cut into 4 equal portions
- 1 teaspoon kosher salt
- 1 teaspoon freshly cracked black pepper
- 1 cup thinly sliced onion
- ¼ cup thinly sliced garlic
- 1 cup dry red wine
- ½ cup balsamic vinegar
- ½ cup plus ½ cup plum preserves
- 1 quart chicken broth
- 2 tablespoons Worcestershire sauce
- 6 sprigs thyme
- 2 cinnamon sticks (about 2 inches each)
- 2 bay leaves
- 2 tablespoons black peppercorns

EDITOR'S NOTE
These succulent, sweet and saucy ribs are great paired with a tangy slaw.

EDITOR'S WINE CHOICE
Concentrated, spiced Barbera d'Alba: 2010 Vietti Tre Vigne

Spareribs are a great cut, and not only because they're inexpensive. They're close to the pig's belly, which means there's a little more fat on them. That helps them stay tender when they're being cooked. The plum glaze here is sweet, to balance the salt.

1. Preheat the oven to 350°F.

2. Heat the canola oil in a large, heavy-bottomed pot (oven-safe) or Dutch oven over medium-high heat. Season the ribs with salt and pepper. Sear the meaty side of the ribs for 1½ to 2 minutes or until golden brown and set aside.

3. Lower the heat to medium and add onions and garlic. Sweat for 2 minutes and add the wine, balsamic vinegar, and ½ cup plum preserves. Simmer for 15 to 20 minutes, or until the liquid has reduced by half.

4. Add the chicken broth, Worcestershire sauce, thyme, cinnamon sticks, bay leaves, and peppercorns. Bring to a low boil and return the ribs to the pot. Cover with lid and braise in the oven for 2 hours or until the meat is tender and pulls away from the bone.

5. Remove from the oven and let the ribs cool slightly, keeping the oven on. Take out the ribs and set aside on a baking sheet at room temperature.

6. Strain the liquid through a fine-mesh strainer into a large, heatproof bowl or saucepan. Skim off and discard the fat. Return the liquid to the heavy-bottomed pot and cook over medium-high heat. Simmer for 30 minutes to reduce the liquid by two-thirds and stir in the remaining ½ cup plum preserves. Simmer and reduce 5 to 10 minutes longer or until the liquid is syrupy.

7. Brush the reduced liquid onto the meaty side of the ribs and bake for 10 minutes. Brush on more glaze, and bake 5 minutes longer. Transfer the ribs to a serving dish and serve with the remaining plum glaze on the side.

BRAISED CAULIFLOWER
with Pickled Mustard Seeds

4 SERVINGS
ACTIVE: 45 MIN; TOTAL: 1 HR 15 MIN

- 1½ tablespoons mustard seeds
- ¼ cup white wine vinegar
- 2 tablespoons sugar
- ¼ cup extra-virgin olive oil
- ½ small yellow onion, diced (1 cup)
- 6 garlic cloves, thinly sliced
- 1½ teaspoons ground cumin
- 1½ teaspoons ground coriander
- 1½ teaspoons Aleppo pepper
- ½ teaspoon ground fenugreek
- 1 cup dry white wine
- 1¼ cups canned crushed tomatoes

Kosher salt

- 1 head of cauliflower, cut into 2-inch florets (about 5 cups)
- ½ cup canned chickpeas, rinsed and drained
- 2 tablespoons fresh lemon juice
- 2 tablespoons mint leaves, thinly sliced

For this fantastic Indian-influenced vegetarian main course, Isabella combines tender cauliflower with chickpeas, tomatoes and quick-pickled mustard seeds that pop in your mouth.

1. Preheat the oven to 375°F. In a small saucepan, combine the mustard seeds with 2 cups of water. Bring to a boil over high heat and simmer for 5 minutes. Drain the seeds in a fine sieve and rinse under cold water; drain well. Transfer the seeds to a heatproof bowl.

2. In the same saucepan, combine the vinegar and sugar with ½ cup of water. Bring to a boil, stirring to dissolve the sugar. Pour the boiling brine over the mustard seeds and let stand at room temperature for about 30 minutes, or until cooled.

3. Meanwhile, in a large, deep ovenproof skillet, heat the olive oil. Add the onion and cook over moderate heat, stirring occasionally, until softened, about 5 minutes. Add the garlic, cumin, coriander, Aleppo pepper and fenugreek and cook, stirring, for 1 minute. Add the wine and cook over high heat until almost evaporated, 6 to 8 minutes. Stir in the tomatoes and 1 teaspoon of salt and bring to a simmer. Cook over low heat, stirring occasionally, until the sauce is thickened, about 10 minutes.

4. Add the cauliflower to the skillet and stir to coat. Transfer the skillet to the oven and braise the cauliflower in the tomato sauce for 20 to 25 minutes, stirring every 5 minutes, until tender. Add the chickpeas and cook until heated through, about 3 minutes longer.

5. Drain the mustard seeds and add them to the cauliflower. Stir in the lemon juice and mint and season with salt. Transfer the braised cauliflower to a bowl and serve.

SERVE WITH Rice, couscous or quinoa.

MAKE AHEAD The braised cauliflower can be refrigerated for up to 2 days.

MIKE ISABELLA ONLINE

mikeisabella.com

f *Chef Mike Isabella*

t *@MikeIsabellaDC*

BOUCHON BAKERY

Thomas Keller & Sebastien Rouxel with Susie Heller, Matthew McDonald, Michael Ruhlman & Amy Vogler

Thomas Keller's cookbooks are famous for their thoroughness, beauty and attention to detail. His latest—featuring breads and pastries from his Bouchon Bakery empire—is no different. This sumptuous 400-page book is an awe-inspiring guide to mastering everything from perfect shortbread (page 128) to French *pâtisserie* classics like *palet d'or,* an ultra-rich chocolate cake (page 132). Throughout, the recipes' specificity is unrivaled: Ingredients are measured down to the tenth of a gram (though volumetric amounts are included as well) and instructions have a military-like precision. For instance, the chocolate in the chocolate chunk cookies (page 136) is to be chopped into ⅜-inch pieces, so get out a ruler. The idea isn't to torture or overwhelm the reader, but to reduce the variables, leading to a more consistently delicious result every single time. PUBLISHED BY ARTISAN, $50

SHORTBREAD

MAKES 24 COOKIES

180	grams (6.3 ounces) unsalted butter, at room temperature
90	grams (½ cup) granulated sugar
2	grams (½ plus ⅛ teaspoon) kosher salt
5.9	grams (1 teaspoon) vanilla paste
270	grams (1¾ cups plus 3 tablespoons) all-purpose flour
24	grams (2 tablespoons) granulated sugar for dusting

AUTHOR'S NOTE

Shortbread will maintain straight edges better if baked in a convection oven rather than in a standard oven.

Traditional shortbread is a rich, crumbly, buttery cookie made with nothing more than flour, butter, and sugar. It delights me that these most basic staple ingredients become so special in your hands when you treat them well and use them in the right proportions.

Shortbread is traditionally baked in a round or square pan, then cut into wedges or rectangles. Sebastien likes to cut the dough first, sprinkle it with sugar, and then bake it, for a more beautiful cookie with a sugary crust. Because of the large amount of butter, the dough should be well chilled before you roll it out; keeping the dough cold will also help the cut cookies retain their shape when baked.

This is a wonderfully versatile dough. For instance, you can roll out the dough, cut out shapes, bake them, and fill them to make sandwich cookies. Or make chocolate shortbread by replacing a quarter of the flour with unsweetened alkalized cocoa powder.

These are also good cookies to frost and decorate for the holidays.

Place the butter in the bowl of a stand mixer fitted with the paddle attachment. Turn to medium-low speed and cream until smooth. Add the 90 grams/½ cup sugar and the salt and mix on medium-low speed for about 2 minutes, until fluffy. Scrape down the sides and bottom of the bowl. Add the vanilla paste and mix on low speed for about 30 seconds to distribute it evenly.

Add the flour in 2 additions, mixing on low speed for 15 to 30 seconds after each, or until just combined. Scrape the bottom of the bowl to incorporate any flour that may have settled there.

Mound the dough on the work surface and, using the heel of your hand or a pastry scraper, push it together into a 5-inch-square block. Wrap in plastic wrap and refrigerate for at least 2 hours, until firm. (The dough can be refrigerated for up to 2 days or frozen for up to 1 month.)

Position the racks in the upper and lower thirds of the oven and preheat the oven to 325°F (convection or standard). Line two sheet pans with Silpats or parchment paper.

Unwrap the dough and place it between two pieces of parchment paper or plastic wrap. With a rolling pin, pound the top of the dough, working from left to right, to begin to flatten it, then turn the dough 90 degrees and repeat. (This will help prevent the dough from cracking as it is rolled.) Roll out to a 9-inch square. If the dough has softened, slide it (in the parchment) onto the back of a sheet pan and refrigerate it until it is firm enough to score. (See Note to Professionals.)

Using a chef's knife and a ruler, score the dough horizontally 3 times to mark four 2¼-inch-wide strips. Then score it vertically 5 times at 1½-inch intervals (for a total of 24 sections). If the dough is not cool to the touch, refrigerate it. Once it is firm, cut through the markings. (The dough can be shaped in advance; see Note on Advance Preparation.)

Dust the tops of the shortbread with the 24 grams/2 tablespoons granulated sugar and arrange on the prepared sheet pans, leaving about ¾ inch between them. Bake until pale golden brown, 13 to 15 minutes in a convection oven, 17 to 19 minutes in a standard oven, reversing the positions of the pans halfway through baking. Set the pans on a cooling rack and cool for 5 to 10 minutes, then transfer the cookies to the rack to cool completely.

The shortbread can be stored in a covered container for up to 3 days.

NOTE TO PROFESSIONALS To ensure a perfectly shaped block of dough, with no waste, we continue to shape the dough as it firms in the refrigerator. We smooth the top with a rolling pin and then push a straightedge against each side of the dough.

NOTE ON ADVANCE PREPARATION The shaped dough can be frozen on the sheet pan—wrapped in a few layers of plastic wrap—for up to 1 month. Transfer to a lined room-temperature sheet pan, and bake from frozen.

Shortbread, page 128

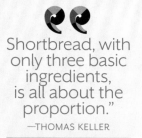

Shortbread, with
only three basic
ingredients,
is all about the
proportion."
—THOMAS KELLER

Glazing devil's food cake for
Palet d'Or, page 132

PALET D'OR

SERVES 8

Devil's Food Cake (recipe follows)

25 grams (0.8 ounce) brune pâte à glacer (see Note on Pâte à Glacer, page 134) or 55 to 70 percent chocolate, melted

CHOCOLATE CREAM

333 grams (1¼ cups plus 3 tablespoons) heavy cream

233 grams (8.2 ounces) 64 percent chocolate, chopped

50 grams (3 tablespoons plus 1 teaspoon) eggs

100 grams (¼ cup plus 3 tablespoons) egg yolks

83 grams (¼ cup plus 3 tablespoons) granulated sugar

CHOCOLATE GLAZE

7.2 grams (3 sheets) silver leaf gelatin (see Note on Gelatin, page 134)

150 grams (½ cup plus 2 tablespoons) heavy cream

225 grams (1 cup plus 2 tablespoons) granulated sugar

180 grams (¾ cup) water

75 grams (¾ cup plus 3 tablespoons) unsweetened alkalized cocoa powder, sifted

Gold leaf for garnishing

AUTHOR'S NOTES

You'll need an 8-by-1⅜-inch cake ring and a pastry bag with a ½-inch plain tip.

For this recipe, we use Cacao Barry brune pâte à glacer, Valrhona Manjari 64 percent chocolate, and Valrhona cocoa powder.

The palet d'or—literally, "gold disk"—conforms to my love of both simplicity and elegance. This beautiful cake looks as if it would be very difficult to make, like a cake you'd see in the fanciest pâtisserie, but it's actually quite simple: two thin layers of devil's food cake, chocolate cream, and a chocolate glaze. It's built within a cake ring, for perfectly straight, smooth, uniform sides.

This is a great example of how to make use of the freezer; the cake is essentially encased in cream, cream that would be impossible to glaze if it were not frozen. Once it's frozen, though, you remove the cake ring and pour the glaze over the cream-covered cake, and it sets up smooth and shiny. The cake can be refrigerated for up to a day and still retain the shine. It's garnished with a few flakes of gold leaf (be sure to use real gold leaf; imitation is not always edible).

Cut two 7¼-inch rounds from the cake. (The trimmings make great snacks.) Using a small offset spatula, spread the pâte à glacer or melted chocolate over each cake round.

Line a sheet pan with a Silpat and position the cake ring toward one end of the pan. Center a cake round (pâte à glacer side down) in the ring. Place the second cake round next to the ring, and freeze for about 1 hour.

FOR THE CHOCOLATE CREAM Whip the cream to soft peaks; refrigerate.

Melt the chocolate in the top of a double boiler. Transfer the chocolate to a large bowl and let cool to 100° to 120°F/37.7° to 48.8°C.

Meanwhile, whisk the eggs, egg yolks, and sugar in the (clean) top of the double boiler over simmering water. Initially the eggs will increase in volume and foam, but after 5 to 7 minutes, the foam will begin to subside and the eggs will thicken. Watch the temperature closely, as the eggs will begin to set if they get too hot; when the temperature reaches 183°F/83.8°C, immediately transfer them to the bowl of a stand mixer fitted with the whisk attachment and whip on medium-high speed for about 7 minutes, until the mixture thickens. When the whisk is lifted, the mixture should form a slowly dissolving ribbon.

Whisk one-third of the whipped cream into the chocolate to combine. Fold in the egg mixture, then fold in the remaining whipped cream. Transfer the chocolate cream to the pastry bag.

Remove the sheet pan from the freezer. Pipe a ring of cream to fill the gap between the edges of the cake and the ring. Then pipe a spiral, beginning in the center of the cake and extending to the edges of the pan. Center the second cake layer over the first layer. Repeat the piping, using enough cream to reach slightly above the rim of the ring. Sweep a long offset spatula over the cream from one side of the ring to the other for a perfectly smooth surface. Refrigerate the excess cream.

Place the sheet pan in the freezer. After several hours, check the cake. If the center has dipped, stir the reserved cream to soften it, then spread it over the top and smooth the surface again. Freeze overnight.

FOR THE CHOCOLATE GLAZE Place the gelatin in a bowl of ice water to soften.

Place the cream, sugar, and water in a large saucepan and bring to a boil. Whisk in the cocoa powder, reduce the heat to keep the mixture at a gentle boil, and cook for about 15 minutes, until the mixture has reduced by about one-third. Test by spooning a small amount onto a plate: run your finger through it—if it runs together, continue to reduce it until your finger leaves a track. Once it has reached the desired consistency, remove the mixture from the heat. Wring the excess water from the gelatin and whisk it into the cocoa mixture.

TO ASSEMBLE THE CAKE Line a sheet pan with parchment paper and set a cooling rack on top. Position the frozen cake, still in the ring, on the rack. Warm the sides of the ring with your hands or with warm towels, if necessary. (Do not use hot water—the cream must remain frozen.) Holding one side of the cake steady, lift up and remove the ring.

Reheat the glaze if necessary until hot, and strain through a fine-mesh strainer into a spouted measuring cup or directly over the cake. In one smooth, quick motion, pour the glaze over the top of the cake, beginning 1½ inches from the edges, allowing the glaze to flow down the sides and into the center to coat. Tap the sheet pan against the work surface to distribute the glaze evenly.

Let the glaze set for a few minutes and then, using a cake lifter or a wide spatula, lift the cake from the rack. If there are any drops of glaze

continued on page 134

PALET D'OR
continued

clinging to the bottom of the cake, carefully scrape them against the rack to remove them, then place the cake on a serving platter.

Using the tip of a paring knife, lift a piece of gold leaf from the package (gold leaf is incredibly light and will want to fold onto itself, so keep it away from drafts) and lower it onto the cake. We like to leave part of the gold leaf standing up, rather than having it all lie flat. (The cake can be refrigerated, uncovered, for up to 1 day, and the glaze will remain shiny.)

TO SERVE Run a slicing knife under hot water and dry it well. Slice the cake, heating the knife again as necessary to keep it clean. A palette knife is the best tool for transferring the slices to plates.

NOTE ON PÂTE À GLACER Pâte à glacer, sometimes referred to as compound chocolate, is used for coating. It can be used on fruits or on ice cream bars or cones, or to decorate cookies or desserts. Pâte à glacer is available in three different flavors—brune (dark), blonde (milk), and ivoire (white)—and it doesn't require tempering.

NOTE ON GELATIN We use only silver-leaf gelatin sheets. Sheet gelatin comes in bronze, silver, or gold, which have increasing strengths; silver is medium strength. Sheet gelatin has a purer flavor than powdered gelatin and is easier to work with.

DEVIL'S FOOD CAKE

This is the ultimate chocolate cake. We use it as the base for the Palet d'Or, but it's fabulous just by itself with some whipped cream or ice cream. Or use it as a component in a parfait. Or make cupcakes with the batter, piping it into regular liners or holiday cupcake papers.

Sebastien wanted the cake to be moist and rich, but not oily from too much butter. He decided to try mayonnaise instead, and the cake was superb. It was a brilliant revelation! Little did he know that chocolate mayonnaise cake was trendy in America, oh, some eighty years ago. It worked great then, and it works great now.

Preheat the oven to 325°F (standard). Line a sheet pan with a Silpat or spray lightly with nonstick spray, line with parchment paper, and spray the parchment.

MAKES 1 SHEET CAKE

101	grams (½ cup plus 3½ tablespoons) all-purpose flour
31	grams (¼ cup plus 2 tablespoons) unsweetened alkalized cocoa powder
2.5	grams (½ teaspoon) baking soda
0.5	gram (⅛ teaspoon) baking powder
1	gram (⅜ teaspoon) kosher salt
56	grams (3½ tablespoons) eggs
126	grams (½ cup plus 2 tablespoons) granulated sugar
2	grams (⅜ teaspoon) vanilla paste
86	grams (¼ cup plus 2½ tablespoons) mayonnaise
105	grams (¼ cup plus 3 tablespoons) water, at room temperature

AUTHOR'S NOTE

For this recipe, we use Valrhona cocoa powder.

Sift the flour, cocoa powder, baking soda, and baking powder into a medium bowl. Add the salt and whisk to combine.

Place the eggs, sugar, and vanilla paste in the bowl of a stand mixer fitted with the whisk attachment and mix on medium-low speed for about 1 minute to combine. Increase the speed to medium and whip for about 5 minutes, until the mixture is thick and pale yellow. Scrape down the sides and bottom of the bowl, then whip on medium-high speed for another 5 minutes, or until the mixture has thickened. When the whisk is lifted, the mixture should form a slowly dissolving ribbon.

Add the mayonnaise and whip to combine. Remove the bowl from the mixer stand and fold in the dry ingredients and water in 2 additions each.

Pour the batter into the prepared pan and, using an offset spatula, spread it in an even layer, making sure that it reaches into the corners. Bake for 10 minutes, or until a skewer inserted in the center comes out clean and the cake springs back when lightly touched. Set on a cooling rack and cool completely.

Lay a piece of parchment paper on the back of a sheet pan. Run a knife around the edges of the cake to loosen it and invert it onto the parchment. Remove the Silpat or parchment from the top of the cake.

Wrapped in a few layers of plastic wrap, the cake can be kept at room temperature for up to 4 hours, refrigerated for up to 3 days, or frozen for up to 2 weeks.

If you will be cutting the cake into shapes, the cake should be frozen before cutting. If frozen, and not being cut into shapes, the cake should be defrosted in the refrigerator still in the plastic wrap (this way, any condensation will form on the outside and not on the cake).

CHOCOLATE CHUNK & CHIP COOKIES

MAKES SIX 4-INCH COOKIES

238	grams (1½ cups plus 3 tablespoons) all-purpose flour
2.3	grams (½ teaspoon) baking soda
3	grams (1 teaspoon) kosher salt
134	grams (½ cup plus 2 tablespoons) lightly packed dark brown sugar
12	grams (1¾ teaspoons) unsulfured blackstrap molasses
104	grams (½ cup plus 1 teaspoon) granulated sugar
107	grams (⅔ cup) ⅜-inch chunks 70 to 72 percent chocolate
107	grams (scant ½ cup) chocolate chips
167	grams (5.9 ounces) unsalted butter, at room temperature
60	grams (3 tablespoons plus 2½ teaspoons) eggs

AUTHOR'S NOTES

You'll need a 2½-inch (#10) ice cream scoop.

For this recipe, we use Valrhona Guanaja 70 percent or Guittard 72 percent chocolate.

Cookies baked in a convection oven will have a more even color and will not spread as much as those baked in a standard oven.

For smaller cookies, divide the dough into 12 equal portions (75 grams each). Bake for 12 to 14 minutes in a convection oven, 16 to 18 minutes in a standard oven.

Bouchon Bakery is well known for its cookies. We love our cookies, and we make them big. The chocolate chunk and chip recipe was one of our first. In most cooking or baking, varying textures is important, and cookies are no different. This is why we use both chocolate chunks and chocolate chips, which behave differently in the dough. The chunks melt, but the chips don't.

I've always believed that when you have a special, expensive ingredient—truffles, for instance, or foie gras—it's important to offer it in abundance so that people know what the fuss is about. Chocolate falls into that category here—these cookies are packed with chocolate. (When we want even more chocolate flavor, as in our Double Chocolate Chunk and Chip Cookies, we replace about 25 percent of the flour with cocoa powder.) We use plenty of brown sugar as well as molasses for a deep, rich flavor. If you like nuts in your cookies, feel free to add them instead of either the chocolate chunks or the chocolate chips.

Place the flour in a medium bowl. Sift in the baking soda. Add the salt and whisk together. Place the dark brown sugar in a small bowl and stir in the molasses and granulated sugar, breaking up any lumps; the mixture will not be completely smooth.

Place the chocolate chunks in a strainer and tap the side to remove any powdered chocolate, which would cloud the cookies. Mix with the chocolate chips.

Place the butter in the bowl of a stand mixer fitted with the paddle attachment. Turn to medium-low speed and cream the butter, warming the bowl if needed (see Note on Pommade, page 138), until it is the consistency of mayonnaise and holds a peak when the paddle is lifted. Add the molasses mixture and mix for 3 to 4 minutes, until fluffy. Scrape down the sides and bottom of the bowl. Add the eggs and mix on low speed for 15 to 30 seconds, until just combined. Scrape the bowl again. The mixture may look broken, but that is fine (overwhipping the eggs could cause the cookies to expand too much during baking and then deflate).

continued on page 138

CHOCOLATE CHUNK & CHIP COOKIES
continued

Add the dry ingredients in 2 additions, mixing on low speed for 15 to 30 seconds after each, or until just combined. Scrape the bottom of the bowl to incorporate any dry ingredients that have settled there. Add the chocolates and pulse on low speed about 10 times to combine. Refrigerate the dough for 30 minutes.

Position the racks in the upper and lower thirds of the oven and preheat the oven to 325°F (convection or standard). Line two sheet pans with Silpats or parchment paper.

Using the ice cream scoop, divide the dough into 6 equal portions, 150 grams each. Roll each one into a ball between the palms of your hands. (The dough can be shaped in advance; see Note on Advance Preparation.)

The cookies are very large; bake only 3 on each pan. With a short end of the pan toward you, place one cookie in the upper left corner, one in the lower left corner, and the third one in the center, toward the right side of the pan. Bring the dough to room temperature before baking.

Bake until golden brown, 14 to 16 minutes in a convection oven, 18 to 20 minutes in a standard oven, reversing the positions of the pans halfway through baking. Set the pans on a cooling rack and cool for 5 to 10 minutes, then transfer the cookies to the rack to cool completely.

The cookies are best the day they are baked, but they can be stored in a covered container for up to 3 days.

NOTE ON POMMADE Before we cream butter for some cookie doughs or some tart doughs, we want the butter to be so soft and creamy that it forms soft peaks and has a consistency like mayonnaise. Typically we warm the mixer bowl with the butter in it, by holding the bowl over a burner, or using a blowtorch against the outside of the bowl, to encourage the softening.

NOTE ON ADVANCE PREPARATION The shaped dough can be refrigerated for up to 2 days before baking. For longer storage, freeze the dough in a covered container or a plastic bag for up to 1 month; the day before baking, place the cookies on a lined baking sheet and defrost in the refrigerator overnight. Bring to room temperature before baking.

GRAPEFRUIT TEA CAKE

8 SERVINGS
ACTIVE: 30 MIN; TOTAL: 1 HR 30 MIN PLUS
2 HR COOLING

SYRUP
- ¾ cup fresh grapefruit juice
- ⅓ cup granulated sugar

CAKE
Unsalted butter, for greasing
- ½ cup all-purpose flour, plus more for dusting
- ½ cup semolina
- 1 teaspoon baking powder
- ½ teaspoon kosher salt
- ½ cup plus 2 tablespoons granulated sugar
- 1 large egg
- ½ cup whole milk
- ⅓ cup olive oil
- 1 tablespoon finely grated grapefruit zest

ICING
- ⅔ cup confectioners' sugar
- 2 tablespoons fresh grapefruit juice

This lovely tea cake is from Sebastien Rouxel, executive pastry chef for the Thomas Keller Restaurant Group. Soaking the cake in a simple grapefruit syrup makes it incredibly moist, with just a hint of fresh citrus flavor.

1. MAKE THE SYRUP In a small saucepan, combine the grapefruit juice and granulated sugar and bring to a simmer. Cook, stirring, until the sugar dissolves. Transfer the syrup to a small bowl and let cool to room temperature, about 30 minutes.

2. MEANWHILE, MAKE THE CAKE Preheat the oven to 325°F. Butter and flour an 8-by-4-inch loaf pan. In a small bowl, sift together the ½ cup of flour, the semolina, baking powder and salt. In a large bowl, whisk the granulated sugar and egg until pale yellow, about 3 minutes. Whisk in the milk, then the olive oil and grapefruit zest. Gradually whisk in the dry ingredients until well incorporated.

3. Pour the batter into the prepared loaf pan. Bake for 30 minutes, then lower the oven temperature to 300°F. Rotate the cake and bake for 20 to 25 minutes longer, until a cake tester inserted in the center comes out clean. Transfer the cake to a rack set over a baking sheet and generously brush the top of the cake with the cooled syrup. Let the cake cool for 30 minutes before unmolding.

4. MAKE THE ICING In a medium bowl, whisk the confectioners' sugar and grapefruit juice until smooth. Spoon the icing over the top of the cake and let stand for at least 2 hours before slicing.

MAKE AHEAD The cake can be kept at room temperature for up to 2 days.

BOUCHON BAKERY ONLINE
bouchonbakery.com
f *Bouchon Bakery*
t *@Chef_Keller*

French Bread Pizza
Sandwiches with
Hot Italian Sausage,
page 142

EMERIL'S
KICKED-UP
SANDWICHES

Emeril Lagasse

"What makes a good sandwich great?" superstar chef Emeril Lagasse asks at the beginning of his 17th cookbook. Over the following 350 pages and 100-plus recipes, Lagasse proves that he knows exactly how to achieve sandwich greatness: with inspired combinations of ingredients, lively condiments and small updates that turn simple deli standards into something sublime. Just a few additions to his egg salad supreme (page 144)—dry mustard, hot paprika, minced shallot and green onion— bring a bit of heat, crunch and depth. His French bread pizza (pictured at left) is unfathomably more delicious than the frozen kind, and intensely flavorful—he starts by topping garlic bread with a 20-minute marinara sauce, then adds three types of cheese and hot Italian sausage. With Lagasse's attention to detail, this kind of sliced-bread genius is easily within your grasp. PUBLISHED BY WILLIAM MORROW, $25

FRENCH BREAD PIZZA SANDWICHES WITH HOT ITALIAN SAUSAGE

4 SANDWICHES, 4 SERVINGS

- 8 tablespoons (1 stick) unsalted butter
- 2 teaspoons minced garlic
- ¼ teaspoon salt
- 1 teaspoon freshly squeezed lemon juice
- 1 tablespoon minced fresh parsley leaves
- 1 loaf French or Italian bread, about 22 inches long
- 1 tablespoon olive oil
- 1½ pounds hot Italian sausage, casings removed and meat crumbled
- 2 cups Quick Tomato Sauce (recipe follows) or other marinara sauce
- 8 ounces mozzarella cheese, grated
- 8 ounces Fontina cheese, grated
- 2 tablespoons chopped fresh thyme leaves
- ½ teaspoon crushed red pepper
- ¼ cup finely grated Parmigiano-Reggiano cheese

Extra-virgin olive oil, for drizzling (optional)

EDITOR'S WINE CHOICE

Berry-rich, medium-bodied Italian red: 2010 Matteo Correggia Barbera d'Alba

Hey, guys, it doesn't get much easier than this. Here we top fresh garlic bread with tomato sauce, cheese, and sausage. Work fast, because your guests will hardly be able to wait for you to bake it with the toppings—the smell from the baking bread alone is enough to make 'em crazy. And go ahead, the buck doesn't stop here: Use your favorite toppings.

1. Preheat the oven to 350°F. Line a baking sheet with aluminum foil or parchment paper for easier cleanup.

2. Melt the butter in a small pan, and combine it with the garlic, salt, lemon juice, and parsley.

3. Halve the bread lengthwise and cut each half in half crosswise. Using your fingers, gently scoop out and discard some of the soft inner part of the thickest portion of the bread, leaving a 1-inch-thick shell. Brush the inside of the bread with the garlic butter. Place the sections, cut side up, on the prepared baking sheet, and bake in the oven until golden, aromatic, and lightly toasted, about 6 minutes. Remove the bread from the oven (leave it on the baking sheet) and raise the oven temperature to 400°F.

4. Heat the olive oil in a medium skillet over medium heat. Add the sausage and cook, stirring as needed, until it is browned and the fat is rendered, about 8 minutes. Using a slotted spoon, transfer the sausage to a paper-towel-lined plate, and set aside.

5. Spoon the tomato sauce evenly over the pieces of bread. Divide the mozzarella and Fontina evenly over the sauce. Top with the sausage, and then garnish with the thyme, crushed red pepper, and Parmesan. Bake for 8 minutes, or until hot and bubbly. Serve immediately, drizzled with extra-virgin olive oil if desired.

1¾ CUPS

- 1 tablespoon olive oil
- 1 onion, chopped
- 3 cloves garlic, chopped
- One 28-ounce can whole peeled tomatoes, drained and pureed
- 1 sprig fresh thyme
- ½ teaspoon salt
- ½ teaspoon freshly ground black pepper
- 1 tablespoon extra-virgin olive oil

QUICK TOMATO SAUCE

Heat the olive oil in a small saucepan over medium heat. Add the onion and garlic, and cook for 3 minutes, until soft. Add the tomatoes, thyme sprig, salt, and pepper, and simmer for 20 minutes. Remove from the heat. Stir in the extra-virgin olive oil, discard the thyme sprig, and set aside until ready to use.

EGG SALAD SUPREME

6 SANDWICHES, ABOUT 3 CUPS FILLING

- 12   hard-boiled eggs
- ½   teaspoon salt
- 1   teaspoon dry mustard
- ½   teaspoon hot Hungarian paprika
- ¼   cup minced shallot
- ¼   cup chopped green onion or fresh parsley leaves
- ¼   cup minced celery
- ½   cup mayonnaise, homemade (recipe follows) or store-bought
- 12   slices white sandwich bread (see Editor's Note)

1½ CUPS

- 1   large egg, at room temperature (see Raw Egg Warning)
- 1   large egg yolk, at room temperature
- 1½   teaspoons freshly squeezed lemon juice, or more to taste
- ½   teaspoon Dijon mustard
- ½ to ¾   teaspoon minced garlic
- ½   teaspoon kosher salt, or more to taste
- ¼   teaspoon freshly ground white pepper or ground cayenne pepper, or more to taste
- 1   cup vegetable oil
- ¼   cup olive oil

EDITOR'S NOTE

Lagasse provides a recipe for white sandwich bread in his book. Alternatively, you can buy a fresh Pullman loaf from a bakery.

Here's a simple, delicious sandwich. The dry mustard and paprika give it a wonderful surprising wasabi-y or horseradish-y accent.

1. Roughly chop the eggs and place them in a mixing bowl. Add the salt, mustard, paprika, shallot, green onion, celery, and mayonnaise. Stir with a rubber spatula or a spoon until very well blended. Transfer to a container, cover, and refrigerate for at least 2 hours and up to 4 days.

2. Spread ⅓ to ½ cup of the egg salad between 2 slices of bread. Repeat with the remaining salad and bread.

HOMEMADE MAYONNAISE

Once you've perfected this simple classic, you'll hesitate about going back to store-bought. My version here has a hint of garlic, but if you're not a garlic lover, simply omit it and the mayonnaise will be just as delicious.

In the bowl of a food processor, combine the egg, egg yolk, lemon juice, mustard, garlic, salt, and pepper. Process on high speed until smooth, light yellow, and frothy, about 1 minute. While the processor is still running, combine the vegetable and olive oils in a measuring cup with a pour spout, and working very slowly, add the oil to the processor in a thin, steady stream, processing until the oil is completely incorporated and a thick emulsion is formed. (It is very important that the oil is added very slowly, especially at the beginning, otherwise the mayonnaise may break.) Transfer the mayonnaise to a nonreactive bowl, and add more salt, pepper, and/or lemon juice if desired. Use immediately, or refrigerate in an airtight nonreactive container for up to 3 days.

RAW EGG WARNING I suggest using caution when consuming raw eggs because of the slight risk of salmonella or other food-borne illness. To reduce this risk, I recommend that you use only fresh, properly refrigerated, clean, grade A or AA eggs with intact shells, and always avoid contact between the yolks or whites and the outside portion of the eggshell.

PHILLY CHEESESTEAK, MY WAY

4 SANDWICHES

Two 1-pound rib-eye steaks
(see Author's Note)

Four 8-inch sections French bread or
po'boy bread

8 slices provolone cheese
(about 8 ounces)

8 slices good-quality American
cheese (about 8 ounces)

¼ cup vegetable oil

4 cups small-diced onion

2 cups sliced green bell pepper

2 teaspoons salt

¾ teaspoon freshly ground
black pepper

¼ cup roughly chopped jarred
cherry (pimento) peppers
or Peppadew peppers (see
Editor's Note)

AUTHOR'S NOTE

*Rib-eye steaks will give you the
tenderest meat, but you can use sirloin
or top round as well.*

EDITOR'S NOTE

*Peppadews are sweet-spicy pickled
peppers from South Africa. They're sold at
specialty stores and many supermarkets.*

EDITOR'S WINE CHOICE

Inky, juicy Malbec: 2010 Luigi Bosca

Most of us don't have a flat-top griddle in our house to make a perfectly authentic-tasting Philly cheesesteak. But I have a great way to mimic the method for this iconic sandwich: Griddle the onions and peppers in a cast-iron skillet instead, and then keep them warm until you're ready to slather them on top of the meat and cheese. Just as you're filling the sandwich, it all melts together—with a few cherry peppers for a twist.

1. Wrap each steak individually in plastic wrap, place them in the freezer, and freeze for about 3 hours; this will make it easier to slice the meat.

2. Remove 1 steak from the freezer and use a very sharp knife to slice it as thin as you can, discarding any pockets of fat. Set aside, and repeat with the other steak.

3. Preheat the oven to 300°F.

4. Slice open the French bread, and set it aside on a large baking sheet.

5. Arrange the cheese in four overlapping piles on a large serving platter, alternating slices of provolone and American.

6. Heat 2 tablespoons of the olive oil in a large cast-iron skillet set over medium-high heat. Add the onion and bell pepper, 1 teaspoon of the salt, and ¼ teaspoon of the black pepper. Cook, stirring occasionally, until the onion is lightly caramelized and tender, about 8 minutes. Stir in the cherry peppers, and then transfer the onion and peppers to the same baking sheet with the bread, and place in the oven to keep warm while you cook the steak.

7. Making 2 sandwiches at a time, increase the heat under the skillet to high and add 1 tablespoon oil. Add half the steak slices, season them with ½ teaspoon salt and ¼ teaspoon pepper, and cook without stirring until most of the meat has browned on one side, about 1 minute. Stir the meat, and then divide it into two cylindrical portions. Lay a shingled pile of cheese over each pile of meat. Remove the baking sheet from the oven and spoon one-quarter of the onion and peppers over each cheese-topped meat pile. Continue to cook in the skillet, undisturbed, for 1 minute longer, or until the cheese begins to melt from the heat of the vegetables. Using a large spatula, transfer each of the meat portions to a bottom half of the bread. Set the 2 filled sandwiches on a small baking sheet and place them in the oven to keep warm. Wipe the skillet clean and repeat to make the other 2 sandwiches.

GRILLED ALMOND BUTTER SANDWICHES

with Bananas & Dark Chocolate

TOTAL: 30 MIN
MAKES 4 SANDWICHES

- 2 cups slivered blanched almonds
- 2 tablespoons grapeseed or canola oil
- 1 teaspoon turbinado sugar, such as Sugar in the Raw

Pinch of kosher salt

- 8 slices of whole wheat bread
- 6 ounces semisweet chocolate, finely chopped (1 cup)
- 4 small bananas, sliced ¼ inch thick
- 4 tablespoons unsalted butter

AUTHOR'S NOTE

The sandwiches can be made with a variety of ingredients. For example, you can replace the chocolate with honey or use cherry or plum jam in place of the bananas and chocolate.

Lagasse upgrades simple peanut butter and banana sandwiches by swapping in homemade almond butter and dark chocolate. Gooey and not too sweet, the sandwiches are fabulous on whole wheat bread.

1. Preheat the oven to 350°F. Spread the almonds on a baking sheet and toast for 6 to 7 minutes, until golden brown. Let cool completely.

2. In a food processor, combine the almonds, grapeseed oil, sugar and salt and blend until smooth, scraping down the side of the bowl as necessary.

3. On a work surface, spread 2 tablespoons of the almond butter on each of 4 slices of the bread. Top with the chopped chocolate and the banana slices and close the sandwiches.

4. In a large nonstick skillet, melt 1 tablespoon of the butter. Add 2 sandwiches and cook until golden, about 2 minutes. Flip the sandwiches, add 1 tablespoon of butter and cook until golden on the second side, about 2 minutes longer. Transfer the sandwiches to a cutting board. Repeat with the remaining butter and sandwiches. Cut the sandwiches in half or quarters and serve hot.

MAKE AHEAD The almond butter can be refrigerated for up to 2 weeks.

EMERIL LAGASSE ONLINE

emerils.com

f Emeril Lagasse

t @Emeril

POLPO

A VENETIAN COOKBOOK (OF SORTS)

Russell Norman

After falling in love with the backstreet bars of Venice known as *bàcari* and their menus of small plates, chef Russell Norman brought the concept to London, creating the hit restaurant Polpo. Its motto: "Venetian snacks adapted for metropolitan sensibilities in a relaxed and slightly jaded urban setting." The best of those dishes are presented in this cookbook, which matches romantic photos of the iconic Italian city with Norman's unpretentious and elemental food based on years of eating there. Throughout, the ingredient lists are often short, as his recipes rely on pure flavors and clever combinations (as in the braised scallops, pancetta and peas, page 152). Still, Norman will stray from tradition to create something as accessible as his crispy-soft roast potatoes and rosemary (page 150), "not a typical Venetian dish, but fast to prepare, very tasty and great to snack on." PUBLISHED BY BLOOMSBURY, $50

ROAST POTATOES & ROSEMARY

FOR 4 TO 6

- 2 kg [about 4½ pounds]
  general-purpose potatoes
  (e.g., Maris Piper, Estima, Desiree;
  see Editor's Note)
- 1 handful of rosemary sprigs,
  leaves picked

Extra-virgin olive oil
Flaky sea salt and black pepper

EDITOR'S NOTE

*If these varieties are not available, Idaho
potatoes work well in this recipe, too.*

Potatoes don't really feature in Italian cooking in the way they do in other European countries. You find potatoes in Italian recipes as an ingredient rather than something to accompany protein—polenta has taken on that mantle.

I did find a recipe for Venetian-style Potatoes, which was simply chopped onions and small-cut potatoes sautéed in butter and olive oil over medium heat for 30 minutes with chopped parsley thrown in at the end. It's actually rather nice.

The recipe below, also using potatoes cut into small, bite-sized pieces, is not a typical Venetian dish, but I like it a lot because it is relatively fast to prepare, very tasty, and great to snack on.

Peel and cut the potatoes into small chunks. Boil in salted water until they are cooked through but holding their shape. Drain in a colander. Shake the potatoes around in the colander until the sides are rough and fluffy. Leave for 10 minutes to cool slightly and lose their excess moisture.

While the potatoes are drying, preheat your oven to 220°C/Gas 7 [425°F]. Heat your roasting tray in the hot oven with the rosemary, several good glugs of olive oil, salt and pepper. Take the tray out, place your parboiled potatoes in and coat well with the oil and rosemary. Roast the potatoes, turning and shaking every 15 minutes until ready. They should take no more than about 45 minutes.

These
potatoes
are crunchy
outside,
fluffy inside.

BRAISED SCALLOPS, PANCETTA & PEAS

FOR 4

8	rashers [slices] of thinly sliced pancetta
2	tablespoons extra-virgin olive oil
16	spring onions
500	grams [about 1 pound] peas—fresh if you can, frozen if not
2	heads of baby gem lettuce, cut into bite-sized pieces
50	grams [about 3½ tablespoons] unsalted butter
12	small scallops (or 6 sliced in half horizontally if very large)

Crusty bread, to serve

EDITOR'S WINE CHOICE

Crisp northern Italian white: 2011 Elena Walch Pinot Grigio

Scallops and peas are perfect companions. This recipe brings a little salty contrast to the sweetness of peas and scallops with the addition of pancetta.

In Venice, the scallops are usually the local variety known as "pilgrims." They are exquisite and relatively small. If you are using the diver-caught scallops, on sale at most good fishmongers I know, then they will be significantly larger. If they are particularly big, simply slice them in half horizontally.

Cut the pancetta into 2-cm [about ¾-inch] strips. Fry in a large pan with the olive oil until browned. Cut the spring onions into 5-cm [about 2-inch] pieces and add to the pan. When they have wilted slightly add all the peas and enough water to cover. Simmer for 3 minutes for frozen peas and 5 to 6 minutes for fresh peas.

Add the chopped baby gem lettuce and the butter and continue to simmer gently. After 1 minute add the scallops and simmer for 1 more minute. Take off the heat and serve almost as a broth in shallow bowls. Have some good crusty bread in the middle of the table to mop up the juices.

PORK & BEEF POLPETTE

FOR 30 BALLS
(3 TO 5 PER PERSON)

- 1 kg minced pork [about 2 pounds ground pork]
- 500 grams minced beef [about 1 pound ground beef]
- 3 medium free-range eggs
- Scant ½ tablespoon fine salt
- 1 teaspoon black pepper
- 150 grams [about 1 cup] breadcrumbs
- Small pinch of dried chilli flakes
- 3 garlic cloves, finely chopped
- ½ handful of flat parsley leaves, chopped
- 1½ litres [about 6⅓ cups] tomato sauce (recipe follows)

EDITOR'S WINE CHOICE
Medium-bodied Chianti Classico:
2007 Fattoria di Ródano

Who doesn't like meatballs? A good meatball is a sublime thing. It has texture and flavour and it's comforting and fun. We often think of it as an American invention. For as long as I can remember, New York has been in the grip of a meatball craze, a sort of revival of the working-class, Depression-era staple that is cheap, easy to make, nutritious and tasty. You can, after all, pretty much mince anything as long as you flavour it with enough salt, pepper and herbs. But meatballs are, of course, as Italian as spaghetti. In Italy they call them polpette.

Talking of spaghetti, you could serve these meatballs with any pasta but they go particularly well with linguine. Just make sure you are generous with the tomato sauce and grate plenty of Parmesan over your individual servings.

We make and serve 25,000 polpette* a year at Polpo. The classic pork and beef is our most popular variety.

Preheat the oven to 220°C/Gas 7 [425°F]. Combine all the ingredients (except the tomato sauce), massage thoroughly and roll into 45-gram [about 2-tablespoon] spheres, like large golf balls. Place the balls on a greased baking tray and roast in the oven for 10 minutes, turning once, until they are starting to brown. Then poach in the tomato sauce in a covered saucepan for 10 minutes.

Serve 3 to 5 balls per person with some lightly toasted focaccia to mop up the juices.

*A word on Italian vocabulary. Our second restaurant was called Polpetto. Many people have informed me that it means meatball. Not so. A polpetta is a meatball, the plural being polpette because it is feminine. Polpetto is a rather cutesy word, not often used, that is a diminutive for baby octopus. The plural here would be polpetti because it is masculine. You will rarely see this in restaurants as Italians generally call small octopuses moscardini. I hope that's all clear now . . .

continued on page 156

No need
to fry these
meatballs;
they brown
in the oven.

PORK & BEEF POLPETTE
continued

FOR 1½ LITRES [ABOUT 6⅓ CUPS]

100	ml [scant ½ cup] extra-virgin olive oil
1	onion, finely sliced
1	garlic clove, chopped
Scant ½ tablespoon fine salt	
¾	teaspoon black pepper
Small pinch of chilli flakes	
750	grams [about 1¾ pounds] fresh tomatoes, quartered
Three	400-gram tins [one and a half 28-ounce cans] of chopped tomatoes
1	small handful of oregano, chopped
Caster sugar [superfine sugar], if necessary	

BASIC TOMATO SAUCE

There was a time when Italian restaurants in London and New York tended to offer a very narrow version of Italian cooking. Often the menu would consist of a variety of pasta dishes with a small range of sauces, nearly all of them tomato-based. We have moved on from this simplistic notion of Italian cuisine but I still have a respectful admiration for the old-school approach of the traditional trattoria where tomato sauce is king. I also love the way New Yorkers refer to these places as "red sauce joints."

A good tomato sauce is such a useful commodity to have to hand and, although the convenience of tinned passata has made shortcuts incredibly tempting, I would still recommend that you make a big batch of this sauce and save what you don't use in the fridge. It will keep for up to a week. (In Italy it keeps longer—you simply scrape the mould off the top before using.)

Heat half the oil in a saucepan on a medium-low flame and in it sweat the onion, garlic, salt, pepper and chilli for 15 minutes. When the onions are glossy and transparent, add the fresh tomatoes and the rest of the oil and cook gently for a further 15 minutes.

Add the tinned tomatoes, bring to a gentle bubble and then simmer on a very low heat for 1 hour.

Take the pan off the heat and add the chopped oregano. You can season the sauce with a little sugar, to taste—it will depend on how sweet your tomatoes are. Transfer to a food blender or use a hand-blender to blitz for a few minutes. If you like, pass through a fine sieve.

RUSSELL NORMAN ONLINE

polpo.co.uk

🅑 *@Ape45l*

BURRATA WITH LENTILS & BASIL OIL

FOR 6

Leaves from a bunch of basil
Flaky sea salt and black pepper
Extra-virgin olive oil

400	grams [about 14 ounces] Puy lentils
2	large carrots, finely chopped
3	celery sticks, finely chopped
1	small onion, finely chopped
3	garlic cloves, finely chopped
5	sprigs of thyme, leaves removed and chopped
100	ml [scant ½ cup] extra-virgin olive oil
25	ml [about 1 tablespoon plus 2 teaspoons] red wine vinegar
1	tablespoon Dijon mustard
1	teaspoon caster sugar [very fine granulated sugar, also known as superfine sugar]
150	grams [about 5 ounces] mature Gorgonzola, cut into very small chunks (see Author's Note)
6	burrata balls

AUTHOR'S NOTE

You should avoid using young, creamy Gorgonzola, as the vinegar in the dressing tends to melt it. Choose the more mature, crumbly variety, which also has more piquancy.

EDITOR'S WINE CHOICE

Fruit-forward, minerally Italian white: 2011 Terredora di Paolo Falanghina Irpinia

Burrata is often confused with mozzarella but they are not the same. Burrata is made in Puglia with milk from Razza Podolica cows (not buffalo) and with added cream, so it is softer and more moist than mozzarella. Burrata's creamy, sweet consistency is the perfect foil to an array of ingredients. It is a delight with bitter cime di rapa [broccoli rabe], for example. This recipe combines it with lentils—a heavenly marriage. Make sure your burrata is of the finest quality and at room temperature. Serving it fridge-cold kills the texture and the flavour.

First make the basil oil by placing most of the basil leaves in a food processor, reserving a few of the smaller prettier ones for decorating at the end. Add a little salt and enough olive oil to make a thin sauce. Whizz for a few seconds and then set aside.

Put the lentils in a saucepan with enough cold water to cover them by about 7 cm [about 2¾ inches]. Don't add salt at this stage as this will toughen the lentils. Bring to the boil and cook for about 45 minutes. Keep checking them—they need to still hold a small bite. When they are done, drain, refresh in cold water, drain again and set aside.

Now, in a large heavy-based pan sweat the vegetables in a few good glugs of olive oil with the thyme leaves, a large pinch of salt and a twist of ground black pepper. When the vegetables are softened and translucent, add the cooked lentils and a splash of water to stop them sticking to the bottom of the pan.

To make the mustard dressing, put the olive oil, red wine vinegar, Dijon mustard, a small pinch of salt, a couple of grinds of pepper and the sugar into a bowl and whisk together. Add the very small chunks of Gorgonzola and mix them into the dressing.

To finish the dish, add 4 tablespoons of the mustard dressing [reserve the rest for another use] to the lentils, check the seasoning and spoon onto a large warm plate. Then tear open your burrata and place on top of the warm lentils. The heat from the lentils will melt the burrata making it even more creamy and soft.

Drizzle some basil oil over the top and scatter with the reserved basil leaves.

Roasted Chicken with
Clementines & Arak, page 164

JERUSALEM

Yotam Ottolenghi & Sami Tamimi

After the success of his groundbreaking 2011 vegetarian cookbook, *Plenty,* London-based, Jerusalem-born chef and restaurateur Yotam Ottolenghi returns with a book that's even closer to his heart. Co-written with his business partner, Sami Tamimi, *Jerusalem* is filled with recipes inspired by the ancient city, a place "where culinary traditions often overlap and interact in upredictable ways, creating food mixes that belong to specific groups but also to everybody else." Ottolenghi is Jewish (of Italian descent) and Tamimi is Palestinian, yet they've created a book with no political agenda—except the hope that food can build bridges. There are exemplary versions of classics such as tabbouleh and hummus, but more exciting are the pair's original ideas, like cauliflower and hazelnuts in a sweet-sour vinaigrette (page 162) or chicken roasted with clementines, fennel and anise liqueur (pictured at left). PUBLISHED BY TEN SPEED PRESS, $35

PARSLEY & BARLEY SALAD

SERVES 4

Scant ¼ cup/40 grams pearl barley
5 ounces/150 grams feta cheese
5½ tablespoons olive oil
1 teaspoon za'atar
½ teaspoon coriander seeds, lightly toasted and crushed
¼ teaspoon ground cumin
Scant 3 ounces/80 grams flat-leaf parsley, leaves and fine stems
4 green onions, finely chopped (⅓ cup/40 grams in total)
2 cloves garlic, crushed
⅓ cup/40 grams cashew nuts, lightly toasted and coarsely crushed
1 green pepper, seeded and cut into ⅜-inch/1-cm dice
½ teaspoon ground allspice
2 tablespoons freshly squeezed lemon juice
Salt and freshly ground black pepper

We started off calling this barley and feta tabbouleh, but the longer we spent with our recipes and sources the more we realized how strongly people feel about the names given to dishes. This is understandable in a place where so much is always at stake.

Still, this recipe is very much inspired by the concept of tabbouleh. It was first cooked for Yotam by Tami Rosenbaum, mother of Yoni, his childhood best friend. Tami is a fantastic cook. She comes from a Yekke family (German Jews), and had a "proper," not particularly Middle Eastern upbringing. Tami studied cookery at secondary school, again receiving traditional training. When Yotam used to visit Yoni as a child, it was the only home of any of his friends where bread rolls— sweet and savory—were baked regularly; schnitzels were made from veal and stuffed with bacon; and all the children played musical instruments seriously—just like back home in Germany. Despite all that, even Tami's food was not immune to local Middle Eastern influences, and many dishes she cooks today manage to fuse together the two worlds in a very delicious way.

Place the pearl barley in a small saucepan, cover with plenty of water, and boil for 30 to 35 minutes, until tender but with a bite. Pour into a fine sieve, shake to remove all the water, and transfer to a large bowl.

Break the feta into rough pieces, about ¾ inch/2 cm in size, and mix in a small bowl with 1½ tablespoons of the olive oil, the za'atar, the coriander seeds, and the cumin. Gently mix together and leave to marinate while you prepare the rest of the salad.

Chop the parsley finely and place in a bowl with the green onions, garlic, cashew nuts, pepper, allspice, lemon juice, the remaining olive oil, and the cooked barley. Mix together well and season to taste. To serve, divide the salad among four plates and top with the marinated feta.

The spice-marinated feta adds bold flavors to this salad.

ROASTED CAULIFLOWER & HAZELNUT SALAD

SERVES 2 TO 4

- 1 head cauliflower, broken into small florets (1½ pounds/ 660 grams in total)
- 5 tablespoons olive oil
- 5 tablespoons/30 grams hazelnuts, with skins
- 1 large celery stalk, cut on an angle into ¼-inch/0.5-cm slices (⅔ cup/70 grams in total)
- ⅓ cup/10 grams small flat-leaf parsley leaves, picked
- ⅓ cup/50 grams pomegranate seeds (from about ½ medium pomegranate)
- Generous ¼ teaspoon ground cinnamon
- Generous ¼ teaspoon ground allspice
- 1 tablespoon sherry vinegar
- 1½ teaspoons maple syrup
- Salt and freshly ground black pepper

Cauliflower, raw or lightly cooked, is a useful salad ingredient, above all in winter when there isn't a great variety of fresh vegetables available. It soaks up flavors particularly effectively and benefits from anything sweet and sharp. This salad is inspired by a recipe from a brilliant Australian chef and food writer, Karen Martini.

Preheat the oven to 425°F/220°C.

Mix the cauliflower with 3 tablespoons of the olive oil, ½ teaspoon salt, and some black pepper. Spread out in a roasting pan and roast on the top oven rack for 25 to 35 minutes, until the cauliflower is crisp and parts of it have turned golden brown. Transfer to a large mixing bowl and set aside to cool down.

Decrease the oven temperature to 325°F/170°C. Spread the hazelnuts on a baking sheet lined with parchment paper and roast for 17 minutes.

Allow the nuts to cool a little, then coarsely chop them and add to the cauliflower, along with the remaining oil and the rest of the ingredients. Stir, taste, and season with salt and pepper accordingly. Serve at room temperature.

Pomegranate seeds add pops of sweet-tart flavor.

ROASTED CHICKEN
with Clementines & Arak

SERVES 4

- 6½ tablespoons/100 ml arak, ouzo, or Pernod
- 4 tablespoons olive oil
- 3 tablespoons freshly squeezed orange juice
- 3 tablespoons freshly squeezed lemon juice
- 2 tablespoons grain mustard
- 3 tablespoons light brown sugar
- 2 medium fennel bulbs (1 pound/500 grams in total)
- 1 large organic or free-range chicken, about 2¾ pounds/1.3 kg, divided into 8 pieces, or the same weight in skin-on, bone-in chicken thighs
- 4 clementines, unpeeled (14 ounces/400 grams in total), cut horizontally into ¼-inch/0.5-cm slices
- 1 tablespoon thyme leaves
- 2½ teaspoons fennel seeds, lightly crushed

Salt and freshly ground black pepper
Chopped flat-leaf parsley, to garnish

EDITOR'S NOTE

The roasted clementine slices are delicious, rind and all. Organic or unsprayed clementines are best if you're going to eat the peels.

EDITOR'S WINE CHOICE

Vibrant, minerally Chablis: 2011 Jean-Marc Brocard Vau de Vey Premier Cru

All the intense flavors lavished on the poor chicken—arak, mustard, fennel, clementines with their skins, brown sugar—somehow manage to come together in a sweetly comforting dish you will always want to come back to. Serve it with plainly cooked rice or bulgur.

Put the first six ingredients in a large mixing bowl and add 2½ teaspoons salt and 1½ teaspoons black pepper. Whisk well and set aside.

Trim the fennel and cut each bulb in half lengthwise. Cut each half into 4 wedges. Add the fennel to the liquids, along with the chicken pieces, clementine slices, thyme, and fennel seeds. Stir well with your hands, then leave to marinate in the fridge for a few hours or overnight (skipping the marinating stage is also fine, if you are pressed for time).

Preheat the oven to 475°F/245°C. Transfer the chicken and its marinade to a baking sheet large enough to accommodate everything comfortably in a single layer (roughly a 12-by-14½-inch/30-by-37-cm pan); the chicken skin should be facing up. Once the oven is hot enough, put the pan in the oven and roast for 35 to 45 minutes, until the chicken is colored and cooked through. Remove from the oven.

Lift the chicken, fennel, and clementines from the pan and arrange on a serving plate; cover and keep warm. Pour the cooking liquid into a small saucepan, place over medium-high heat, bring to a boil, and then simmer until the sauce is reduced by one-third, so you are left with about ⅓ cup/80 ml. Pour the hot sauce over the chicken, garnish with some parsley, and serve.

TOMATO & ALMOND TARTS

8 SERVINGS
ACTIVE: 45 MIN; TOTAL: 1 HR 30 MIN

Sunflower or canola oil, for greasing
- ¾ cup unsalted roasted almonds
- 1¼ sticks (10 tablespoons) unsalted butter, at room temperature
- 2 large eggs, beaten
- 1¼ cups fresh bread crumbs
- 2 garlic cloves, minced
- ½ cup fresh ricotta cheese
- ¼ cup freshly grated Parmigiano-Reggiano cheese
- 2 tablespoons thyme leaves

Flaky sea salt, preferably Maldon, and freshly ground black pepper
- One 14-ounce package all-butter puff pastry, thawed
- 2 pounds medium tomatoes, cut into ⅓-inch-thick slices
- 12 anchovies in oil, drained and torn
- 2 tablespoons olive oil

EDITOR'S WINE CHOICE
Fragrant, cherry-inflected rosé: 2012
Unti Vineyards

In this clever recipe, Ottolenghi spreads a tasty mix of ground almonds, eggs, garlic and cheese over puff pastry before piling on juicy tomatoes, creating a layer of rich, nutty custard.

1. Preheat the oven to 425°F. Lightly grease 2 large baking sheets with sunflower oil.

2. In a food processor, pulse the almonds until finely ground. Transfer to a bowl.

3. In a medium bowl, using an electric mixer, beat the butter until fluffy. Beat in the eggs (the mixture may break, but it will become creamy once you add the bread crumbs). Add the ground almonds, bread crumbs and garlic and beat until blended. Stir in the ricotta, Parmesan, 1 tablespoon of the thyme and ½ teaspoon of sea salt; season with black pepper.

4. On a lightly floured work surface, using a lightly floured rolling pin, roll out the puff pastry to a 9-by-20-inch rectangle, about ⅛ inch thick. Cut in half crosswise to form 2 rectangles, then transfer to the prepared baking sheets. Spread the almond mixture evenly over the pastry, leaving a 1-inch border around the edges. Lay the tomato slices on top in 3 long rows, overlapping them slightly. Sprinkle with the anchovies and the remaining 1 tablespoon of thyme. Drizzle the tarts with 1 tablespoon of the olive oil and season with sea salt and black pepper.

5. Bake the tarts for 15 minutes. Lower the oven temperature to 350°F, shift the baking pans and bake for about 15 minutes longer, until the pastry is golden and cooked through. Let the tarts cool slightly, then drizzle with the remaining 1 tablespoon of olive oil and serve.

YOTAM OTTOLENGHI ONLINE
ottolenghi.co.uk

f *Ottolenghi*

t *@ottolenghi*

THE SMITTEN KITCHEN COOKBOOK

Deb Perelman

Massively popular food blogger Deb Perelman is the kind of cookbook author we love best—she truly sweats the small stuff, fanatically poring over each detail of every recipe until it's perfect. Her dishes take you from morning to night, weekday to weekend, and they're always easy, approachable and fun. She makes a breakfast casserole, for instance, with bagels and cream cheese, baking it like a bread pudding, then serves it with a side of lox (page 168). And for her terrific blueberry cornmeal butter cake, she fuses standard cornbread with a blueberry buckle (page 172). Perelman's fresh take on familiar American dishes will make this cookbook an instant favorite. PUBLISHED BY ALFRED A. KNOPF, $35

NEW YORK BREAKFAST CASSEROLE

YIELD: SERVES 8 TO 10

- 8 cups bagels cut into 1-inch cubes (from approximately 1½ pounds or 570 grams bagels; see Author's Note)
- 8 ounces (225 grams) cream cheese, chilled, cut into irregular small bits
- ¼ medium red onion, halved lengthwise, thinly sliced (quarter-moons)
- 1½ cups (1 pint or 10 ounces) tomatoes, preferably grape or cherry tomatoes, cut in half, or quartered if on the large side
- 8 large eggs
- 2⅓ cups (555 ml) milk or half-and-half
- 1 teaspoon table salt
- Freshly ground black pepper
- Capers, for serving
- Lox or bacon, for serving

AUTHOR'S NOTE

Bagel sizes tend to be very inconsistent, making it difficult to estimate the number you will need. You might need up to a dozen freezer-aisle bagels or merely four or five large ones from a bagel shop. Do your best to eyeball what you'll need, and if you overestimate, well, nobody ever complained about a freezer full of bagels.

I'm not sure how it is where you live, but in New York City there are few more popular breakfasts than (1) an egg and cheese on a roll or (2) cream cheese and lox on a bagel. You can get either made to order frighteningly cheap anywhere—the deli, the bodega, some bars, the average corner store, where you can stock up on beer, lottery tickets, or cat litter along with breakfast. The randomness of these transactions is one of my favorite things about New York.

Does New York need an all-purpose breakfast vehicle like the one below? Arguably, no. But I came up with it one day as an attempt at a Yankee spin on the kinds of breakfast casseroles I've had in the South—usually with Tater Tots, lots of cheese, and bacon or ham; and, yes, they are insanely delicious—and got back to that corner-store breakfast (minus the pack of cigarettes and bottle of vitaminwater). I found it to be better balanced than your average egg sandwich—which always feels too heavy on the bread for me—and was delighted to discover that, in the oven, bits of cream cheese puff and bronze like tiny marshmallows. Plus, as I always prefer, it serves a crowd, and can be assembled in advance, even the night before it is needed.

PREPARE CASSEROLE Spread a third of the bagel cubes in a 9-by-13-inch pan (or other 4-quart baking dish, if necessary). Dot the bagels with a third of the cream-cheese bits, and mix in the red onion and cherry tomatoes. Repeat in two more alternating layers. Whisk eggs with milk, salt, and freshly ground black pepper. Pour the egg mixture over bagel-and-cheese mixture, and feel free to turn any seedy sides of the bagel croutons faceup, in order to pretty up the dish. Cover tightly with plastic wrap, and refrigerate overnight.

TO COOK The next morning—I mean, whenever you are forced from bed—remove casserole from the fridge and preheat your oven to 350°F. Bake on a tray, uncovered, in the middle of the oven until it has puffed, turned golden brown, and cooked through (a knife inserted into the center of the casserole and rotated slightly shouldn't release any liquid), for 1 to 1¼ hours. Let it rest 10 minutes before serving.

TO SERVE Serve in big scoops with a sprinkle of capers and a side of lox. Or bacon.

Use your
favorite type
of bagel or
mix and
match flavors.

EMMENTALER ON RYE

with Sweet & Sour Red Onions

YIELD: 2 SANDWICHES

ONIONS

- 1 tablespoon olive oil
- 1 tablespoon unsalted butter
- 1 large red onion, halved and thinly sliced (about 2 cups)
- 2 teaspoons brown sugar, light or dark
- ¼ teaspoon table salt, plus more to taste
- 1 tablespoon balsamic vinegar

Freshly ground black pepper

SANDWICHES

- Four ½- inch-thick slices rye bread
- 2 tablespoons (30 grams) butter, salted or unsalted, softened
- ¾ cup (about 3 ounces or 85 grams) grated Emmentaler or another Swiss cheese

---

EDITOR'S WINE CHOICE

Earthy, berry-rich Sonoma Pinot Noir: 2011 Hirsch Vineyards The Bohan–Dillon

Oh, stop giving me that look. I know my tastes in grilled cheese are weird. My husband says so all the time. He says that normal people embrace, not fight, those good old jellied, individually wrapped orange squares of American "singles." Normal people enjoy an occasional slice of white bread, or at least a soft whole wheat, in their cheese sandwiches. Normal people leave it at that: Grilled cheese was never broken, so why try to fix it? I've found that if you call it a "panini," people let you put whatever you want between your slices of bread. Vegetables and sweet things and nontraditional cheeses are allowed to melt and muddle together in peace. If it helps, you can pretend this is a panini. But I hope you trust that there is great deliciousness within: Those onions are cooked slow and low until sweet and tart and resonating with immense flavor. Swiss cheeses have a vaguely bitter nuttiness that goes dreamily with this, and rye, well, I know you probably don't like the caraway seeds; it seems nobody does. So, if you can't find seedless rye, and you can't find the best substitute, which is a seedless pumpernickel, you can use plain old white or whole-wheat bread. But I think you're missing out.

COOK ONIONS Heat the olive oil and 1 tablespoon butter in a large skillet over medium-high heat. Add the onion, and sauté for 5 minutes. Add the brown sugar and salt, lower the heat to medium-low, and cook another 10 minutes, stirring occasionally. Add the vinegar, and scrape any stuck onion bits from the bottom of pan with a spoon. Simmer for 1 to 2 minutes, until the onion mixture thickens, and season to taste with black pepper. Cool to lukewarm, or store in an airtight container in the refrigerator until needed, up to 5 days. You should have just shy of ½ cup of cooked onions.

ASSEMBLE THE SANDWICHES Generously butter one side of each slice of bread; these will be the outsides of your sandwiches. Arrange one slice, buttered side down, on a plate. Spread thickly with jammy onions (about 2 tablespoons per sandwich; you'll have extra). Sprinkle with half the grated cheese. Arrange a second slice of bread on top of the cheese, buttered side facing up. Repeat with the remaining slices to make a second sandwich.

COOK SANDWICHES Heat a heavy 12-inch skillet over medium-low heat. Once it's hot, arrange your sandwiches in the pan, and cook them until crisp and deep golden brown, about 5 minutes per side. If you are making a larger batch and want to keep them warm and melty, arrange them in a single layer on a baking sheet in a 200°F oven. When ready to eat, slice the sandwiches in half. Don't expect leftovers.

BLUEBERRY CORNMEAL BUTTER CAKE

YIELD: 16 SQUARES OF CAKE

- 8 tablespoons (115 grams or 1 stick) unsalted butter, at room temperature, plus more for pan
- 1 cup (125 grams) all-purpose flour, plus more for pan
- ½ cup (60 grams) cornmeal
- 2 teaspoons baking powder
- ½ teaspoon table salt
- 1 cup (200 grams) sugar
- 2 large eggs
- ¼ teaspoon vanilla extract
- ¼ teaspoon freshly grated lemon zest
- ⅓ cup (80 grams) sour cream
- 2 cups (190 grams) blueberries, rinsed and patted dry

STREUSEL

- ½ cup (100 grams) sugar
- 6 tablespoons (45 grams) all-purpose flour
- 2 tablespoons (15 grams) cornmeal
- ¼ teaspoon ground cinnamon
- Pinch of table salt
- 2 tablespoons (55 grams) unsalted butter, cut into small pieces

This recipe started with a whim: I imagined the place where a dense, buttery blueberry buckle would intersect with the kind of sweet, cakey cornbread that would make every Southerner I know shudder to hear it called "cornbread," and I wanted to go there. And what fun I had trying! There were versions with less lemon, some vanilla, buttermilk in place of milk, then sour cream for buttermilk, less liquid, more blueberries, more streusel, a crunchier streusel, a slip of cinnamon, a square cake instead of a round. Each time, I planned my next tweak, hit the market for more berries, and went at it again. Are we friends? You've probably had this cake twice.

A summer later, I was still playing with this cake, and it was time to accept the truth: We just loved it so much that I created excuses to make it some more. It's that kind of cake—dense and buttery, dotted with dreamy berries, portable, quick to make, and infinitely snacky— and I hope it won't be long until your version of this page is as spattered with berry, batter, and grit as mine.

Preheat your oven to 350°F. Line the bottom of an 8-inch square pan with parchment, then either butter and flour the bottom and sides, or coat them with a nonstick spray.

Whisk the flour, cornmeal, baking powder, and salt in medium bowl, and set aside. Using an electric mixer, beat the butter with sugar in large bowl until pale and fluffy, for at least 2 minutes. Beat in the eggs one at a time, scraping down the bowl between additions, then add the vanilla and zest. Add a third of flour mixture, all of sour cream, and another third of the flour, beating until just blended after each addition. Scrape down sides of bowl. Mix the remaining third of the flour mixture with the blueberries. Fold the blueberry-flour mixture gently into the cake batter.

Spread the cake batter in the prepared cake pan. Use your original dry-ingredients bowl (see how we look out for your dishpan hands?) to combine the dry topping ingredients with a fork. Mash in the butter with your fork, fingertips, or a pastry blender. Scatter the topping over the batter.

Bake the cake until the top is golden brown and the tester inserted into center comes out clean, about 35 minutes. Cool the cake in the pan on a rack for 5 minutes. Run the spatula around the edges of the cake to loosen it, then flip out onto a cooling rack.

VIETNAMESE HOME COOKING

Charles Phan with Jessica Battilana

When Charles Phan arrived in the US as a Vietnamese refugee in the 1970s, he was not a chef, just a talented home cook who mastered his craft by preparing meals for his family of 10. Today Phan has a San Francisco restaurant empire, with museum cafés, a bourbon bar and his flagship, the Slanted Door, the pioneering restaurant that introduced diners to vibrant and refined Vietnamese food prepared with a local, organic sensibility. His debut book includes Slanted Door favorites like super-tender shaking beef, made with grass-fed filet mignon. But most recipes are humbler and draw from his repertoire of family meals: bok choy and shiitake stir-fried with rice wine, garlic and fish sauce (page 180); a warming beef stew fragrant with star anise (page 178). Mirroring his cooking philosophy, they're "interesting without being challenging; simple, honest and straightforward, yet incredibly flavorful." PUBLISHED BY TEN SPEED PRESS, $35

ROASTED EGGPLANT & LEEK SALAD

SERVES 6 AS A SIDE DISH OR
PART OF A MULTICOURSE MEAL

- 4 Rosa Bianca or globe eggplants (about 3½ pounds total)

Kosher salt

- 12 baby leeks, white and light green parts only, halved lengthwise
- 4 tablespoons canola oil

Freshly ground black pepper

- 1½ cups loosely packed fresh cilantro leaves, coarsely chopped
- ½ cup Spicy Soy Sauce (recipe follows)
- 1 tablespoon freshly squeezed lime juice

EDITOR'S NOTE

Phan makes his own roasted chile paste for the Spicy Soy Sauce and includes the recipe in his book. Alternatively, jarred versions are available at Asian markets. Phan recommends using a brand made without preservatives.

MAKES ABOUT 1½ CUPS

- ¾ cup sugar
- ½ cup light soy sauce
- 3 tablespoons distilled white vinegar
- 2 tablespoons roasted chile paste (see Editor's Note)

Eggplant is eaten throughout Vietnam, usually either fried or grilled. Grilling gives it a silky texture and a smoky flavor that contrasts well with the leeks, which become sweeter when cooked. This salad is good on its own, or alongside any simple grilled meat.

1. Trim the stem end of each eggplant, peel and slice lengthwise into 1-inch slices. Sprinkle with salt and set aside to drain, 1 hour. After an hour, pat slices dry with a paper towel.

2. While the eggplant slices are draining, prepare a medium fire for direct-heat grilling in a charcoal grill (you should be able to hold your hand 1 inch above the grate for only 4 to 5 seconds).

3. When the coals are ready, drizzle the leeks with 2 tablespoons of the oil and sprinkle with salt and pepper. Place the leeks on the grate and cook, turning as needed, for about 15 minutes, until soft and charred in spots. Transfer to a plate, cover with plastic wrap, and let steam while you cook the eggplant.

4. Drizzle the eggplant slices on both sides with the remaining 2 tablespoons oil, then sprinkle on both sides with salt and pepper. Grill the slices, turning occasionally, for about 20 minutes, until very soft and browned.

5. Remove the eggplant slices from the grill. When cool enough to handle, cut into ½-inch cubes and transfer to a serving bowl. Cut the leeks crosswise into 1-inch-thick slices and add to the eggplant. Add the cilantro and toss to combine.

6. In a small bowl, whisk together the spicy soy sauce and lime juice. Pour over the eggplant-leek mixture and toss to coat evenly. Season with additional salt and pepper and serve.

SPICY SOY SAUCE

In a bowl, stir together the sugar, soy sauce, vinegar, and ½ cup water until the sugar has dissolved. Stir in the roasted chile paste.

LEMONGRASS BEEF STEW

SERVES 6 AS A MAIN COURSE

- 3 pounds boneless beef short ribs, cut into 1½-inch cubes
- 4 tablespoons canola oil
- 1 teaspoon kosher salt
- ½ teaspoon freshly ground black pepper
- 2 cups diced yellow onions
- 2 teaspoons minced garlic
- ¼ cup finely minced lemongrass
- 3 tablespoons tomato paste
- 2-by-1-inch piece fresh ginger, peeled and smashed
- 2 whole star anise pods
- 1 or 2 Thai chiles, stemmed, plus 1 teaspoon minced, for garnish
- 6 cups beef stock
- 3 carrots, peeled and cut into 2-inch lengths
- 8 ounces daikon radish, peeled and cut into 1-inch lengths
- About 2 tablespoons fish sauce
- ¼ cup finely sliced fresh Thai basil, for garnish

EDITOR'S BEER CHOICE
Citrusy, balanced farmhouse-style ale: Ommegang Hennepin

Obviously this dish is imported from France, but it has a very Vietnamese sensibility, seasoned with lemongrass, ginger, Thai chile and fish sauce. You can make the stew with beef chuck or brisket, but I like to use boneless short ribs. Once an overlooked cut of meat, short ribs are now on menus across the country (and, sadly, are no longer as cheap as they once were). The meat is generously marbled with fat, which breaks down during the braising process, yielding a velvety sauce and extremely tender texture.

This stew is brothier and more soup-like than Western versions, and I often serve it over rice noodles. But if you prefer a thicker sauce, you can remove the meat and vegetables at the end and boil the sauce over high heat until it has reduced and thickened to your desired consistency, then serve it with bowls of steamed rice or with a chunk of baguette.

1. Place the beef in a bowl. Drizzle with 1 tablespoon of the oil, sprinkle with the salt and pepper, and stir to coat. Let stand while you prepare all of the other ingredients.

2. In a large Dutch oven or heavy-bottomed pot, heat the remaining 3 tablespoons oil over high heat. When the oil is hot, working in batches, add the beef and cook, turning as needed, for about 8 minutes, until browned on all sides. As each batch is ready, transfer it to a rimmed baking sheet.

3. Decrease the heat to medium and add the onion to the now-empty pot. Cook, stirring frequently, for about 10 minutes, until the onion is a deep golden brown. Stir in the garlic and cook, stirring, for 30 seconds more. Add the lemongrass, tomato paste, ginger, star anise, and whole chile to taste and stir to combine. Transfer the mixture to a large clay pot.

4. Add the beef and any accumulated juices to the clay pot and pour in the stock. Bring the liquid to a boil over medium heat, decrease the heat so the liquid is at a gentle simmer, cover, and cook, stirring occasionally, for 1½ hours, until the meat is just tender.

5. Add the carrots and daikon, re-cover, and cook for 30 minutes longer, until the vegetables are cooked through and the meat is very tender. Remove from the heat; stir in the fish sauce, 1 tablespoon at a time, to taste.

6. Serve the stew directly from the clay pot. Top each serving with some of the basil and minced chile.

Thai basil
and chile
garnishes are
a must.

BOK CHOY WITH BABY SHIITAKE MUSHROOMS

SERVES 2 TO 4 AS PART OF
A MULTICOURSE MEAL

- 3 tablespoons canola oil
- 1 teaspoon minced garlic
- ¼ pound fresh baby shiitake mushrooms, stems removed, or ¼ pound fresh regular-size shiitake mushrooms, stemmed, caps thinly sliced
- 2 pounds bok choy, rinsed and cut into 3-inch lengths
- 2 tablespoons rice wine
- 1½ tablespoons fish sauce
- 1 tablespoon chicken stock or water

Bok choy and shiitake mushrooms, flavored with rice wine, fish sauce, and garlic, is a pretty common stir-fry combination, but this recipe works just as well with an equal amount of snow or snap peas or thinly sliced summer squash. It's also especially good with Brussels sprouts, provided you have the patience to separate every leaf. Rinse the bok choy in water before you stir-fry it; the little bit of moisture that clings to the vegetable helps it steam-cook as you stir-fry.

1. Heat a wok over high heat until very hot; the metal will have a matte appearance and a drop or two of water flicked onto its surface should evaporate on contact. Add the oil and heat until the oil is shimmering but not smoking.

2. Add the garlic, cook 5 seconds, then add the shiitakes and stir-fry 30 seconds, until just softened. Add the bok choy and rice wine and mix together with the mushrooms and garlic.

3. Add the fish sauce and chicken stock and cook until the bok choy is just tender, about 1 to 2 minutes, stirring frequently. If after 2 minutes the bok choy is still crunchy, cover the wok with a lid and let cook until tender.

4. Remove from the heat, transfer to a bowl, and serve immediately.

GINGERED CHERRY TOMATOES
with Buttermilk Sorbet & Mint

8 SERVINGS
ACTIVE: 45 MIN; TOTAL: 1 HR 15 MIN PLUS
3 HR FREEZING

BUTTERMILK SORBET

- 1 cup sugar
- 1½ cups plus 3 tablespoons buttermilk
- ⅓ cup plain whole-milk yogurt
- ⅓ cup corn syrup, agave nectar or rice syrup
- ½ teaspoon finely grated lemon zest
- ½ vanilla bean, split and seeds scraped

Pinch of kosher salt

GINGERED TOMATOES

- One 6-inch piece of fresh ginger, peeled and thinly sliced
- ⅛ teaspoon pure vanilla extract
- ½ vanilla bean, split and seeds scraped
- 1 pound Sweet 100 cherry tomatoes, halved lengthwise
- 1 tablespoon cornstarch
- 2 tablespoons coarsely chopped mint, for garnish

Slanted Door pastry chef Chucky Dugo created this ultra-refreshing dessert that pairs sweet cherry tomatoes with homemade buttermilk sorbet. If you don't want to make your own sorbet, the gingered tomato compote pairs well with plain or vanilla frozen yogurt.

1. MAKE THE BUTTERMILK SORBET In a medium saucepan, combine the sugar and 1 cup of water and bring to a boil. Simmer over moderate heat, stirring, until the sugar dissolves, about 2 minutes. Transfer the simple syrup to a measuring cup. You should have about 1½ cups.

2. In a blender, combine the buttermilk, yogurt, corn syrup, lemon zest, vanilla seeds, salt and ½ cup plus 3 tablespoons of the simple syrup (reserve the remaining simple syrup for the tomatoes). Puree until smooth. Freeze the mixture in an ice cream maker according to the manufacturer's instructions. Transfer the sorbet to a plastic container and freeze until firm, at least 3 hours.

3. MEANWHILE, MAKE THE GINGERED TOMATOES In a medium saucepan, combine ¾ cup of the reserved simple syrup with the ginger, vanilla extract and vanilla seeds. Bring to a boil and simmer for 1 minute. Transfer the mixture to a blender and puree until smooth. Strain the ginger syrup through a fine sieve set over a small saucepan, pressing on the solids. Discard the solids.

4. Place the tomatoes in a medium bowl set in an ice bath. In a small bowl, whisk the cornstarch with 1 tablespoon of cold water. Bring the ginger syrup to a boil. Whisk in the cornstarch slurry and simmer until thickened, about 1 minute. Pour the ginger mixture over the tomatoes and toss to coat well. Stir until chilled.

5. Spoon the tomatoes into serving bowls and top with scoops of sorbet. Garnish with the mint and serve.

CHARLES PHAN ONLINE

charlesphan.com

f The Slanted Door

STANDARD BAKING CO.

PASTRIES

Alison Pray & Tara Smith

From a small, modest shop in Portland, Maine, Standard Baking Co. turns out some of the country's most acclaimed baked goods. In their first cookbook, owner Alison Pray and pastry chef Tara Smith provide clear, easy-to-follow recipes for their stellar cakes, cookies and morning pastries, bringing together refined European baking traditions and simpler American classics. Home bakers can tackle the five-page recipe for croissants or make the soft, crumbly granola bars (page 184) in less than 40 minutes, start to finish. The rustic apple tart—folds of buttery dough encasing a mound of fresh apples—falls somewhere in between the two worlds, "like a somewhat refined cousin of American apple pie" (page 188). It's the authors' personal favorite, adaptable to almost any fruit in any season, and an indispensable addition to the home baker's repertoire. PUBLISHED BY DOWN EAST BOOKS, $30

FRUIT & NUT GRANOLA BARS

MAKES THIRTY 1-BY-5½-INCH BARS

- 1 cup (2 sticks) unsalted butter
- 2 cups packed light brown sugar
- 1½ cups peanut butter, natural salted
- 1 cup light corn syrup
- 2 tablespoons vanilla extract
- 7 cups rolled (not instant) oats
- One 12-ounce package small chocolate chips
- 1½ cups dried cranberries
- 1 cup hulled sunflower seeds
- ½ cup pumpkin seeds, toasted (see Toasted Nuts, page 186)
- ½ cup sesame seeds
- ½ cup chopped pecans, toasted (see Toasted Nuts, page 186)

When we cut the granola bars in the morning we always cut the outside edges off first. The trimmings are placed on a plate on the staff break table. They disappear in minutes! These hearty bars feature many of the nuts, seeds, and dried fruits that are staples in the bakery. Any combination of inclusions can be used as long as the amount of dry ingredients stays the same.

1. In a small saucepan, melt the butter over low heat and set it aside to cool (it should cool completely before using or it will melt the chocolate chips).

2. Preheat the oven to 375°F. Prepare a rimmed 13-by-18-inch baking sheet by lining it with parchment paper and spraying the sides with nonstick cooking spray.

3. In a large bowl, combine the brown sugar, peanut butter, corn syrup, and vanilla.

4. In another large bowl, combine the oats, chocolate, cranberries, sunflower seeds, pumpkin seeds, sesame seeds, and pecans.

5. Add half of the dry ingredients and half of the melted butter to the peanut butter mixture. Mix and knead with your hands to combine.

6. Add the remaining dry ingredients and the rest of the butter and mix until all of the ingredients are thoroughly incorporated.

7. Spread the mixture out onto the prepared baking sheet and press it down to fill the pan. Cover the mixture with another sheet of parchment paper and use a rolling pin to make sure it is pressed firmly to a uniform thickness.

8. Bake for 10 to 11 minutes, rotating the pan halfway through the baking time. The edges will be a light golden brown. The mixture will look under-baked in the center, but will set up after cooling.

9. Transfer the pan to a wire rack and let it cool for several hours before cutting.

continued on page 186

FRUIT & NUT GRANOLA BARS
continued

10. To cut, run a knife around the outside edge to loosen it from the pan and then flip the pan over onto a cutting board. Using a very sharp knife, cut into any size you like. A ruler and a small paring knife work well to score the top of the granola into strips. Use a large sharp knife to cut straight down through the bars on the score marks.

TOASTED NUTS

Follow these directions when a recipe calls for toasted nuts.

1. Preheat the oven to 350°F.

2. Spread the nuts in a single layer on a baking sheet and bake for 8 to 12 minutes, stirring once or twice to evenly toast. The nuts will darken in color and give off a toasted aroma. Watch carefully as they can burn quickly.

PUMPKIN CREAM SCONES

MAKES 12 SCONES

FOR THE GARNISH
- ⅓ cup granulated sugar
- ⅛ teaspoon ground cinnamon
- ⅓ cup pumpkin seeds

- 2½ cups all-purpose flour
- ¼ cup packed dark brown sugar
- 1 tablespoon plus ½ teaspoon baking powder
- ½ teaspoon salt
- 1¾ teaspoons ground cinnamon
- 1¼ teaspoons ground ginger
- 1¼ teaspoons ground nutmeg
- 1 teaspoon ground allspice
- ½ cup plus 2 tablespoons (1¼ sticks) unsalted butter, cut into ½-inch cubes, chilled
- ⅓ cup finely diced crystallized ginger
- 1 egg
- ¾ cup pumpkin puree
- ⅓ cup half-and-half
- 2 tablespoons molasses

Just as the leaves turn to gold and crimson, the smell of warm pumpkin scones is the bakery's own sign of autumn's approach. These seasonal scones are so comforting on a chilly fall morning, with just the right amount of warm spices and pieces of ginger.

1. Position a rack in the center of the oven and preheat the oven to 400°F. Line a baking sheet with parchment paper.

2. Make the cinnamon sugar garnish. In a small bowl, combine sugar and cinnamon and set aside.

3. In a large bowl, whisk together the flour, brown sugar, baking powder, salt, cinnamon, ground ginger, nutmeg, and allspice. Break up any remaining lumps with your fingertips.

4. Add the cubed butter and, using your fingertips, work it into the flour mixture until a few pea-size chunks of butter remain. Add the crystallized ginger and toss until it's evenly distributed.

5. In a separate bowl, whisk together the egg, pumpkin puree, half-and-half, and molasses. Pour this mixture into the dry ingredients and, using your hands or a rubber spatula, fold everything together until the dry ingredients are evenly moistened. It's important not to over mix at this stage or the scones will be tough.

6. With an ice cream scoop, drop golf ball–size mounds onto the baking sheet, about 2½ inches apart.

7. Top each scone with a few pumpkin seeds and dust with cinnamon sugar. Bake for 23 to 25 minutes, rotating the baking sheet after 12 minutes for even baking. They will be golden brown and feel firm in the center.

8. Remove from the oven and transfer the scones to a wire rack to cool slightly before serving.

RUSTIC APPLE TART

MAKES ONE 8-INCH TART OR
FOUR 4-INCH TARTS

FOR THE EGG WASH
- 1 egg

Pinch salt

- ¼ cup sugar
- 2 tablespoons all-purpose flour
- ½ teaspoon ground cinnamon
- ⅛ teaspoon freshly grated nutmeg
- 4 medium (about 1½ pounds) apples (Gravenstein or other tart baking variety; see Editor's Note)
- 1 recipe Rustic Tart Dough, rolled out and chilled (recipe follows)
- 1 cup Streusel (recipe follows)

EDITOR'S NOTE

Other tart baking apples that are great for this recipe include Granny Smith and Honeycrisp.

This beautiful tart has lovely folds of flaky, buttery dough enveloping a mound of fresh seasonal fruit. A sprinkle of streusel adds the final touch. This lovely pastry conjures up images of a farmhouse lunch table in the height of harvest time. We love substituting plums for the apples in the summer. Amazing flavor and a gorgeous crimson color! And just think . . . no pie pan to wash!

When properly made, the apple slices will retain their shape after baking, but be very tender, not firm or crisp. Depending on the variety and freshness of your apples, the fruit may need to be sliced thinner or wider to achieve the desired texture.

1. Position a rack in the center of the oven and preheat the oven to 425°F. Line a baking sheet with parchment paper.

2. In a small bowl, make the egg wash by beating the egg, 2 teaspoons of water, and salt with a fork.

3. In a large bowl, combine the sugar, flour, cinnamon, and nutmeg.

4. Peel, core, and slice the apples into ½-inch-thick slices. Toss the apples in the spice mixture until the slices are evenly coated. Remove the small circles of tart dough from the refrigerator and place them on a lightly floured work surface. If you are making a large tart, place the large tart circle on the prepared baking sheet. Use a pastry brush to lightly brush the egg wash around the outside inch of the tart circles.

5. Divide the apples among the four small tarts, piling them in the center, leaving a 2-inch border around the edge. For the large tart, pile the apples into the center, leaving a 3-inch border around the edge.

6. For small tarts, fold a 3-inch portion of the dough over the apples, then fold the next 3 inches up, overlapping the last portion by an inch. Continue to fold the dough up around the apples until you overlap the first fold. Place tarts evenly spaced on the prepared baking sheet. For a large tart, fold up using 4-inch folds.

7. Lightly brush the outside surface of the tart with the egg wash. Top each small tart with ¼ cup of streusel, gently squeezing and pressing it into the tart to hold it in place. Top the large tart with 1 cup of streusel.

continued on page 190

The secret
to the tender,
flaky crust is
cream cheese.

8. Bake both the large and small tarts for 10 minutes, rotate the baking sheet, and reduce the oven temperature to 375°F. Bake the small tarts for another 25 minutes. Bake the large tart for another 35 minutes, or until the pastry is a dark golden brown and the folds of tart dough no longer have a translucent appearance.

9. Remove from the oven and carefully slide the parchment paper off of the baking sheet and onto a wire rack. Serve warm from the oven with crème fraîche, whipped cream, or ice cream. If serving at room temperature, cool completely on the wire rack.

RUSTIC TART DOUGH

One of our flakiest pastry doughs, we use it for hand-formed galettes, called Rustic Tarts, in the bakery, but it would work just as well in a traditional tart ring or as a pie dough. The discs or rolled-out rounds can be stored in the refrigerator, wrapped tightly with plastic wrap, for up to 3 days or frozen for up to 2 weeks. To use the frozen dough, transfer it to the refrigerator to defrost the night before you plan to make your tart.

**MAKES ONE 8-INCH TART
OR FOUR 4-INCH TARTS**

- 1 cup plus 1 teaspoon all-purpose flour
- ½ teaspoon salt
- ⅛ teaspoon baking powder
- 6 tablespoons unsalted butter, cubed and chilled
- ⅓ cup cream cheese, cubed and chilled
- 1 tablespoon plus 1 teaspoon ice cold water

MAKING THE DOUGH

1. In a large bowl, whisk together the flour, salt, and baking powder. With your fingertips or a pastry cutter, blend the butter into the dry ingredients until it's reduced to pea-size chunks.

2. Add the cream cheese to the flour mixture and blend it in with your fingertips until the mixture has the consistency of a coarse meal. Add the water to the mixture and, using a fork or your fingertips, gently toss all of the ingredients together until most of the dry particles are moistened. It will look crumbly and not quite hold together at this point.

3. Carefully form the dough mixture into a loose ball and gently flatten it into a disc. If making small tarts, divide the dough into four equal portions, then form them into discs. Wrap the discs in plastic wrap and place them in the refrigerator to chill and rest for at least an hour or overnight.

TO ROLL OUT THE DOUGH

1. Place the dough disc on a lightly floured work surface. Starting from the center of the disc, using a rolling pin, roll outward toward the edges, lifting the dough and giving it a quarter turn occasionally to keep it from sticking to the work surface.

2. Roll the dough into a circle about ⅛ inch thick. For a large hand-formed tart, roll it out to 11 inches in diameter, for a small tart about 7 inches in diameter. If the dough has warmed and becomes difficult to work with, place it in the refrigerator for a few minutes to firm up before continuing.

3. Place the rolled-out dough on a baking sheet lined with parchment paper, cover it with plastic wrap, and transfer to the refrigerator for at least 1 hour to chill.

STREUSEL

Streusel is a crumbly topping made of few ingredients—flour, sugar, salt, and butter. How can such a simple concoction add so much to the cakes, tarts, and pastries it adorns? This component recipe is a good example of how wonderful ingredients are when brought simply together in an uncomplicated way.

1. In a large bowl, whisk together the granulated sugar, brown sugar, salt, and flour.

2. Add the butter. Blend it into the flour mixture using your fingers or a pastry blender until it's evenly moistened and resembles coarse crumbs.

3. Can be used immediately or transferred to a tightly covered storage container and kept refrigerated until ready to use. The streusel can be stored in the refrigerator for up to 3 days or in the freezer for up to 3 weeks.

MAKES ABOUT 2 CUPS STREUSEL

- ¼ cup granulated sugar
- ¼ cup packed dark brown sugar
- ⅛ teaspoon salt
- 1½ cups all-purpose flour
- 7 tablespoons unsalted butter, melted and cooled

FRENCH PUFFS

MAKES 24 PUFFS

2⅔ cups all-purpose flour
¾ teaspoon salt
1½ teaspoons baking powder
¼ teaspoon baking soda
1 teaspoon freshly grated nutmeg
¾ cup (1½ sticks) unsalted butter, room temperature, plus more for greasing pan
⅓ cup granulated sugar
⅓ cup packed dark brown sugar
2 eggs, room temperature
1 teaspoon vanilla extract
1 cup buttermilk, room temperature

FOR THE TOPPING

¼ teaspoon vanilla extract
4 tablespoons butter, melted
¼ cup sugar
1½ teaspoons ground cinnamon

The hint of fresh nutmeg, tangy buttermilk, and dusting of cinnamon sugar may conjure up cake doughnut daydreams, but baked in this diminutive shape, this little cake is at home on the fanciest of brunch tables. To get a nice, even coating of cinnamon sugar, it's best to allow a few minutes for the puff to absorb the melted butter.

1. Position a rack in the center of the oven and preheat to 425°F. Lightly butter a 24-cup mini-muffin tin.

2. In a large bowl, whisk together the flour, salt, baking powder, baking soda, and nutmeg.

3. In the bowl of a stand mixer fitted with the paddle attachment, cream together the butter and sugars on medium speed until smooth. Reduce to low speed and beat in the eggs one at a time. Add the vanilla and half the buttermilk, beating to combine well after each addition. Stop the mixer occasionally to scrape down the sides of the bowl and paddle using a plastic scraper or rubber spatula.

4. On low speed slowly add half the dry ingredients and beat until just incorporated.

5. Add the remaining buttermilk followed by the rest of the dry ingredients. Mix until the batter is smooth and all the ingredients are fully combined.

6. Scoop the batter into the prepared muffin tins, about two heaping tablespoons per cup. The batter will mound up over the top of the cups. Bake for 14 minutes, rotating the tray halfway through the baking time. The cakes will feel firm when pressed gently on the tops.

7. Remove from the oven and place on a cooling rack to cool for a few minutes. While the puffs are still warm, add the vanilla to the melted butter, dip the tops of each puff and set aside. In a small bowl, combine the sugar and cinnamon, then roll each puff in the cinnamon sugar until it's coated with a thin, uniform layer. These are heavenly when served still warm from the oven.

PEANUT BUTTER–CHOCOLATE CHIP FRIDAYS

MAKES 24 COOKIES
TOTAL: 45 MIN PLUS COOLING

- 1 cup all-purpose flour, plus more for dipping
- ½ teaspoon baking soda
- ¾ teaspoon salt
- 1 stick unsalted butter, at room temperature
- 1 cup packed dark brown sugar
- ⅔ cup creamy natural peanut butter
- 1 large egg, at room temperature
- 1 teaspoon pure vanilla extract
- 3½ ounces bittersweet or milk chocolate, chopped (⅔ cup)

Standard Baking Co. doesn't sell peanut butter cookies, but, says Smith, "We all crave them!" So she and Pray created Peanut Butter Fridays, when they mix up a small batch of these cookies for the staff. "We always bake one tray lightly for the fans of soft cookies and make one dark batch for the crunchy-cookie lovers," she says.

1. Preheat the oven to 350°F and set the racks in the upper and lower thirds of the oven. Line 2 baking sheets with parchment paper.

2. In a medium bowl, whisk the 1 cup of flour with the baking soda and salt. In a large bowl, using an electric mixer, beat the butter and brown sugar at medium-high speed, scraping down the bowl a few times, until light and fluffy, about 3 minutes. Beat in the peanut butter. Add the egg and vanilla and beat at low speed just until incorporated. Beat in the dry ingredients, scraping down the bowl as needed, until thoroughly blended. Fold in the chocolate.

3. Using a 2-tablespoon ice cream scoop, place 12 balls of dough onto each of the prepared baking sheets, about 1½ inches apart; the cookies will spread slightly. With the tines of a fork dipped in flour, press a crosshatch pattern into the top of each cookie.

4. Bake the cookies for about 12 minutes, or until golden, shifting the baking sheets halfway through for even baking. Transfer the cookies to a rack to cool.

MAKE AHEAD The cookies can be stored at room temperature for up to 3 days.

STANDARD BAKING CO. ONLINE

f *Standard Baking Co.*

GRAN COCINA LATINA

Maricel E. Presilla

It took Maricel Presilla almost 30 years to research this definitive volume on the food and culinary history of Latin America. With nearly a thousand pages and over 500 recipes, *Gran Cocina Latina* is encyclopedic, but it isn't dry. Presilla, who runs two fantastic Latin restaurants in Hoboken, New Jersey (and also has a PhD in medieval history), demystifies the cuisine of this sprawling region, weaving in personal stories along the way. There are recipes for some of Latin America's most famous dishes, like juicy Argentinean grilled skirt steak served with a smoky red chimichurri sauce (page 202), as well as more obscure ones, like a Peruvian-style white bean casserole with fresh tuna steak cooked in a piquant, cumin-inflected Andean pepper sauce (page 198), a New World dish with Old World flavors.

PUBLISHED BY W. W. NORTON & CO., $45

JICAMA STICKS WITH CHILE & LIME
Botana de Jícama con Chile y Limón

SERVES 6

1 pound jicama, peeled
  (see Author's Note)
Juice of 2 limes (about ¼ cup)
Juice of ½ bitter orange (about
  1 tablespoon)
1 tablespoon distilled white vinegar
¼ teaspoon ground dried chile,
  cayenne, or red pepper flakes
¼ teaspoon salt
⅛ teaspoon freshly ground
  black pepper
1 teaspoon finely chopped cilantro,
  optional
1 teaspoon sugar (only if the jicama
  is very fresh and firm)

AUTHOR'S NOTE

*Some jicamas, especially large ones,
tend to be fibrous. Look for a
medium-size jicama with dense
and crunchy flesh.*

AUTHOR'S DRINK CHOICE

*A shot of an aged tequila, such as
Patrón, Herradura, or Corazón, or a
margarita on the rocks*

*In Querétaro, Mexico, next to many old churches you will find women
selling crunchy jicama botanas. I never cease to be amazed at their art.
They can turn the humblest vegetable or fruit into a magnificent still
life, cutting the burly jicamas into perfect long strips and seasoning
them lightly with citrus fruit and a sprinkling of hot pepper. Inspired
by these Mexican botanas, I like to arrange long strips of jicama in
tequila shot glasses and bring them to the table as an amuse-bouche.*

*Jicama is a vine of the legume family that grows a large edible root
shaped like a turnip. Beneath the tan skin, the root flesh has a
crunchy texture, not unlike that of water chestnuts. Neutral-flavored
with a touch of sweetness that offsets its subtle starchy quality,
jicama absorbs the heat of the chile and the tang of the citrus juice
to make for a crisp and refreshing starter.*

Cut the jicama lengthwise into ½-inch-thick slices, then cut the slices
into ½-inch-wide sticks. Place them in a medium bowl and toss with
the rest of the ingredients. Arrange in small 2-ounce tequila shot
glasses, standing up like breadsticks, and moisten with the juices of
the marinade.

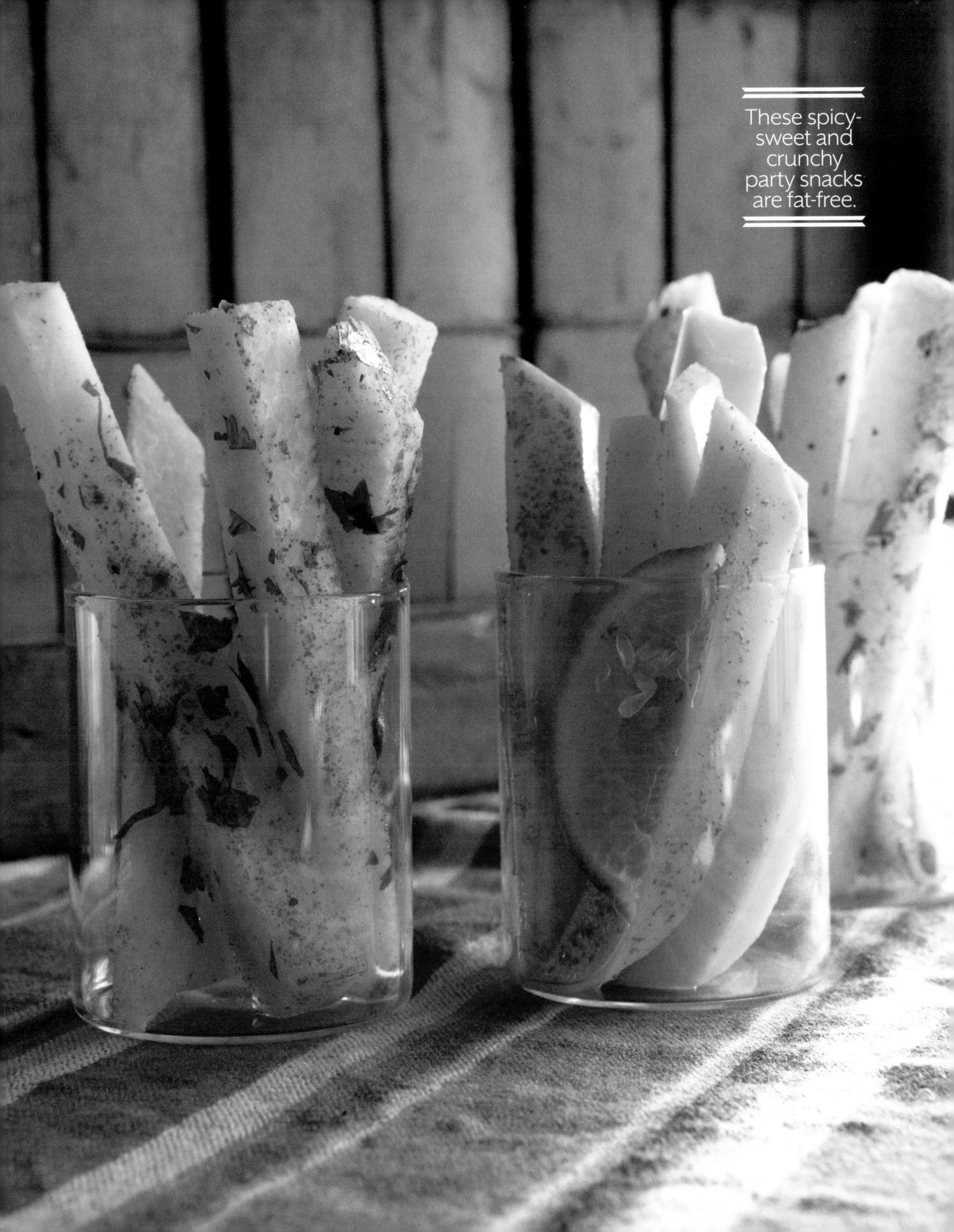

These spicy-sweet and crunchy party snacks are fat-free.

TUNA & WHITE BEANS PERUVIAN STYLE

Atún con Frijoles Blancos a la Peruana

SERVES 6

FOR THE BEANS

- 8 ounces dried Great Northern beans (about 1 cup; see Author's Note)
- 1 large yellow onion (12 ounces)

FOR THE TUNA

- 2 garlic cloves, mashed to a paste with a mortar and pestle or finely chopped and mashed
- 2 teaspoons ground dried *mirasol* pepper, homemade (recipe follows) or store-bought, or ½ teaspoon ground cayenne
- Juice of ½ medium lime (about 1 tablespoon)
- 1 teaspoon extra-virgin olive oil
- 1 teaspoon salt
- 1 teaspoon ground cumin
- 1 pound fresh tuna steak

FOR THE COOKING SAUCE

- 6 dried *mirasol* peppers, stemmed and seeded
- 2 tablespoons extra-virgin olive oil
- 4 garlic cloves, finely chopped
- 1 small red onion (4 ounces), finely chopped
- 1 teaspoon ground cumin
- 1 teaspoon salt
- 2 tablespoons finely chopped cilantro
- ¼ cup cider vinegar

AUTHOR'S NOTE

For a shortcut, use a 15-ounce can of white beans, drained.

AUTHOR'S WINE CHOICE

A Spanish Tempranillo such as Sierra Cantabria Crianza

Tuna is as versatile as pork, and has a similar affinity for white beans and assertive seasonings such as a cooking sauce (aderezo) flavored with golden dried mirasol *peppers. You only need crusty bread and a lively red wine to turn this robust white bean casserole into a complete meal.*

COOKING THE BEANS Place the beans and onion in a large stockpot with 3 quarts water and bring to a boil over high heat. Lower the heat and simmer, covered, adding more water if the beans dry out. Cook only until the beans are tender but retain their shape, 1 to 1½ hours. Discard the onion. Drain the beans and reserve. Makes about 3½ cups.

SEASONING THE TUNA In a medium bowl, whisk together the garlic, ground *mirasol* or cayenne pepper, lime juice, olive oil, salt, and cumin. Add the tuna and toss to coat evenly. Let rest for at least 15 minutes.

PREPARING THE COOKING SAUCE Place the *mirasol* peppers and 3 cups water in a small saucepan. Bring to a boil over medium heat and cook until soft, 15 to 20 minutes. Drain, reserving ½ cup of the cooking liquid. Place the peppers in a blender or food processor with the reserved cooking liquid and process to a smooth puree.

Heat the oil in a 12-inch sauté pan or skillet. Add the garlic and sauté until golden, about 40 seconds. Add the red onion, *mirasol* pepper puree, cumin, and salt. Cook for 3 minutes, stirring, until the onion is translucent. Stir in the cilantro and vinegar and cook for 2 more minutes.

FINISHING THE DISH Add the tuna to the cooking sauce and cook briefly, depending on how rare you like it. Stir in the reserved beans and cook just until heated through, about 5 minutes.

SERVING AND STORING Serve warm, not hot, as a main course for a light meal. The dish will keep, well covered, in the refrigerator for a couple of days.

GROUND ANDEAN PEPPERS

AJÍ MOLIDO

MAKES 1 CUP

24 dried *mirasol* peppers (about 6 ounces), stemmed and seeded

Many Peruvian and Bolivian recipes call for a fine powder of mirasol *pepper (dried* ají amarillo*) called* ají molido. *The pepper is ground by machine, so the powder is usually very fine. Several Peruvian companies in the United States import* ají molido, *but I prefer to grind my own so I can be assured of its freshness.*

If the peppers are still pliable and a bit fresh, spread on a cookie sheet and dry in a 200°F oven for 1 to 2 hours, or until brittle. Let cool completely.

Chop the peppers with a knife, or crush to small bits between two pieces of wax paper using a rolling pin or a mallet, or with mortar and pestle. The smaller the bits, the easier they will be to grind. Grind to a powder in a spice mill. I like a coarse texture. Grind twice or longer if you want to obtain a very fine powder.

STORING Keep in a tightly covered container in a cool, dark place.

USES Stir into soups or stews or sprinkle on finished dishes for instant heat and color.

VARIATION For ground *panca* peppers, *ají panca molido*: Substitute 5 ounces dried *ají panca* peppers (about 24 peppers).

CLAM, PORK & WHITE BEAN STEW WITH SMOKED PAPRIKA & GARLIC SAUCE

Cazuela de Almejas, Cerdo y Frijoles Blancos con Salsita de Pimentón Ahumado

SERVES 6 TO 8

FOR THE BEANS

- 8 ounces dried Great Northern beans (about 1 cup)
- 1 medium yellow onion (8 ounces), peeled and quartered
- 2 bay leaves

FOR THE STEW

- 4 dozen Manila clams, scrubbed and rinsed
- 2 tablespoons extra-virgin olive oil
- 6 garlic cloves, finely chopped
- 1 medium yellow onion (8 ounces), finely chopped (about 1 cup)
- 2 teaspoons hot *pimentón* (Spanish smoked paprika)
- 1 teaspoon ground cumin
- 6 medium plum tomatoes (about 1 pound), peeled, seeded, and finely chopped
- 2 celery stalks, finely chopped
- 2 medium carrots (8 ounces), peeled and cut into ¼-inch dice
- 1 pound boneless pork shoulder or butt, cut into 1-inch dice
- ¼ cup dry white wine
- 1 teaspoon cider vinegar
- 1¼ teaspoons salt
- 1 pound green cabbage, coarsely shredded
- 8 ounces Caribbean pumpkin (*calabaza*) or kabocha or Hubbard squash, peeled, seeded, and cut into ½-inch dice
- ¼ cup finely chopped flat-leaf parsley

FOR THE SAUCE

- ¼ cup extra-virgin olive oil
- 6 garlic cloves, peeled and minced
- 1 tablespoon sweet *pimentón*
- 1 tablespoon cider vinegar
- ½ cup chicken broth, homemade or store-bought
- ¼ teaspoon salt

Like a red dress that transforms a plain woman into a siren, a sultry sauce of smoked paprika, olive oil, garlic, and vinegar turns this soothing, homespun stew into something irresistibly alluring. The moment you add it, you will find your hand reaching for a spoon and your mouth begging for a bite. I like to serve the stew in deep earthenware bowls with a crusty bread.

COOKING THE BEANS Put the beans, onion, and bay leaves in a heavy pot, add enough cold water to cover by 1 inch, and simmer over low heat, adding up to 8 more cups of cold water to cover the beans as they dry out. Never allow the beans to boil. It takes a long time to cook the beans by this Catalan method, but they will come out tender and perfect in shape. Drain and reserve.

OPENING THE CLAMS Place 1 cup water in a large skillet. Bring to a boil. Lower the heat, add the clams, and remove them to a bowl with tongs as they open. Strain the broth and set aside for another use.

MAKING THE STEW In a large, heavy pot, heat the oil over medium-high heat. Sauté the garlic until golden, about 40 seconds. Add the onion and cook until translucent, about 8 minutes. Stir in the paprika and cumin and cook 1 minute. Add the tomatoes, celery, and carrot, and cook 5 minutes. Add the pork, wine, vinegar, and salt, lower the heat, and simmer, covered, 30 minutes. Add the cabbage, squash, and parsley and cook until the vegetables are soft but still whole, 15 to 20 minutes.

MAKING THE SAUCE While the stew simmers, heat the oil and sauté the garlic for about 40 seconds. Add the paprika and cook, stirring, 1 minute. Stir in the vinegar, broth, and salt. Cook 2 minutes and remove from the heat.

FINISHING THE STEW Add the beans and opened clams with their juice to the stewed pork and vegetables. Stir in the sauce and cook over medium heat until the stew is hot, 5 to 6 minutes.

SERVING Serve immediately with crusty bread. A side of white rice is a good accompaniment.

WHAT TO DRINK A dry, spicy rosé with backbone, like Montes Cherub Rosé of Syrah from Archangel Estate in Marchigüe, Chile.

GRILLED SKIRT STEAK WITH ARGENTINEAN CHIMICHURRI

Entraña con Chimichurri Argentino

SERVES 4

- 4 skirt steaks (about 1 pound each), trimmed (see Author's Note)

Coarse salt

- 1 recipe Red Chimichurri (recipe follows)

AUTHOR'S NOTE

Latin American butcher shops sell long skirt steaks that can be as long as 27 inches and weigh close to 2 pounds. Halve and trim each steak to a manageable size before cooking. I like my skirt steak long (about 14 inches) and on the generous side, ranging between 14 ounces and 1 pound.

EDITOR'S WINE CHOICE

Juicy, violet-scented Malbec: 2011 Don Miguel Gascón

MAKES ABOUT 2 CUPS

- ½ cup fresh cilantro, finely chopped
- 1 large head garlic (about 12 large cloves), peeled and finely minced
- 1 small yellow onion (about 5 ounces), minced (about 1 cup)
- 1 tablespoon dried oregano, lightly crushed
- 1 tablespoon *pimentón* (Spanish smoked paprika, hot or sweet)
- 1 tablespoon crushed hot red pepper flakes or Argentinean *ají molido* (ground red pepper)
- ½ cup red wine vinegar
- ½ cup extra-virgin olive oil
- 1 teaspoon freshly ground pepper

Salt to taste

Skirt steak, commonly known by the generic name of churrasco, *is a long, thin, and deeply flavorful strip of meat with well-defined open fibers cut from the diaphragm muscle of the cow, just below the ribs. Popularized by Argentinean and Hispanic Caribbean restaurants in the United States, it is by far the most requested cut of meat in any Latin restaurant today. While Argentineans simply salt it and grill it and then lavishly smother it with chimichurri sauce at the table, Hispanic Caribbean cooks like to marinate it with some of the sauce before pan-frying it, broiling it, or cooking it on the barbecue grill or a la plancha (on the griddle).*

Light a grill or preheat a broiler on medium-high heat. Season the steaks with salt and brush with some of the chimichurri sauce. Grill or broil the steaks about 4 inches from the source of heat for 4 to 5 minutes on each side, or until medium rare. Let stand for 5 minutes before serving. If you wish, thinly slice the steaks across the grain at an angle before serving.

SERVING Bring to the table with a bowl of Red Chimichurri. Serve with rice and beans.

RED CHIMICHURRI

CHIMICHURRI ROJO

A blend of Spanish smoked paprika (pimentón) and hot ground pepper gives this chimichurri a sultry reddish hue. I also love how the onion and cilantro work together with these seasonings to make a deeper sauce that adds more than acidity and a garlicky touch to grilled meats.

Mix all the ingredients by hand in a small bowl, whisking to blend well, or mix in a food processor by pulsing until the ingredients are finely chopped but not pureed. Serve at room temperature. It will keep in the refrigerator, in a well-sealed glass container, for 2 to 3 weeks.

SAUTÉED FENNEL WITH ARGENTINEAN SAUSAGE

Hinojo Salteado con Chorizo Argentino

6 SERVINGS
TOTAL: 40 MIN

- ½ cup extra-virgin olive oil
- 6 garlic cloves—4 thinly sliced, 2 minced
- 1 small yellow onion, halved lengthwise and thinly sliced crosswise
- ¼ cup grated *panela* (see Note), dark brown sugar or muscovado sugar
- 3 fennel bulbs (about 2¼ pounds)—quartered, cored and thinly sliced, fronds chopped for garnish
- 2 tablespoons Spanish sherry vinegar, plus more for seasoning
- ½ teaspoon smoked hot paprika, preferably pimentón de la Vera
- 1 teaspoon anise seeds or fennel seeds

Sea salt
- 1 pound Argentinean or sweet Italian sausages

Freshly ground pepper

AUTHOR'S WINE CHOICE
Bodegas Escorihuela Gascón Syrah from Mendoza, Argentina, which has a subtle hint of anise

These golden brown sausages are delicious with the sweet sautéed fennel. Presilla likes to serve the dish as a substantial appetizer or a light supper with salad and bread. It would also be fantastic piled onto a roll and eaten like a hoagie.

1. In a large skillet, heat ¼ cup of the olive oil. Add the sliced garlic and cook over moderate heat, stirring, until lightly golden, about 20 seconds. Add the onion and cook, stirring occasionally, until softened, about 5 minutes. Stir in the *panela* and cook, stirring, until it dissolves. Add the sliced fennel and cook for 5 minutes. Add the 2 tablespoons of vinegar, the paprika and anise seeds and cook, stirring occasionally, until the fennel is crisp-tender, about 5 minutes longer. Season the fennel with salt and sherry vinegar, cover and keep warm.

2. Light the broiler and position an oven rack 6 inches from the heat. Place the sausages on a small rimmed baking sheet and drizzle with 2 tablespoons of the olive oil. Broil for 10 minutes, turning frequently, until golden all over. Halve the sausages lengthwise, sprinkle with the minced garlic and drizzle with the remaining 2 tablespoons of olive oil. Season with pepper. Broil for 4 to 5 minutes longer, until the sausages are golden brown and cooked through.

3. Spoon the sautéed fennel onto plates and top with the sausages. Garnish with the chopped fennel fronds and serve.

NOTE *Panela* is a dense, dark brown Latin American cane sugar that's formed into disks, squares or cones and then grated. It's available at Latin markets and *thelatinproducts.com*.

MARICEL PRESILLA ONLINE
maricelpresilla.com

f *Maricel Presilla*

t *@MaricelPresilla*

Gingerbread Icebox Cake with Mascarpone Mousse, page 206

VINTAGE CAKES

Julie Richardson

When Julie Richardson discovered a drawerful of old dessert recipes left in a filing cabinet by the former owners of her acclaimed Baker & Spice Bakery in Portland, Oregon, she got out her mixer and began testing them. The results inspired *Vintage Cakes,* a charming collection of early- to mid-20th-century American heirloom cakes. To appeal to today's palates, Richardson adapted the original recipes: She cut back on sugar, swapped out margarine and Crisco for butter and even reverse-engineered instant ingredients to make wholesome equivalents from scratch. There are airy chiffon cakes, elegant rolled cakes and "little cakes" like her adorable malted milk chocolate cupcakes, each topped with a malted milk ball (page 212). Dreamy photos take you back to a time "when a cookie was a 'cooky,' housewives were disciples of Betty Crocker and no one had heard of Martha Stewart." PUBLISHED BY TEN SPEED PRESS, $24

GINGERBREAD ICEBOX CAKE
with Mascarpone Mousse

8 TO 10 SERVINGS

BAKE TIME/WAFERS: 12 TO 14 MINUTES

PAN: A BAKING SHEET OR TWO, EITHER LIGHTLY GREASED OR LINED WITH PARCHMENT PAPER

WAFERS

- 4¾ cups (23¾ ounces) all-purpose flour
- 1 tablespoon ground ginger
- 1 tablespoon ground cinnamon
- 1 teaspoon ground cloves
- ¾ teaspoon baking soda
- ¼ teaspoon baking powder
- ½ teaspoon fine sea salt
- ¾ cup (6 ounces) unsalted butter, at room temperature
- ¾ cup (5⅔ ounces) firmly packed brown sugar
- 2 eggs
- ¾ cup (9 ounces) unsulfured blackstrap molasses

MOUSSE

- 1 pound mascarpone, cold
- 1½ cups heavy cream, cold
- ⅓ cup (2⅓ ounces) sugar
- 2 tablespoons pure vanilla extract, or ¼ cup brandy

Store-bought confections like Tastykakes, Entenmann's, and Ivins' were treats we could not find on the grocery store shelves as kids growing up in rural Vermont. Instead, we waited eagerly for a visit from my grandmother, who would drive eight hours north from Philadelphia with her trunk packed full of boxed goodies. My oldest brother always settled into the Ivins' Famous Spiced Wafers, which appeared every autumn at the Acme grocery chain in Philly. This cake was created with the spice flavor of those wafers in mind (never fear if you don't have a source for Ivins', as this recipe uses homemade spice cookies, rolled as thin as possible to resemble wafers). Note that this cake needs to rest overnight to allow the flavors to meld and the cookies to soften.

To make the wafers, center an oven rack and preheat the oven to 350°F.

Sift together the flour, ginger, cinnamon, cloves, baking soda, baking powder, and salt into a bowl, then whisk the mixture by hand to ensure that the ingredients are well mixed.

In the bowl of a stand mixer fitted with the paddle attachment, mix the butter and brown sugar on medium speed until well combined. Add the eggs one at a time, scraping down the sides and bottom of the bowl between additions. Blend in the molasses. Add the dry ingredients all at once and combine on low speed, scraping down the bowl as needed to create a unified dough. Divide the dough in four quarters and shape each piece into a rough rectangle about 1 inch thick. Wrap each piece tightly in plastic wrap and refrigerate the dough until it is firm enough to roll out, about 2 hours.

On a lightly floured surface, roll out the dough with a rolling pin to ⅛ inch thick or even a bit thinner (use a ruler; you can never go too thin, but you will need to reduce your baking time if you roll the dough thinner than ⅛ inch). Using a 2½-inch round cookie cutter, cut out disks and place them 1 inch apart on the prepared baking sheet.

Gather up the scraps and reroll. If the dough gets too warm and hard to handle, pop it back in the refrigerator to firm up before continuing. You will need 70 wafers to assemble the cake. If you have extra dough, use it to cut some festive cookies to embellish the top of the cake, or chill it to make more gingerbread wafers later; the dough will keep in the refrigerator for up to 5 days or in the freezer for 2 months.

Bake the wafers until golden around the edges and firm on top, 12 to 14 minutes. Let the wafers cool on their baking sheet until cool enough to handle, then remove them to a wire rack to cool completely.

Once the wafers are baked, make the mascarpone mousse. Place a mixing bowl or the bowl of a stand mixer and its whisk attachment in the freezer for 5 minutes to chill. Blend the mascarpone, cream, and sugar in the cold bowl on low speed until combined. Increase the speed to medium high and whip just until the cream becomes thick and fluffy and holds a stiff peak (warning: overmixing will cause the contents to curdle). Blend in the vanilla or brandy on low speed until just incorporated.

To assemble the cake, spread about 2 tablespoons of the cream on a flat serving plate. Arrange 6 wafers touching side by side in a circle plus 1 wafer in the middle. Spread a heaping ½ cup of mousse atop the wafers, almost covering them but leaving a smidge of room at the edge of the circle. Repeat with another 7 wafers and more mousse, offsetting the wafers from the previous layer so they do not stack right on top of each other. Repeat until you have ten layers of wafers staggered with ten layers of mousse (not counting your initial dollop on the plate), topping the last layer of wafers with all the mousse that is left in the bowl. Cover loosely with plastic wrap and refrigerate for at least 12 hours. Serve chilled, and if you made any decorative cookies, arrange them on the top.

This cake keeps for up to 3 days refrigerated in an airtight container.

ITALIAN CREAM CAKE

8 TO 12 SERVINGS

BAKE TIME: 25 TO 30 MINUTES

PAN: THREE 8-BY-2-INCH ROUND CAKE PANS, GREASED

- 2 cups (10 ounces) all-purpose flour
- ¾ teaspoon baking soda
- ½ teaspoon fine sea salt
- 1½ cups (10½) ounces sugar
- ½ cup (4 ounces) unsalted butter, at room temperature
- ½ cup canola oil
- 2 teaspoons pure vanilla extract
- 4 eggs, at room temperature
- 1 cup buttermilk, at room temperature
- ½ cup heavy cream, cold
- 1½ cups (6 ounces) lightly packed sweetened shredded coconut
- 1 cup (4 ounces) toasted chopped pecans

Chocolate Ganache (recipe follows)

- ¼ cup (1 ounce) sifted confectioners' sugar, for dusting (optional)

This cake is no more Italian than French toast is French. This white cake flavored with coconut and pecans originated in the South. Even people who don't like coconut love this cake! Traditionally, it's made with cream cheese frosting, but my twist is to layer this cake up with a chocolate ganache enriched with toasted pecans instead.

Center an oven rack and preheat the oven to 350°F.

Sift together the flour, baking soda, and salt in a bowl, then whisk the mixture to ensure that the ingredients are well distributed.

In the bowl of a stand mixer fitted with the paddle attachment, cream the sugar and butter together on medium-high speed until fluffy, about 5 minutes. As you make the batter, stop the mixer frequently and scrape the paddle and the sides of the bowl with a rubber spatula. With your mixer on low speed, drizzle the oil and the vanilla into the mixture until well combined. Blend in the eggs one at a time, adding the next one as soon as the previous one has disappeared into the batter. With the mixer on low speed, add the flour mixture in three parts, alternating with the buttermilk in two parts, beginning and ending with the flour. After each addition, mix until just barely blended and stop and scrape down the bowl. Stop the mixer before the last of the flour has been incorporated and complete the blending by hand with a rubber spatula to ensure you do not overbeat the batter.

In a separate bowl, whisk the heavy cream to soft peaks with a hand whisk. Gently fold the cream into the cake batter, followed by the shredded coconut and ½ cup of the pecan pieces, reserving the other ½ cup to blend into the ganache.

Divide the batter evenly among the prepared pans (approximately 1 pound and 3 or 4 ounces per pan) and smooth the tops. Bake until the center springs back when lightly touched, 25 to 30 minutes.

Remove the pans from the oven and promptly run a thin knife around the edges of the pans to help the cake retract evenly from the sides. Cool the cakes in their pans on a wire rack for 30 minutes. Flip the cakes out of the pans and let them continue to cool on the rack, top side up, until they reach room temperature.

While the cake is cooling, mince the remaining ½ cup of pecans and mix them into the ganache.

To assemble the cake, lay one cake top side up on a flat plate. Spread the cake with a ¼-inch-thick layer of ganache (approximately one-third of the ganache), spreading it slightly over the edge of the cake. Place the next layer of cake on top of the ganached layer, again top side up. Spread it with another third of the ganache as you did with the bottom layer. Lay the third layer of cake top side up, align the layers, and slather on the remainder of the ganache.

Just before serving, and only if your cake is firmly planted on the plate (or a cardboard round) and won't slide, carefully tilt the cake ever so slightly and dust the sides of the cake with the confectioners' sugar tapped from a fine mesh sieve, rotating the cake to dust the sides evenly. Serve at room temperature.

Under a cake dome or loosely wrapped, this cake keeps for up to 3 days at cool room temperature.

continued on page 210

ITALIAN CREAM CAKE
continued

MAKES ABOUT 1½ CUPS (ENOUGH TO LIGHTLY
GLAZE OR FROST AN 8- OR 9-INCH CAKE)

1 or 1¼ cups heavy cream, depending on
    the type of chocolate

8 ounces semisweet or bittersweet
    chocolate, chopped or chips

AUTHOR'S NOTE

*If you are using the ganache as a
frosting (rather than a glaze), make it at
least 2 or 3 hours before you'll need it, as
it takes time to reach a spreading
consistency.*

CHOCOLATE GANACHE

Measure the chocolate into a small heat-resistant bowl. If you are using semisweet chocolate, use 1 cup of cream. If you are using bittersweet chocolate, use 1¼ cups of cream. Heat the cream in a saucepan over medium heat, stirring occasionally. When the cream begins to simmer, quickly remove the pot from the heat and pour it over the chocolate. Swirl the bowl to ensure that all the chocolate is coated with the hot cream.

Cover the bowl with a lid to trap the heat, and let it rest for 5 minutes. Remove the lid and begin to slowly whisk the mixture, starting with small circles in the middle and working your way outward until you have a smooth, glossy frosting.

If you intend to use the ganache as a glaze, let it cool at room temperature for about 30 minutes. Pour the liquid ganache over your cake while the ganache is still warm but not hot. If the ganache thickens too much, rewarm it by placing it over (not in) simmering water.

If you plan to use the ganache as a frosting (not a glaze), you can leave the ganache at room temperature, stirring occasionally, until it reaches spreading consistency. The time varies for this depending on your room temperature, but plan for 2 to 3 hours. Alternatively, you can pop it into the refrigerator to hurry this process, gently stirring it with a spatula every 10 minutes or so until it stiffens up to spreading consistency. If the ganache ever becomes too hard to spread, simply put it somewhere warm to soften.

Covered with plastic wrap at room temperature, this frosting keeps for up to 3 days.

This feathery cake is reminiscent of an Almond Joy candy bar.

MALTED MILK CHOCOLATE CUPCAKES

24 CUPCAKES

BAKE TIME: 24 TO 26 MINUTES

PAN: MUFFIN TINS FOR 24 STANDARD (⅓-CUP) CUPCAKES, LINED WITH PAPER CUPS

2	cups (10 ounces) all-purpose flour
2	cups (14 ounces) sugar
2	teaspoons baking powder
1	teaspoon fine sea salt
1	cup (5 ounces) malted milk powder (not Ovaltine)
6	ounces unsweetened chocolate, chopped
½	cup (4 ounces) unsalted butter
¼	cup canola oil
1¾	cups whole milk, at room temperature
3	eggs, at room temperature
2	teaspoons pure vanilla extract
	Malted Milk Chocolate Frosting (recipe follows)
24	malted milk balls for garnish (optional)

AUTHOR'S NOTE

Make the frosting ahead of time, as it takes about 2 hours to chill to a spreading consistency.

Malted milk powder first arrived on the scene in 1897 as a health aid, but soon became a popular ingredient in chocolate milkshakes at the Walgreen's pharmacy soda fountains in Chicago. More than one hundred years later, here's my recipe for malted milk chocolate cupcakes. You can usually find malted milk powder in the baking aisle of your local grocery store (though sometimes it's on the shelf next to the cocoa and coffee). A few things to note: the frosting will take about three hours to make from start to finish, so plan accordingly. Also use paper cupcake cups and your cupcakes will be perky and presentable; without them, the cupcakes turn out on the flatter side.

Center an oven rack and preheat the oven to 350°F.

In the bowl of a stand mixer, sift together the flour, sugar, baking powder, and salt. Add the malted milk powder and whisk the mixture by hand to ensure that the ingredients are well mixed.

Melt the chocolate and butter in a heat-resistant bowl set over a pot of simmering water. Once both are melted, remove the bowl from the heat and stir in the oil until the mixture is uniform. Scrape the chocolate mixture into the bowl of dry ingredients, pour in 1 cup of the milk, and blend with the paddle attachment on low speed until incorporated, scraping the bottom well to incorporate any dry-ingredient patches. Once combined, kick up the mixer to medium-high speed for 1 minute. Stop the mixer and scrape the paddle, sides, and bottom of the bowl. Whisk together the remaining ¾ cup of milk, the eggs, and the vanilla in a separate bowl and add half this mixture into the batter on low speed. Scrape down the sides of the bowl and add the second half of the mixture, blending until well combined.

Pour the thin batter into the paper-lined pans, filling the cups to just below the rim. Place the tins in the middle of the oven and bake until the cupcakes are perky and firm on the top, 24 to 26 minutes. Cool the cakes in their tins on a wire rack until they reach room temperature.

Once cool, frost the cupcakes with the frosting and place a malted milk ball on top for decoration. These cupcakes are best the day they are made but keep for 3 days in an airtight container at room temperature.

continued on page 214

MALTED MILK CHOCOLATE CUPCAKES
continued

MAKES ABOUT 4 CUPS (ENOUGH TO FROST
24 CUPCAKES)

- 12 ounces milk chocolate,
chopped or chips
- 1 cup (5 ounces) malted milk
powder
- 1 cup heavy cream
- ½ cup (4 ounces) unsalted butter,
at room temperature, and cut into
small cubes

MALTED MILK CHOCOLATE FROSTING

Put the chocolate into the mixing bowl of a stand mixer. Put the malted milk powder into a small saucepan and whisk in the heavy cream ½ cup at a time to prevent the malt from forming clumps. Place the saucepan on the stove over medium heat, stirring often, until the cream begins to bubble around the edge of the pan. (Malted milk powder is essentially sugar, so it will burn unless you keep stirring the cream.) Pour the cream over the chocolate and swirl the bowl so that all the chocolate is coated with the hot cream. Place a lid or plastic wrap over the bowl and let it sit for 5 minutes. Remove the lid or wrap and slowly begin to whisk the mixture, starting with small circles in the middle and working your way outward until you have a smooth, glossy frosting. Cover the bowl with plastic wrap and place in the refrigerator to chill for about 2 hours.

To finish the frosting, remove the bowl from the refrigerator and fit it into the stand mixer. Beat the butter into the frosting with the whisk attachment: begin adding a few butter pieces on low speed, then add more as soon as the butter has been incorporated into the frosting. Once the butter has all been added, mix the frosting on medium-high speed until it is thick and creamy. If the frosting seems too soft, just pop it back into the refrigerator to chill before frosting the cupcakes.

Covered with plastic wrap at room temperature, this frosting keeps for up to 3 days. Refrigerated, it lasts for 7 days.

BANANA BUCKWHEAT BUNDT CAKE

with Maple Glaze

10 TO 12 SERVINGS
ACTIVE: 45 MIN; TOTAL: 2 HR PLUS
2 HR COOLING

CAKE

- 2 sticks unsalted butter, at room temperature, plus more for the pan
- 1 cup walnuts (3½ ounces), optional
- 2½ cups all purpose flour
- ⅔ cup buckwheat flour
- 1 teaspoon fine sea salt
- 1 teaspoon baking powder
- ½ teaspoon baking soda
- 1 cup buttermilk, at room temperature
- 3 large overripe bananas, mashed (1⅓ cups)
- 2 cups granulated sugar
- 4 large eggs

GLAZE

- 2 tablespoons unsalted butter
- ¼ cup pure Grade B maple syrup
- ¼ cup heavy cream
- Pinch of sea salt
- 1½ cups confectioners' sugar, sifted

By combining earthy buckwheat flour with bananas, walnuts and maple syrup, Richardson reconceives the flavors in banana buckwheat pancakes as an elegant, wholesome bundt cake.

1. MAKE THE CAKE Preheat the oven to 350°F and butter a 10-inch nonstick bundt pan. Spread the walnuts on a small baking sheet and toast for about 8 minutes, until golden and fragrant. Let cool, then coarsely chop.

2. In a medium bowl, sift the flours, sea salt, baking powder and baking soda. Whisk to blend well. In another medium bowl, whisk together the buttermilk and bananas.

3. In a large bowl, using an electric mixer, beat the 2 sticks of butter and the sugar at medium speed until fluffy, about 5 minutes, scraping down the side of the bowl frequently. Beat in the eggs 1 at a time, beating well between additions. At low speed, beat in the flour mixture in 3 additions, alternating with the banana mixture and beginning and ending with the flour. Fold in half of the nuts, if using.

4. Spoon the thick batter into the prepared bundt pan and tap the pan on the counter to release any air bubbles. Bake for 45 to 50 minutes, until the cake is golden and a wooden skewer inserted in the center comes out just barely clean. Let the cake cool in the pan on a rack set over a baking sheet or wax paper for 30 minutes. Turn out the cake and set it back on the rack right side up.

5. MEANWHILE, MAKE THE GLAZE In a small saucepan, combine the butter, maple syrup, cream and salt. Bring to a boil and simmer, stirring, until thickened, about 1 minute. Let cool for 5 minutes. In a medium bowl, whisk the confectioners' sugar with the maple mixture until smooth. Spoon the glaze over the cake and immediately garnish with the remaining nuts, if using. Let cool completely, about 2 hours, before serving.

MAKE AHEAD The cake can be stored at room temperature for up to 3 days.

JULIE RICHARDSON ONLINE

bakerandspicebakery.com

f Baker & Spice Bakery

t @BakerandSpice

"I've been lucky enough to witness many taco revelations, the moments when visitors to Mexico bite into one that changes their lives."

—ROBERTO SANTIBAÑEZ

TACOS, TORTAS & TAMALES

Roberto Santibañez with JJ Goode

In his 2011 cookbook, *Truly Mexican,* chef Roberto Santibañez demystified the complex world of Mexican adobos, moles and salsas. Here, he turns his focus to something simpler, "the food that Mexicans eat every single day of our lives": tacos, tamales and the overstuffed sandwiches called *tortas*. These are humble dishes that are within the reach of any home cook. The components are easy to mix and match: You can stuff his succulent slow-cooked pork (page 226), for instance, into a tortilla, a roll or a tamale. The recipes are further customizable with his many salsas, some calling for just four ingredients. Santibañez's preparations of common street snacks and meals are incredibly satisfying, even when they stray from tradition—like his pachola burger, packed with chiles, cumin and garlic (page 222). It's the kind of food you want to pick up with both hands and devour. PUBLISHED BY JOHN WILEY & SONS, $20

BASIC TAMALES

MAKES 24 TAMALES

EQUIPMENT: STAND MIXER WITH WHISK ATTACHMENT

2 to 3 cups filling

- 10 ounces (1⅓ cups) golden-colored pork lard or vegetable shortening, chilled
- 5¾ cups tamale flour (masa harina para tamales; see Author's Note)

Generous 2 tablespoons kosher salt

- 1½ teaspoons baking powder
- 6 cups Spice-Infused Water (recipe below right) or room-temperature water
- 48 dried corn husks, soaked in warm water for ½ hour and drained well

---

AUTHOR'S NOTE

Fresh masa—starchy corn treated with calcium hydroxide (slaked lime) then ground into a dough—is wonderful but difficult to find in the U.S. So this book calls for the easy-to-find powdered dried masa called masa harina. Tamales and tortillas require a slightly different grind of masa harina, a coarser grind for the former than for the latter. The bag you buy should specify which of the two it's meant to make.

Put the lard in the bowl of a stand mixer fitted with the whisk attachment. Beat the lard on high until it's white, fluffy, and tripled in volume (it'll look like vanilla icing), 7 to 8 minutes.

Meanwhile, combine tamale flour, salt, and baking powder in a large bowl and stir well. Add the water and mix well with your hands until you have a smooth dough. (The dough should be moist but not at all wet. If it's dry, very gradually knead in water.)

Lower the speed to medium-high and add the dough by the Ping Pong ball–sized piece until it's all added. Keep beating for another 5 minutes or so. To test that the batter is light and fluffy enough, fill a glass with water and drop in ½ teaspoon of the batter. If it doesn't sink rapidly to the bottom (or better yet, it floats), then you're ready to move to the next step. If not, keep beating.

Fill and steam according to the instructions that follow. They'll take about 45 minutes.

SPICE-INFUSED WATER

Combine 2 teaspoons aniseed, 2 teaspoons cumin seeds, and 10 to 20 tomatillo husks with 7 cups of water in a medium pot. Bring the water to a boil, cook for 10 minutes, then strain it into a large container. Measure 6 cups of the liquid (adding a little fresh water or pouring out a little water, if necessary). Let the liquid come to room temperature.

FILLINGS FOR TAMALES

Nearly anything delicious can serve as the filling for tamales, including many of the meat and vegetable options in the torta and taco chapters. Each tamale requires just a tablespoon or two of the filling, so for twenty-four tamales, you'll need two to three cups. Here are just some ideas:

- ➤ 2½ cups shredded chicken and Tomato-Habanero Salsa (recipe follows)
- ➤ ¾ pound goat cheese, diced; 12 canned pickled jalapeños, cut into strips; and 24 epazote leaves (optional)
- ➤ Refried beans
- ➤ Carnitas (page 226)

continued on page 220

PHOTOGRAPH BY ERIC WOLFINGER

BASIC TAMALES
continued

WRAPPING TAMALES IN CORN HUSKS

Soak the corn husks in warm water for at least ½ hour. Drain well before using. You can keep the wrapped, uncooked tamales in the fridge for up to a day before steaming them. They'll take a little longer to cook if you steam them straight from the fridge.

FOR CLASSIC WRAPPING

For each tamale, put about ⅓ cup batter in the center of the concave side of one corn husk. Spread to flatten it evenly so it forms a rough square. Put a tablespoon or two of the filling in the middle of the square.

Fold the long sides of the husk to enclose the filling in the batter, then fold the pointed end over the seam side. Put the package seam side down on another corn husk so that the open end of the package faces the pointed end. Fold the long sides of the second husk to enclose the package and fold the pointed end over the seam side. Turn the tamale over so the package stays closed. Repeat with the remaining batter, filling, and corn husks.

FOR "CANDY-WRAPPING"

Tear a few corn husks into long, thin strips for tying. You'll need two strips per tamale.

For each tamale, put about ¼ cup batter in the center of the concave side of one corn husk and spread to flatten it evenly so it forms a rough square.

Fold the long sides of the husk to enclose the filling in the batter, then one end at a time, gather the ends and tie each one tightly with a strip of husk to form a shape that looks like a large piece of candy. Repeat with the remaining batter, filling, and corn husks.

STEAMING TAMALES

The method for steaming tamales is the same for each version. Here's how to do it: fit the tamales in a dedicated tamale steamer or deep steamer basket of a pasta pot. Fill the pot with about 2 inches of water, and place a coin in the pot so you can tell if the water has evaporated (you will hear the coin start to jiggle when the water boils and you'll know you need to add more water when the jiggling noise stops). Bring the water to a boil.

Place the tamale-filled steamer basket in the pot, then cover the tamales with additional corn husks and a tight-fitting lid. (Covering the pot with two layers of heavy-duty foil, instead of a lid, will do, too.)

Steam the tamales, adding more boiling water if you no longer hear the coin jiggle, until you can easily and cleanly peel the husk from the tamale, about 45 minutes to 1¼ hours. Leave the tamales in the covered pot with the heat off for 15 minutes before serving.

TOMATO-HABANERO SALSA

CHILTOMATE PARA TACOS

MAKES ABOUT 2 CUPS

1½	pounds tomatoes (about 5 medium), cored
2 to 3	fresh habanero chiles, stemmed
¼	medium white onion, roughly chopped
1	small garlic clove, peeled
1¾	teaspoons kosher salt
2	tablespoons olive or vegetable oil

Preheat the oven to broil or 500°F.

Put the tomatoes, cored sides up, on a large foil-lined baking sheet and roast until the tops have blackened and the tomatoes are cooked to the core, 20 to 30 minutes.

Preheat a pan over medium-low heat. Roast the chiles until they're softened and blackened in spots, 8 to 12 minutes.

Peel the tomatoes, then puree the tomatoes, habaneros, onion, garlic, and salt in a blender until smooth.

Heat the oil in a medium saucepan over medium heat. Add the tomato mixture and gently simmer, stirring occasionally, until the flavors have come together, about 10 minutes. Let cool and season to taste with salt.

MAKE AHEAD This salsa keeps in the fridge for up to three days or in the freezer for up to one month.

PACHOLA BURGERS
Hamburguesas Estilo Bisteces de Metate

MAKES 4

- 1½ ounces guajillo chiles (about 6; see Note on Dried Chiles, page 225), wiped clean, stemmed, slit open, seeded, and deveined
- 2 medium garlic cloves, peeled
- 1 tablespoon apple cider vinegar
- 1 tablespoon kosher salt
- ¾ teaspoon ground cumin
- 1 tablespoon plus 1 teaspoon olive or vegetable oil
- 2 pounds ground beef (preferably 20 percent fat)
- ½ cup finely diced red onion
- ½ cup lightly packed chopped cilantro
- 5 large spearmint leaves, finely chopped
- 4 large hamburger buns

AUTHOR'S NOTE
For an even better burger, ask your butcher to grind the beef to order. My favorite lean-meat-to-fat ratio for burgers is 80 percent to 20 percent.

EDITOR'S WINE CHOICE
Robust, dark cherry–rich Spanish red: 2009 Morlanda Mas de Subirà

Passing by hot dog vendor after hot dog vendor on the streets of New York City sometimes makes me wonder: in such a burger-crazy town, why can't you find carts hawking hamburguesas? Rather than sit-down sustenance, hamburgers in Mexico are mainly found in squares and road-side stalls. My version of this sizzling street treat is inspired by a Mexican dish called pachola or bisteces de metate, a patty of ground beef mixed with guajillo chile, garlic, and cumin—not served on a bun but instead alongside salsa, beans, and tortillas. Yet once it's grilled and topped with avocado slices and a drizzle of salsa or some pickled jalapeños, you have a burger that drowns out the memory of nearly all that came before it.

MAKE THE PATTIES Soak the chiles in a bowl of cold water for 30 minutes, then drain well, discarding the water.

Combine the chiles with the garlic, vinegar, salt, cumin, and ¼ cup of fresh water in a blender and blend until very smooth, poking and prodding if necessary to get the chiles to blend. Don't be tempted to add more water.

Heat 1 tablespoon of the olive oil in a small pan over medium heat until it shimmers. Pour in the chile mixture, then swish 1 tablespoon of fresh water in the blender to get as much of the chile puree as possible. Pour it, too, into the pan.

Cook at a simmer, stirring constantly to prevent scorching, until the mixture thickens to the texture of tomato paste and the color turns slightly darker, 3 to 5 minutes. Let the chile puree cool completely.

Combine the cooled chile sauce with the beef, onion, cilantro, and mint in a large bowl. Mix it all together with your hands until the ingredients are well distributed, no more than 30 seconds. Form 4 patties, each about ¾ inch thick.

continued on page 224

The pickles and chiles in the tartar sauce add a tart, spicy punch.

PACHOLA BURGERS
continued

MAKES ABOUT 2 CUPS

1½ cups diced seeded tomatoes
⅓ cup finely chopped red onion
Heaping ¼ cup chopped cilantro
2 teaspoons finely grated lemon zest
2 tablespoons plus 1 teaspoon freshly squeezed lemon juice, or more to taste
1½ tablespoons finely chopped fresh serrano or jalapeño chiles (including seeds), or more to taste
1½ teaspoons kosher salt

MAKE THE BURGERS Rub a large heavy skillet (or the grates of a grill) with the remaining teaspoon of oil. Heat the skillet over medium-high heat until the pan smokes, then lower the heat to medium. Cook the patties until a deep brown crust forms on both sides and the burgers are cooked to your liking, 4 to 5 minutes per side for medium doneness. (Remember, the chile mixture gives the interior of the burgers a reddish color that shouldn't be mistaken for rare meat.) Transfer the patties to a plate to rest for 5 minutes.

Briefly toast the buns, if you'd like, top them with the burgers, and add slices of ripe Mexican Hass avocado, Pico de Gallo with Lemon Zest (recipe follows), and Mexican Tartar Sauce (recipe follows) or mayonnaise.

PICO DE GALLO WITH LEMON ZEST
PICO DE GALLO CON LIMÓN AMARILLO

Pico de gallo, also known as salsa mexicana, *has become a common sight on tables in the U.S., and it's easy to see why. The highly seasoned mixture of raw, chopped ingredients improves just about any meal with its lively acidity, lip-tingling heat, and crisp texture. This version swaps the classic lime for lemon to great effect. Whenever I take a bite I have a heretical thought: This is so delicious that maybe we Mexicans should use only lemons!*

Combine all the ingredients in a large bowl and stir thoroughly. Season to taste with more chile, lemon juice, and salt. I like to let the salsa sit for at least 30 minutes before serving.

MAKE AHEAD You can make this salsa up to a few hours before you plan to serve it.

MAKES 1 CUP

- ½ cup mayonnaise
- ¼ cup finely chopped drained dill pickles
- 3 tablespoons finely chopped drained canned pickled jalapeños
- 2 tablespoons finely chopped red onion
- 1 teaspoon Dijon mustard
- ½ teaspoon freshly ground black pepper

MEXICAN TARTAR SAUCE

SALSA TARTARA

I just love to slather this creamy, crunchy, spicy sauce on shrimp and fish, either tucked into tacos or just piled on a plate.

Combine the ingredients in a bowl and stir until the ingredients are well distributed. Season to taste with salt.

MAKE AHEAD The sauce keeps in the fridge for up to two days.

NOTE ON DRIED CHILES

Look for dried chiles that are supple, not brittle; more or less unbroken; and have minimal pale spots.

Store dried chiles in an airtight resealable bag, and keep them in a cool, dry place for up to six months.

Trick: Can only find brittle dried chiles? Try this: Put them in an airtight resealable bag with a square of just-damp paper towel and by the next day, they'll be supple.

➤ **ANCHO** Slightly spicy and fleshy with a prune-like sweetness

➤ **ÁRBOL** Fiery with a subtle acidity and nutty quality
(Note: Don't be fooled by chiles that are labeled "árbol" but bear little resemblance in flavor to the real thing. Look for longer, more cylindrical, less wrinkly chiles from Mexico, with at least some stems attached.)

➤ **GUAJILLO** Mild and fruity with a hint of citrus

➤ **CHIPOTLE** Smoky, spicy, and subtly sweet
(Note: There are two main varieties of chipotles available in the U.S. For the purposes here, look for chipotles moras, which are small and dark purple, rather than elongated, tobacco-colored chipotles mecos. The two are not interchangeable.)

CARNITAS (SLOW-COOKED PORK) TACOS

Tacos de Carnitas

MAKES 24 TACOS

FOR THE CARNITAS

- 8 medium garlic cloves, peeled
- ½ medium white onion, roughly chopped
- 1 tablespoon dried Mexican oregano
- ½ teaspoon dried thyme
- 5 teaspoons kosher salt
- 5 pounds boneless pork shoulder, cut into 2-inch chunks
- 3 dried bay leaves
- 1 cup Coca-Cola

EDITOR'S NOTE

The tender shredded pork shoulder can just as easily be tucked into rolls for tortas (Mexican sandwiches) or layered with cheese to make quesadillas.

EDITOR'S BEER CHOICE

Crisp Mexican pilsner: Pacifico

Restaurants and stands throughout Mexico, especially in Michoacán, Mexico City, and Guanajuato, specialize in this pork-lover's fantasy, meat simmered until the liquid evaporates and all that's left is fat. This fat then fries the pork, giving the pieces savory, crisp edges. To make it, many cooks in my home country put an entire pig, butchered into parts, in a giant copper pot to bubble away and customers order by calling out their favorites, perhaps the cueritos (soft, sticky bits of skin), pierna (leg), or even surtida, a mixture of different parts. Because I suspect you might not have an enormous copper pot in your cupboard—I know I don't!—I've come up with an incredibly easy way to recreate the flavors of true carnitas with the help of my Guanajuato-born friend, Anita Andrade, an incredible cook who works with me at my restaurants. The secret weapon? Coca-Cola.

Preheat the oven to 450°F.

Blend the garlic, onion, oregano, thyme, salt, and ½ cup of water in a blender until fairly smooth.

Combine the pork and bay leaves in a 6-quart Dutch oven or deep baking dish that can hold the pork in no more than 2 layers. Pour the blended mixture and the Coca-Cola over the pork and stir and toss well.

Cover the pot and cook in the oven until the pork is very tender, about 2 hours. The sides of the pot might look dark. That's just fine.

Uncover the pot and return it to the oven. Continue cooking, tossing well and scraping the bottom of the pot every 10 minutes, until the pork is slightly crispy on the outside and deep golden brown, about 30 minutes. Coarsely shred the pork.

MAKE AHEAD You can make carnitas up to three days before you plan to serve them.

Serve alongside 24 warm corn tortillas and lime wedges and top with chopped white onion, chopped cilantro, and Fresh Green Salsa (recipe follows), Jalapeño & Pineapple Salsa (recipe follows), or Pico de Gallo with Lemon Zest (page 224).

continued on page 228

CARNITAS (SLOW-COOKED PORK) TACOS
continued

MAKES ABOUT 1½ CUPS

- ½ pound tomatillos (5 or 6), husked, rinsed, and coarsely chopped
- ½ cup coarsely chopped cilantro
- 2 fresh jalapeño or serrano chiles, coarsely chopped (including seeds), or more to taste
- 1 large garlic clove, peeled
- 2 tablespoons chopped white onion
- 1½ teaspoons kosher salt

MAKES 2½ CUPS

- 6 ounces fresh serrano or jalapeño chiles, roughly chopped (including seeds)
- ⅓ cup finely chopped white onion
- 2 small garlic cloves, peeled
- 1 cup low-sodium chicken stock
- ¾ cup diced (¼-inch) cored peeled pineapple (about ¼ ripe pineapple)
- ¼ cup olive or vegetable oil
- 1¼ teaspoons kosher salt

FRESH GREEN SALSA
SALSA VERDE CRUDA

Tart and fiery, this classic bright-green salsa shows off the flavor of tomatillos and the lovable grassy sharpness of fresh unripe chiles. Serve it with anything that would benefit from lively contrast, such as rich Carnitas Tacos.

Put the tomatillos in a blender first, then add the remaining ingredients. Pulse a few times, then blend until the salsa is very smooth, at least 1 minute. Season to taste with additional chile and salt, and blend again.

AVOCADO POWER! Want a more velvety version with the same thrilling flavors? Just double the amount of chiles, bump up the salt by ½ teaspoon, add ½ cup water, and scoop in the flesh of a large, ripe Hass avocado before you blend.

JALAPEÑO & PINEAPPLE SALSA
SALSA DE JALAPEÑOS CON PIÑA

My friend and star assistant Maria Barrera, who shared and helped test recipes for this book, grew up in the mountains of Guerrero eating this salsa at home and at her cousin's taco stand in the town of Tlapa. Savory and spicy, the salsa also provides sweetness with every chunk of pineapple. The addition of chicken stock, common in Guerrero, adds a welcome richness.

Blend the jalapeños, onion, garlic, and most of the chicken stock until smooth, then pour the mixture into a small saucepan or pot. Swish the remaining stock in the blender, then pour it in too.

Add the pineapple, oil, and salt, set the pan over medium-high heat, and bring the mixture to a boil. Boil for a minute or so, stirring frequently. Pour it into a bowl and let it cool completely. Season to taste with salt.

MAKE AHEAD This salsa keeps in the fridge for up to three days.

ROASTED-PLUM SALSA

Salsa de Ciruela

MAKES 1½ CUPS
TOTAL: 50 MIN

1   pound ripe black or red plums
2   jalapeños or serranos, stemmed
3   garlic cloves
1   teaspoon kosher salt

Cooks in Mexico will use just about anything in salsa as long as it's flavorful, Santibañez says. He adores this gorgeous purple-red plum salsa. Black plums lend a lovely deep red color, but red plums work well, too.

1. Light the broiler. Line a rimmed baking sheet with foil. Place the whole plums on the baking sheet and broil 6 inches from the heat for about 10 minutes, turning frequently, until the skins are blackened and blistered. Turn the oven to 500°F and roast the plums for 15 minutes, until they are very soft. Let cool slightly, then slip off the charred skins. Halve, pit and chop the plums.

2. Meanwhile, in a small cast-iron skillet, cook the jalapeños and garlic over moderately high heat, turning occasionally, until the garlic is tender and charred and the jalapeños are blistered and blackened in spots, about 8 minutes for the garlic and 15 minutes for the jalapeños.

3. In a blender, combine about ½ cup of the chopped plums with the charred garlic and jalapeños. Add the salt and puree until smooth. Add the remaining plums and pulse a few times to create a slightly chunky salsa.

SERVE WITH Pork chops, grilled skirt steak or roasted chicken.

MAKE AHEAD The salsa can be refrigerated for up to 2 days.

ROBERTO SANTIBAÑEZ ONLINE

robertosantibanez.com

f *Roberto Santibañez*

t *@FondaRestaurant*

The Sussman brothers: Eli (left) and Max

> "If you think you're only an 'American food' person, stop being so boring. And if you say that you just can't do it, well, you're just flat out wrong."
> —MAX & ELI SUSSMAN

THIS IS A COOKBOOK

RECIPES FOR REAL LIFE

Max Sussman & Eli Sussman

This cookbook has recipes for every occasion in the life of a post-college foodie: brunches, date nights, backyard parties and late-night munchies. But even more grown-up cooks will find plenty to love in this debut from the twentysomething Sussman brothers, who have worked in some of Brooklyn's best kitchens, including Roberta's and Mile End Delicatessen. They translate the neo-rustic Brooklyn restaurant aesthetic into a mishmash of ethnic dishes, like chilaquiles topped with tangy tomatillo salsa (page 234), a Southwestern-style steak rubbed with a super-simple spice mix (page 236) and chicken schnitzel coated with an extra-crispy crust of salt-and-vinegar potato chips (page 238). Max is confident that this book will help anyone cure what he calls our national "epidemic of bad food consumption."

PUBLISHED BY OLIVE PRESS, $23

LATKES WITH LOTS OF SAUCES

SERVES 4 TO 6

FOR THE LOX SAUCE
- 1 **cup (8 ounces/250 grams) sour cream**
- 3 **ounces (90 grams) lox, diced**
- 1 **tablespoon minced fresh chives**

FOR THE APPLESAUCE
- 1 **cup (9 ounces/280 grams) applesauce**
- 1 **tablespoon ground cinnamon**
- 1 **tablespoon light brown sugar**
- 1 **tablespoon granulated sugar**
- 1 **teaspoon ground ginger**

- 4 **russet potatoes, peeled**
- 1 **yellow onion, minced**
- 3 **large eggs, lightly beaten**
- ¼ **cup (1½ ounces/45 grams) plus 2 tablespoons all-purpose flour**
- 2 **tablespoons minced fresh chives**
- 1 **garlic clove, minced**

Salt and freshly ground pepper
Olive oil for frying

EDITOR'S WINE CHOICE
Refreshing, strawberry-scented sparkling rosé: 2010 Raventós i Blanc de Nit Cava

Our dad makes these every year on Hanukkah. And he makes a huge mess. He puts newspapers on the floor, uses every burner, and the whole house smells bad for a week. But they are super delicious and we had to include them in our book. We make them almost every weekend. We had our dad test the recipe.

1. Preheat the oven to 200°F (95°C). Fit a baking sheet with a wire rack and set aside.

2. To make the sauces, stir together the ingredients for each in separate small bowls. Transfer to serving dishes and refrigerate.

3. Using the large holes on a box grater, shred the potatoes into a large bowl of water. Drain the potatoes and rinse under cold running water. Drain again thoroughly, squeezing to remove as much liquid as possible. Transfer the potatoes to a clean kitchen towel and squeeze to dry even further, and then place in a large bowl. Wrap the minced onion in a double thickness of paper towels, squeeze to remove as much moisture as possible, and add to the bowl. Add the eggs, flour, chives, garlic, and salt and pepper to taste and stir to mix well.

4. Pour the oil into a large frying pan to a depth of about ½ inch (12 mm) and heat over medium heat. Using your hands, scoop up a portion of the potato mixture and shape it into a ball slightly larger than a golf ball. Flatten into a very thin pancake, still blotting with paper towels as needed to remove any remaining moisture, and place in the hot oil. Repeat to add 2 or 3 more latkes to the pan, making sure not to overlap them or crowd the pan. Cook until golden brown on the first side, about 3 minutes. Using a slotted spatula, turn the latkes and cook until golden brown on the second side, 2 to 3 minutes longer. Transfer to the wire rack on the baking sheet and place the baking sheet in the warm oven. Repeat to cook the remaining latkes, adding them to the oven as they are finished. When all of the latkes are cooked, serve right away with the sauces.

CHILAQUILES WITH TOMATILLO SALSA

SERVES 4

FOR THE TOMATILLO SALSA

3	pounds (1.5 kg) tomatillos
½	yellow onion, cut into big chunks
1	jalapeño
2	garlic cloves
2	tablespoons extra-virgin olive oil

Salt

Leaves from 1 bunch fresh cilantro, roughly chopped

2	tablespoons olive oil
4	large eggs
2	cups (12 ounces/375 grams) leftover or store-bought roasted chicken, shredded (optional)
1	large bag tortilla chips, preferably thick-cut

Crumbled queso fresco for serving

You are hungover. You have chips. You want to eat some breakfast. We have the solution. Continue reading below.

1. To make the tomatillo salsa, preheat the oven to 400°F (200°C). Peel the papery husks off the tomatillos and rinse under warm water to remove the sticky coating. Put the tomatillos in a large bowl along with the onion, jalapeño, garlic, extra-virgin olive oil, and salt to taste. Toss to mix well. Spread in a single layer on a baking sheet and roast until the skins of the tomatillos and jalapeño are blistered and tender, 20 to 25 minutes. Let cool slightly, then remove the stem from the jalapeño, along with some or all of the seeds if you want a milder salsa. Transfer the jalapeño and the rest of the contents of the baking sheet to a food processor and process to a coarse purée. Transfer to a bowl and let cool, then stir in half of the cilantro. Taste and adjust the seasoning. Set aside.

2. In a large sauté pan, warm the olive oil over medium heat. Carefully crack the eggs into the pan without breaking the yolks. Cook, without disturbing, until the whites are just set, about 5 minutes. (This is called sunny-side up eggs.)

3. To assemble the chilaquiles, warm the tomatillo salsa and the chicken, if using, in a saucepan until the salsa is just simmering. Spread the chips on a serving platter and arrange a layer of the salsa and chicken, if using, on top. Sprinkle with some crumbled queso fresco and half of the remaining cilantro. Carefully slide the fried eggs on top. Garnish with more queso fresco and cilantro and serve right away.

Max and Eli top this dish with sunny-side up eggs.

GRILLED FLANK STEAK
with Chile Spice Rub

SERVES 4

FOR THE SPICE RUB

- 2 tablespoons kosher salt
- 2 teaspoons ground cumin
- 2 teaspoons ground coriander
- 1 teaspoon paprika
- 1 teaspoon freshly ground black pepper
- 1 teaspoon garlic powder
- 1 teaspoon cayenne pepper

- 1 flank steak, about 3 pounds (1.5 kg)

Oil for grill

EDITOR'S NOTE

Make an extra-large batch of the spice rub; it's great to have on hand for chicken and pork as well.

EDITOR'S WINE CHOICE

Rich, coffee-scented Malbec: 2012 Durigutti

Take a piece of meat, season it well, and put it on the grill. Turn it over a few times. Don't overcook it. Then let it rest before slicing it against the grain. If you can master this basic technique and follow the steps below, you are going to be able to cook a steak way better than any of your friends. —Max

1. In a baking dish large enough to fit the steak, stir together all the ingredients for the spice rub. Add the steak and turn to coat thoroughly with the rub, pressing with your fingers to help it adhere to the meat as needed. Cover and let marinate in the fridge for at least 1 hour and up to 6 hours. When you are ready to cook, let the steak come to room temperature while the grill is heating.

2. Build a hot fire in a charcoal grill or preheat a gas grill to high. Using a grill brush, scrape the heated grill rack clean. Rub the grill rack with oil.

3. Place the flank steak directly over a hot area of the grill and let it sit for about 3 minutes. Rotate the steak 90 degrees, and again don't move it for another few minutes. Turn the steak and repeat the process to grill the second side: 3 minutes without disturbing, rotate, 3 more minutes. An instant-read thermometer inserted into the thickest part will read 130°F (54°C) for medium-rare. Finish cooking on a cooler part of the grill if you like your steak medium.

4. Cover the steak loosely with foil and let rest for 10 minutes. Carve it against the grain into slices about ½ inch (12 mm) thick and serve.

A spice rub transforms this budget-friendly cut.

CHICKEN SCHNITZEL

SERVES 4

4 boneless, skinless chicken breast halves (about 6 ounces/185 grams each)

3 cups (4½ ounces/140 grams) packed salt-and-vinegar potato chips

2 cups (8 ounces/250 grams) unseasoned dried bread crumbs

2 cups (10 ounces/315 grams) all-purpose flour

4 large eggs

Salt

Canola or grapeseed oil for frying

1 tablespoon unsalted butter

Thyme Spaetzle (recipe follows) for serving

EDITOR'S WINE CHOICE

Bright, red-berried Beaujolais: 2010 Georges Descombes Morgon Vieilles Vignes

Who doesn't love chicken schnitzel? Maybe people who don't like puppies or rainbows. I don't know any of them and I don't ever want to. We use salt-and-vinegar potato chips to add a nice tangy element. —Max

1. Wrap a chicken breast half in plastic wrap and place it on a work surface. Using a rolling pin or a small, heavy frying pan, pound the chicken breast to an even thickness of about ¼ inch (6 mm). Repeat to pound the remaining breast halves.

2. Put the potato chips and bread crumbs in a food processor and pulse until finely ground and well mixed. Spread the crumb mixture on a large plate. Spread the flour on another large plate. In a wide, shallow bowl, beat the eggs with a pinch of salt.

3. Dredge a piece of chicken in the flour, then dip into the eggs, turning to coat, and then press each side in the crumb mixture to cover completely. Place on a baking sheet. Repeat to coat the remaining chicken pieces.

4. Set up 2 large frying pans and pour oil into each to a depth of ¼ inch (6 mm). Warm the oil over medium heat, and then place 2 breaded chicken breasts in each pan and cook until golden on the first side, about 4 minutes. Add ½ tablespoon butter to each pan, let melt, and tilt the pan to distribute it evenly. Turn the chicken breasts and add more oil if the pan seems dry. Cook until golden brown on the second side and opaque throughout, about 4 minutes longer. Serve right away with the spaetzle.

continued on page 240

Any kind of chips will work for the coating.

CHICKEN SCHNITZEL
continued

1½ cups (7½ ounces/235 grams) all-purpose flour

Salt and freshly ground pepper

2 large eggs

¼ cup (2 fluid ounces/60 ml) half-and-half or whole milk

3 tablespoons unsalted butter

1 tablespoon minced fresh thyme

THYME SPAETZLE

1. In a large bowl, combine the flour, 1 teaspoon salt, and ½ teaspoon pepper and stir to mix well. In a separate bowl, whisk together the eggs and half-and-half. Form a well in the dry ingredients and pour in the egg mixture. Stir the wet ingredients into the dry, gradually pulling the flour mixture into the well, and mix until the dough is smooth. Let the dough rest at room temperature for 20 minutes.

2. Bring a pot of generously salted water to a boil over high heat. Take up a large slotted spoon. Pull off a portion of the dough and, using the back of a soupspoon, push it through the holes or slots of the large spoon into the boiling water. Repeat 2 times for one batch of spaetzle; you don't want to crowd the pot. When the spaetzle float to the surface, scoop them out, transfer to a colander placed in the sink, and rinse quickly under cool running water. Repeat to cook the remaining dough.

3. When all of the spaetzle has been boiled and rinsed, melt the butter in a large frying pan over medium heat. When the butter is hot and foamy, add the spaetzle and stir to coat evenly. Stir in the thyme. Sauté the spaeztle until they begin to brown and crisp slightly, 1 to 2 minutes. Serve right away.

FLUKE CEVICHE WITH PLANTAINS & RADISHES

10 HORS D'OEUVRE SERVINGS
TOTAL: 25 MIN

- ¼ cup fresh lime juice
- ⅓ cup chopped cilantro
- 1 jalapeño, seeded and minced

Kosher salt

- Two 4-ounce skinless fluke fillets, halved lengthwise and sliced crosswise ¼ inch thick
- One 2-ounce bag round plantain chips (about 30 chips)
- 4 radishes, thinly sliced

Extra-virgin olive oil, for drizzling

EDITOR'S WINE CHOICE
Spritzy, lime-scented Vinho Verde: 2012 Vera

Delicate fluke takes on a bright, clean, fresh flavor in just 10 minutes when it's marinated in lime juice, jalapeño and cilantro. Max and Eli fry their own plantain chips, but to make these hors d'oeuvres super-fast, you can use store-bought chips.

1. In a large bowl, combine the lime juice, cilantro and jalapeño; season with salt and mix well. Add the fluke and toss to coat. Let stand for 10 minutes.

2. Drain the fluke and season with salt. Top each plantain chip with a radish slice and some of the fluke ceviche. Drizzle with olive oil and serve immediately.

MAX & ELI SUSSMAN ONLINE

thesussmanbrothers.com

f *Max and Eli Sussman*

t *@TheSussmans*

MICHAEL SYMON'S
CARNIVORE

Michael Symon with Douglas Trattner

Celebrity chef and *The Chew* cohost Michael Symon is an unabashed meat lover. In his second cookbook, he shares 120 recipes that capture the lively Mediterranean-influenced, meat-focused cooking that has made his flagship Lola restaurant a hit in his hometown of Cleveland. Symon covers practically every type of meat, from lean chicken breast to smoky ham hocks to robust, venison-like elk chops. But instead of pairing them with heavy sauces or decadent sides, Symon deftly deploys ingredients meant to "counter meat's inherent richness, fattiness and intenseness." Tomatoes, jalapeño pepper and crispy lemon-herb bread crumbs perk up succulent braised chicken thighs (page 248), while a generous showering of fresh torn mint plays off the lushness of his ground lamb Bolognese with cavatelli pasta (page 246). PUBLISHED BY CLARKSON POTTER, $35

SPICY SRIRACHA CHICKEN WINGS

SERVES 5

- 5 pounds chicken wings, split
- ¼ cup coriander seeds, crushed
- 1 teaspoon cumin seeds, crushed
- 1 teaspoon ground cinnamon
- 2 tablespoons kosher salt
- ¼ cup extra-virgin olive oil
- ¾ cup Sriracha sauce
- 12 tablespoons (1½ sticks) unsalted butter, melted
- ½ cup chopped fresh cilantro

Grated zest and juice of 3 limes
Vegetable oil, for deep-frying

EDITOR'S BEER CHOICE

Refreshing, crisp pilsner: Victory Prima Pils

These are the wings we make and sell at B Spot, and they are super popular despite being super spicy. If you don't have a bottle of Sriracha on hand, get one. It is an amazing and amazingly versatile condiment that goes great in soups, on sandwiches, and on pretty much everything else! It is what gives these wings their signature kick.

1. In a very large bowl, toss to combine the wings, coriander, cumin, cinnamon, salt, and olive oil. Cover and refrigerate for at least 4 hours or overnight.

2. Preheat the oven to 375°F.

3. Arrange the wings on 3 large rimmed baking sheets and roast for 30 minutes, or until firm but not fully cooked through. (If you would prefer not to deep-fry the wings as this recipe states, continue baking for an additional hour, or until the wings are crisp and golden brown.)

4. Meanwhile, in a mixing bowl, stir to combine the Sriracha, melted butter, cilantro, and lime zest and juice.

5. In a deep-fryer or very large pot, heat 8 inches vegetable oil to 375°F.

6. In batches, fry the wings for 5 minutes, or until crisp and golden brown. When done, remove the wings from the oil, shaking off as much oil as possible. As each batch is cooked, toss the wings in the Sriracha-butter sauce, remove, and transfer to a platter.

7. Serve hot, with plenty of napkins.

These wings
can also
be baked
instead
of deep-fried.

LAMB BOLOGNESE WITH CAVATELLI

SERVES 8

1 tablespoon olive oil
2 pounds ground lamb
Kosher salt
1 cup diced red onion
3 garlic cloves, minced
1 cup finely diced peeled carrot
1 cup finely diced celery
1 cup dry red wine
One 28-ounce can whole plum
  tomatoes, with juice
1 bay leaf, preferably fresh
6 sprigs fresh oregano
2 pounds fresh cavatelli
1 cup fresh mint, torn
½ cup freshly grated Parmesan
  cheese (see Editor's Note)
2 tablespoons unsalted butter

EDITOR'S NOTE
Pecorino Romano cheese is a great alternative to Parmesan. It has a bolder flavor and is less expensive than Parmigiano-Reggiano.

EDITOR'S WINE CHOICE
Earthy, red-berried Sangiovese: 2010 Arnaldo Caprai Montefalco Rosso

For such a satisfying comfort food, Bolognese is a remarkably straightforward sauce to make. Whenever possible, try and make the sauce the day ahead, which gives the flavors a chance to really meld together. If I find myself with a huge cache of great lamb, I'll make a double batch of this sauce and freeze half of it for another night. While Bolognese is traditionally served with tagliatelle, for this recipe I like to pair the sauce with ricotta cavatelli, like we do at Lola. It's also great with gnocchi. The fresh mint at the end really brightens up the whole dish.

1. Put a large saucepan over medium-high heat. Add the olive oil and lamb along with a large pinch of salt. Cook the lamb until browned, about 10 minutes. Remove from the pan and set aside.

2. Add the onion and garlic to the pan and cook for 3 minutes, until softened. Add the carrots and celery and cook for another 3 minutes. Deglaze the pan with the red wine, using a wooden spoon to scrape up the tasty bits on the bottom of the pan. Cook until nearly evaporated.

3. Return the lamb to the pan along with the tomatoes and their juice. Bring to a simmer, breaking up the tomatoes with a spoon. Add the bay leaf and oregano and taste and adjust for seasoning. Simmer for about 2 hours, skimming off any excess fat that collects on the top. Remove the bay leaf and oregano sprigs.

4. When the sauce is ready, bring a large pot of salted water to a boil. Drop the fresh cavatelli into the water and cook until they float, 1 to 2 minutes. Remove from the water with a slotted spoon and add to the sauce. If the sauce is too thick, add ¼ cup of the pasta water. Remove from the heat and stir in the mint, Parmesan, and butter. Serve immediately.

Use
American
lamb for
a stronger,
gamier flavor.

BRAISED CHICKEN THIGHS WITH SPICY KALE

SERVES 6

Kosher salt
- 6 bone-in, skin-on chicken thighs
- 2 tablespoons olive oil
- 2 cups thinly sliced red onions
- 2 cups large-diced peeled carrots
- 1 jalapeño, sliced into rings
- 4 garlic cloves, sliced
- 1½ cups dry white wine
- One 12-ounce can crushed San Marzano tomatoes
- 2 bay leaves, fresh or dried
- 2 pounds kale, roughly chopped
- ½ cup toasted fresh bread crumbs (see Editor's Note)
- Grated zest of 2 lemons
- ½ cup chopped fresh flat-leaf parsley
- 2 tablespoons extra-virgin olive oil

EDITOR'S NOTE

In place of toasted fresh bread crumbs, you could top the dish with panko for extra crunch.

EDITOR'S WINE CHOICE

Juicy, medium-bodied Côtes du Rhône: 2011 Eric Texier Rouge

In the restaurant biz, it isn't too often that you get a couple of nights off to spend with visiting friends. But last winter, we got to do just that when our dear friends Laurence Kretchmer and his wife, Becca Parish, came to stay with us in Cleveland, bringing along their lovely young daughter, Delilah. After a few days of hitting the town, we decided to stay in for dinner. While Kretchmer is a front-of-the-house guy, he wanted to prove to me he had chops in the kitchen. I'm not sure how famous his "famous" chicken and kale is outside his own family, but I can tell you it's delicious. (And I may have made it once or twice after he left town.)

1. If you have the time, liberally salt the chicken the night before and refrigerate overnight.

2. Allow the chicken to come to room temperature for half an hour before cooking. Pat the chicken dry.

3. Preheat the oven to 375°F.

4. In a large Dutch oven, heat the olive oil over medium heat. When the oil is hot, put the chicken skin-side-down into the pot. Cook for 3 to 4 minutes, until the chicken is well browned. Flip the pieces and cook for 3 to 4 minutes to brown the other sides. Remove the chicken from the pot and set aside on a plate.

5. Add the onions and a good pinch of salt to the pot and cook for 1 minute. Add the carrots, jalapeño, and garlic and cook for 2 minutes. Pour in the wine and scrape up the tasty browned bits from the bottom of the pan using a wooden spoon. Cook for about 4 minutes, or until the wine is reduced by half. Add the tomatoes and bay leaves and bring to a simmer.

6. Adjust for seasoning, adding salt if needed, and then add the kale. Cover the pot and cook for 5 minutes. Remove the lid and stir. Put the chicken thighs on top of the kale, put the lid back on, and put in the oven for 20 minutes, until the chicken is cooked through.

7. Meanwhile, in a small bowl, combine the bread crumbs, lemon zest, parsley, and extra-virgin olive oil.

8. Remove the chicken from the oven and discard the bay leaves. Top the chicken with the bread crumb mixture. Serve family-style right from the pot.

BRAISED HALIBUT
with Peas, Morels & Mint

4 SERVINGS
TOTAL: 40 MIN

- 1 stick unsalted butter, cut into tablespoons
- 1 small shallot, finely chopped (3 tablespoons)
- ½ pound fresh morels, well cleaned, or 1½ ounces dried morels, reconstituted in boiling water
- ¾ cup mushroom stock or broth
- 1 pound fresh young peas, shelled (1 cup)
- Four 6-ounce skinless halibut fillets
- Kosher salt and freshly ground pepper
- 2 tablespoons chopped mint

EDITOR'S WINE CHOICE
Fresh, floral Grüner Veltliner: 2011 Weininger Herrenholz

In Symon's elegant one-pan dish, mild, meaty halibut simmers with fresh peas and woodsy morels in a rich broth. If fresh morels aren't available, you can use reconstituted dried morels.

1. In a large saucepan, melt 2 tablespoons of the butter. Add the shallot and morels and cook over moderate heat, stirring occasionally, until softened, about 5 minutes. Stir in the stock and peas. Season the halibut fillets on both sides with salt and pepper and add them to the saucepan. Bring to a simmer and cook over low heat for 3 minutes. Turn the fillets and cook until the halibut just flakes, 3 to 5 minutes longer. Using a spatula or slotted spoon, transfer the fish to shallow serving bowls.

2. Whisk the remaining 6 tablespoons of butter into the sauce, 1 tablespoon at a time, and season with salt and pepper. Stir in the mint. Top the fish with the sauce and serve.

MICHAEL SYMON ONLINE
lolabistro.com

f *Lola Bistro*

t *@chefsymon*

Soy-Sake Salmon with Almond Fried Rice, page 252

SIMPLY MING IN YOUR KITCHEN

Ming Tsai & Arthur Boehm

If you've ever read a recipe and wished you could watch the chef actually make the dish, this is the book for you. In this latest cookbook from Ming Tsai, chef at Blue Ginger in Wellesley, Massachusetts, and host of PBS's *Simply Ming*, each recipe has an accompanying video and downloadable shopping list on his website. The food bears Tsai's signature East-meets-West spin: The spicy kick of chiles in his New Mexico–style pork stew is mellowed by miso and sweet potatoes (page 258); trout almondine is reimagined as almond fried rice topped with salmon fillets marinated in soy sauce, sake and lime juice (pictured at left). And throughout there are "Ming's tips," like using fishing line to cut goat cheese into perfect rounds for his shiitake and goat cheese crostini, and removing the tough inner core of lemongrass before chopping it to flavor a light, silky panna cotta. PUBLISHED BY KYLE BOOKS, $35

SOY-SAKE SALMON
with Almond Fried Rice

SERVES 4

Four 6-ounce skinless center-cut
        salmon fillets
½   cup plus 1 tablespoon
       naturally brewed soy sauce
       (see Note on Soy Sauce)
½   cup sake
2   tablespoons honey
Juice from 2 limes
1   cup slivered almonds
3   large eggs
Kosher salt and freshly ground black
       pepper
6   tablespoons canola oil
1   tablespoon minced ginger
2   bunches scallions, white and
       green parts, sliced ¼ inch thick,
       1 tablespoon of the greens reserved
6   cups cooked and cooled jasmine
       or basmati rice or other long-grain
       rice (see Ming's Tips)
2   tablespoons unsalted butter

AUTHOR'S DRINK CHOICE
*A chilled sake, like Ty Ku Black, or a
crisp Chardonnay, like Éric Chevalier,
from France*

I had my first trout almondine in the only French restaurant in Dayton, Ohio, my home town. I loved the contrast of the crunchy almonds and buttery fish. I honor that classic combo of fish and almonds in this recipe, but use salmon, a richer, more luscious fish, instead of trout. The salmon gets a piquant sweet-sour marinade that's also used to make a pan sauce. The almonds go into the rice, which also includes spring onions and scrambled eggs. This is a homey dish that's also great for casual entertaining.

1. Put the salmon in a deep plate. In a small bowl, combine the ½ cup soy sauce, sake, honey and lime juice. Pour over the salmon and marinate for at least 15 minutes and up to 1 hour.

2. In a wok, toast the almonds over medium heat, stirring constantly, until golden, 3 to 5 minutes. Transfer to a small bowl and set aside.

3. Line a large plate with paper towels. In a small bowl, beat the eggs and season with salt and pepper.

4. Heat the wok over high heat. Add 4 tablespoons of the oil and swirl to coat the pan. When the oil is almost smoking, add the eggs, which will puff. Stir to scramble, about 10 seconds, and transfer to the paper towels to drain.

5. Reduce the heat to medium-high. Add 1 tablespoon of the oil to the pan and swirl to coat the pan. Add the ginger and scallions and sauté, stirring, for about 30 seconds. Season with salt and pepper, add the rice, almonds, eggs and remaining 1 tablespoon soy sauce, and stir to blend, breaking up the eggs. Adjust the seasoning, if necessary, and transfer to a large bowl.

6. Remove the salmon from the marinade and pat dry. Reserve the marinade.

7. Heat a large sauté pan over medium-high heat. Add the remaining tablespoon oil and swirl to coat the bottom. When the oil is hot, add the salmon nicest side down and cook until golden, about 1 minute. Flip the salmon, lower the heat to medium-low and cook for 2 minutes. Increase the heat to medium and turn the salmon on one edge and cook for 2 minutes more. Turn onto the remaining edge and cook until medium, 2 minutes more. Transfer to a plate.

8. Wipe out the pan. Add the marinade and bring to a simmer over medium heat. Add the reserved scallions and reduce the marinade by half, 1 to 2 minutes. Remove from the heat and whisk in the butter. Taste to adjust the seasoning.

9. Spread the rice on a platter or divide it among individual plates and top with the salmon. Drizzle the fish with the pan sauce and serve.

MING'S TIPS

➤ If you get tail-end fillets, sauté them on 2 sides only, not on their edges.

➤ To store cooked rice to be used for fried rice, spread it out in a thin layer on a clean baking sheet. Refrigerate, uncovered, overnight and break up any clumps before adding to a stir-fried rice recipe. If short on time, place the baking sheet in the freezer for 30 minutes, checking the rice periodically to make sure it doesn't freeze.

NOTE ON SOY SAUCE The indispensable Chinese and Japanese seasoning, soy sauce has been used for millennia. I call for naturally brewed "regular" soy sauce, which is sometimes called light or thin to distinguish it from darker or thicker kinds. Soy sauce is made from a soybean, flour and water mixture and should be naturally fermented or brewed rather than synthetically or chemically produced. Look for "naturally brewed" on the label and read ingredient listings. Avoid soy sauces that contain hydrolized soy protein, corn syrup and caramel color—a sure sign of an ersatz sauce. Japanese Kikkoman soy sauce is a standby, but I prefer an organic brand like Wan Ja Shan.

TO SEE A VIDEO OF THIS RECIPE GO TO *ming.com/inyourkitchen/ recipe28*

SOY-SAKE ROASTED CHICKEN 'N' EGGS

SERVES 6

  2 cups naturally brewed soy sauce
  2 cups sake, preferably Ty Ku Silver
  ½ cup dark brown sugar
  1 tablespoon minced garlic
  1 tablespoon minced ginger
  6 chicken legs
  6 chicken thighs
 12 large eggs
  2 bunches scallions, white and
    green parts, cut into ½-inch
    lengths
One 10-ounce bag shredded carrots
  1 small head red cabbage,
    thinly sliced
Juice and zest of 2 lemons, 1 teaspoon
    zest reserved for garnish
  6 cups 50-50 white and brown rice
    (see Editor's Note)

EDITOR'S NOTE

Tsai serves this dish with "50-50" rice that he makes by soaking 1½ cups brown rice in water for 1 hour, then cooking it with 1½ cups white rice that has been well rinsed. Alternatively, you can use either all white or all brown rice here.

AUTHOR'S DRINK CHOICE

A chilled sake, like Ty Ku Silver

I'm known for my East-West cooking. This dish, however, draws on two Asian cuisines, Japanese and Chinese. The braising liquid contains soy and sake—the Japanese part—and the eggs, which are cracked and cooked in the liquid, are Chinese-inspired. Served with roasted chicken and a tasty slaw, the eggs are wonderfully flavored and beautiful too— once shelled, they show a mosaic pattern made by the soy. As a kid, I enjoyed similar eggs for Easter while my friends ate the candy kind. Nobody envied my eggs, but once you taste their descendants in this terrific dish, you'll understand why I loved Easter.

1. In a medium bowl, combine the soy sauce, sake, brown sugar, garlic and ginger; stir to combine. Reserve ½ cup of the marinade; set aside. Put the chicken in a large bowl and pour the marinade over it. Turn to coat it evenly with the marinade, cover and refrigerate for 1 hour.

2. Fill a large bowl with ice and add water. Bring a stock pot half full of water to a boil. Add the eggs, cook for 3½ minutes and transfer to the bowl. When the eggs are cold, remove and crack the shells gently. Set aside. Dry the pot.

3. Preheat the oven to 400°F and place a baking sheet large enough to hold all the chicken on the middle rack. Drain the chicken, reserve the marinade and transfer the chicken to the baking sheet—the chicken will sizzle. Roast until cooked through, turning the chicken once, about 35 minutes. Glaze with the ½ cup reserved marinade after 10 minutes, after the chicken is turned, and 5 minutes before it's cooked through.

4. In the meantime, add the remaining marinade to the pot and bring to a boil over medium heat. Return the eggs to the pot, add the scallions and carrots, cover and simmer over low heat for 30 minutes. Using a slotted spoon, transfer the eggs to a medium bowl.

5. In a large bowl, combine the cabbage, lemon juice and all but the reserved zest, the cooked carrots and scallions, and toss. Let sit for 10 minutes.

6. Peel the eggs. Place a mound of the cabbage mixture in individual serving bowls. Top each with a chicken leg and thigh and 2 of the eggs. Garnish with the lemon zest and serve with bowls of the rice.

TO SEE A VIDEO OF THIS RECIPE GO TO *ming.com/inyourkitchen/recipe54*

Underneath
the chicken
is a crisp,
lemony slaw.

ONION-BURGER "HOT DOGS"

with Sweet Chile Relish

MAKES 8

3 tablespoons canola oil
2 large onions, minced
Kosher salt and freshly ground black
    pepper
1 tablespoon minced garlic
1 large red bell pepper, minced
1 tablespoon sambal (see Note on
    Sambal) or hot sauce, or to taste
2 tablespoons agave syrup (see
    Note on Agave Syrup) or honey
½ cup rice vinegar
1 tablespoon cornstarch mixed with
    1 tablespoon cold water
2 pounds ground beef
4 tablespoons unsalted butter
8 hot dog buns

AUTHOR'S WINE CHOICE
*A Syrah blend, like Arrogant Frog Croak
Rotie Syrah Viognier, from France*

I'm a golfing fiend. For a while, I spent as much time as I could golfing at the Olympic Club in San Francisco. One of its attractions, besides the course itself, was its signature dish, hot dog–shaped burgers served in hot dog buns, garnished with a fantastic chile sauce. Here's my version, which makes another great party nibble. The burger shape is the same, but I've upped the ante by adding onions to the beef and making sure the sauce has an intense spicy-sweet tang. Serve this with your favorite chips.

1. Heat a large heavy skillet over medium heat. Add 1 tablespoon of the oil and swirl to coat the pan. When the oil is hot, add the onions, season with salt and pepper, and brown, without stirring, 5 to 6 minutes. Turn and brown for another 3 to 4 minutes. Transfer half the onions to a large bowl and cool.

2. Meanwhile, add the garlic to the skillet, season with salt and pepper, and sauté, stirring, for 1 minute. Add the red pepper and sauté, stirring, for 30 seconds, then add the sambal and agave, stir, and add the vinegar. Bring to a simmer, whisk in the cornstarch slurry, and simmer until the relish is thickened, about 30 seconds. Transfer to a bowl and cool to room temperature. Wipe out the skillet.

3. Put the beef in a large bowl and add the reserved onions, season with salt and pepper, and combine lightly. Very gently shape the beef mixture into 8 thick ovals the length of the buns, and flatten the tops. Season with salt and pepper. Heat the skillet over medium-high heat, add the remaining 2 tablespoons oil, and swirl to coat the pan. When the oil is hot, add the beef patties and cook, turning once, about 4 minutes per side for medium-rare, 1 minute more per side for medium, and 1 minute more per side for medium-well.

4. Meanwhile, heat 2 tablespoons of the butter in a medium pan over medium-high heat. When the butter has melted, add half the hot dog buns crumb side down and toast, moving them in the butter, until brown and crisp, about 1 minute. Repeat with the remaining 2 tablespoons butter and buns.

5. Transfer the "hot dogs" to the buns and cover generously with the relish. Transfer to a platter and serve.

MING'S TIPS

➤ You can make the relish and store it overnight, refrigerated.

➤ You can toast the rolls without butter in a toaster, toaster oven, or under the grill, if you like.

NOTE ON SAMBAL A fiery, chile-based condiment from Southeast Asia, the type I use, and which you're most likely to find, is *sambal oelek*. It's usually made from chiles, vinegar, sugar and salt and is without other ingredients, such as garlic and shrimp paste, found in other sambal types.

NOTE ON AGAVE SYRUP Produced in Mexico and South Africa, this product of the agave plant, which is also used to make Tequila, is similar to honey, but lighter and more "neutral" in taste. There are two kinds of the syrup, sometimes sold as agave "nectar," light and dark. The former is milder, and the one I recommend for the recipes in *Simply Ming in Your Kitchen.*

TO SEE A VIDEO OF THIS RECIPE GO TO *ming.com/inyourkitchen/recipe5*

CHILE MISO PORK STEW

SERVES 6 TO 8

- 4 jalapeño peppers
- 3 green bell peppers
- 1 tablespoon paprika
- 1 tablespoon chile powder
- 1 tablespoon natural onion powder
- 1 tablespoon natural garlic powder
- 2 tablespoons kosher salt, plus additional for seasoning
- 2 pounds pork butt (shoulder), cut into 1-inch cubes
- 3 tablespoons canola oil, plus additional if needed
- 2 large onions, cut into 1-inch pieces
- 1 tablespoon minced garlic
- 2 quarts fresh chicken stock or low-sodium bought
- 4 tablespoons *shiro miso* (see Note on Miso)

Freshly ground black pepper

- 2 large sweet potatoes, peeled and cut into ½-inch dice
- 2 cups shelled edamame

Crusty bread

AUTHOR'S DRINK CHOICE
A lager, like Yanjing, or an off-dry Riesling, like Leitz Eins Zwei Dry

I first enjoyed pork stew in Santa Fe. It was made with Hatch green chiles, remarkable because their initial heat decrescendos to a lovely sweetness. They're difficult to find, though, and jalapeños work beautifully in the stew too. I include miso for the same reason I put it in other dishes—as a natural flavor enhancer. Added too are sweet potatoes and edamame for great textural contrast. Serve the stew with crusty whole-wheat bread and you're in business.

1. Turn a gas burner to high. Skewer the jalapeños on a metal skewer and place on the burner. Allow the peppers to bubble and turn black, 2 to 3 minutes. When one side is charred, protecting your fingers with a potholder or kitchen towel, turn the skewer and char the peppers on the second side, 2 to 3 minutes. Alternatively, char the peppers under the broiler. Transfer to a brown paper bag, close the bag and let sit to steam for 5 to 10 minutes. This helps loosen the skin. Remove the peppers from the bag, and with your fingers or a damp paper towel, rub off the skin. Remove and discard the stem, seeds and veins. Repeat the procedure with the bell peppers, turning them with tongs until they're blistered on all sides. Cut the peppers into 1-inch pieces and transfer them and the chiles to a plate. Set aside.

2. In a medium bowl, combine the paprika and the chile, onion and garlic powders. Add the 2 tablespoons salt and mix well. Add the pork, toss to coat it well, and transfer to the refrigerator to flavor for at least 1 hour or overnight.

3. Heat a small stock pot or heavy soup pot over medium-high heat. Add 1 tablespoon of the oil and swirl to coat the bottom. Add half the pork and brown on all sides, 4 to 5 minutes. Transfer the pork to a plate and set aside. Repeat with another tablespoon of oil and the remaining pork.

4. Wipe out the pot and heat over medium-high heat and add the remaining 1 tablespoon oil. Swirl to coat the bottom and when the oil is hot, add the onions and garlic and sauté, stirring, until browned, 5 to 6 minutes. Add the peeled peppers, return the pork to the pot. Add the stock and bring to a simmer. Place the miso in a strainer, dip it into the stock and whisk to dissolve the miso into the soup. Adjust the seasoning with salt and pepper and simmer until the pork is tender, about 1½ hours.

5. Add the sweet potatoes and edamame and simmer until the sweet potatoes are tender, 15 to 20 minutes. Transfer to individual bowls and serve with the bread.

MING'S TIPS

➤ If you can find Hatch green chiles, fresh, frozen, or canned, use 2 cups chopped instead of the jalapeños. If using the canned kind, drain the chiles first.

➤ You can make this dish in a pressure cooker to save time. Follow the instructions up to the final simmering and lock the lid in place according to the manufacturer's instructions. When the steam begins to hiss out of the cooker, reduce the heat to low, just enough to maintain a very weak whistle, and cook for 30 minutes. Release the pressure, add the potatoes and edamames, lock on the lid, and cook for another 15 minutes.

NOTE ON MISO The defining ingredient of the eponymous Japanese soup, miso is a savory seasoning paste made from rice, barley, and/or soybeans. For the recipes in this book, I call for *shiro miso,* which is made from rice. It's available in cans, jars, tubs and plastic bags, and is best stored in the fridge, where it lasts up to 3 months.

TO SEE A VIDEO OF THIS RECIPE GO TO *ming.com/inyourkitchen/ recipe25*

MING TSAI ONLINE

ming.com

[f] *Ming Tsai*

[t] *@chefmingtsai*

MAC & CHEESE, PLEASE!

Laura Werlin

It takes an award-winning cheese expert like Laura Werlin to put together an insanely delicious collection of 50 mac and cheese recipes. Werlin includes every kind imaginable, from stovetop to oven, fancy to low-brow—even gluten-free. Her classic version is a good starting point, using a mix of Gruyère and cheddar for deep flavor and oozing texture (page 262). Once you've mastered the basics you can explore Werlin's more gonzo creations, like a Super Bowl–ready nacho mac and cheese filled with Tex-Mex ingredients and topped with crushed tortilla chips (page 268). The spicy "home fries" mac and cheese (page 265) is a "potato-on-pasta splurge worth its weight in carbs," she says. There's also a terrific section that expertly guides readers through the world of cheeses, from the best melters and graters to the creamiest varieties around. PUBLISHED BY ANDREWS MCMEEL, $17

CLASSIC MAC & CHEESE

SERVES 6

- 1 tablespoon plus 1 teaspoon kosher salt
- 8 ounces small elbow macaroni
- 5 tablespoons salted butter, plus more for baking dish
- 2 cups coarse, fresh bread crumbs (preferably homemade; see Turning Bread Into Crumbs, page 264)
- 2 ounces Parmigiano-Reggiano or Pecorino Romano cheese, finely grated (about 1 cup)
- ¾ cup finely diced yellow onion (about ½ medium onion)
- 2 tablespoons all-purpose flour
- 2 cups whole or reduced-fat milk
- 1 cup heavy cream
- 6 ounces medium or aged cheddar cheese, preferably orange, coarsely grated (2 cups)
- 6 ounces Gruyère cheese, coarsely grated (2 cups)
- ½ teaspoon mustard powder
- ¼ teaspoon cayenne pepper
- ⅛ teaspoon ground or freshly grated nutmeg

EDITOR'S NOTE

Instead of elbow macaroni, you could substitute other short pasta shapes, such as shells, penne or ziti.

EDITOR'S WINE CHOICE

Raspberry-rich Oregon Pinot Noir: 2010 Scott Paul La Paulée

This is a classic mac & cheese in every way but it includes onion. I like the sweetness the onions add, but if you prefer, simply leave them out. The dish will likely make it into your regular mac & cheese repertoire either way.

Preheat the oven to 375°F. Butter an 8-inch square (1½-quart) baking dish or pan (or six 8-ounce ramekins). Set aside.

Fill a 4- to 5-quart pot about three-quarters full with water and add 1 tablespoon of the salt. Bring to a boil and add the pasta. Cook, stirring once or twice, until tender but firm, about 4 minutes, and drain. Reserve the pot.

While the pasta is cooking, in a medium skillet, melt 2 tablespoons of the butter in a medium skillet over medium heat. Turn off the heat and add the bread crumbs and Parmigiano-Reggiano. Stir until mixed well. Set aside.

Using the same pot you used to cook the pasta, melt the remaining 3 tablespoons butter over medium heat. Add the onion and cook, stirring occasionally, until soft and translucent, about 5 minutes. Slowly whisk in the flour and stir constantly until the onion is coated with the flour, 30 to 45 seconds. Continue stirring for about 2 minutes more, or until the mixture starts to darken slightly and smell a bit nutty. Slowly whisk in the milk, cream, and the remaining 1 teaspoon salt and cook until the mixture is just beginning to thicken and bubble around the edges, 5 to 7 minutes. It should be similar in texture to cake batter. If it's soupy, continue cooking until it thickens. Add 1½ cups of the cheddar, the Gruyère, mustard powder, cayenne, and nutmeg and stir until the cheeses have melted and the sauce is smooth but not too runny. Again, it should be similar in texture to cake batter. If it's soupy, continue cooking, stirring constantly, until it thickens.

Add the pasta and stir to combine. Pour into the prepared baking dish. Sprinkle with the remaining ½ cup of cheddar and top with the bread crumb mixture. Place the dish on a rimmed baking sheet and bake until bubbling and golden brown, about 30 minutes. Let cool for 15 minutes before serving.

continued on page 264

A mix of cheeses makes this creamy and flavorful.

CLASSIC MAC & CHEESE
continued

ADD-INS

> **BACON** Cook 6 to 8 slices bacon. Crumble and add after the cheeses have been added and the sauce is smooth, and/or

> **OVEN-ROASTED TOMATOES** Add after the cheeses have been added and the sauce is smooth, and/or

> **ARUGULA** Add 6 cups, a handful at a time, after the cheeses have been added and the sauce is smooth, and/or

> **ROASTED RED PEPPERS** Add ¾ cup coarsely chopped peppers from a jar along with the pasta.

TURNING BREAD INTO CRUMBS

Although a food processor is the easiest way to make your own bread crumbs, it's not the only way. If you are using a food processor, then simply put four sandwich-size slices of bread, crusts removed (optional), into the work bowl and whirl away. You'll end up with 2 cups crumbs, which is what you'll need for the 1½-quart pan that's specified in almost all of the recipes in *Mac & Cheese, Please!* If you don't have a food processor, then you're best off letting your bread get stale by tearing it into pieces, putting it on a baking sheet, and leaving it out overnight. Once it's dry, you can put it in a resealable plastic bag and run a rolling pin or heavy can over it to crush the bread into crumbs. The more rustic, the better, so don't worry if the crumbs aren't uniform.

If you don't have all night to wait, then put the torn-up pieces of bread in a very low oven for 20 to 30 minutes. You don't want to toast the bread; you just want to dry it out.

Finally, if all else fails, then yes, you can toast the bread. Just do so as lightly as possible—long enough to dry it out but not so long that it darkens too much. Remember, these crumbs are going to get baked on top of the macaroni and cheese, so if you start with bread that's too toasted, it will likely burn once it's cooked again. Let the toasted bread cool and then crush away.

SPICY "HOME FRIES" MAC & CHEESE

SERVES 6

1 tablespoon plus ½ teaspoon kosher salt, plus more as needed
8 ounces small or medium shell pasta
¼ cup plus 2 tablespoons olive oil
1 pound small red potatoes, cut into ¼-inch chunks (do not peel)
Freshly ground black pepper
1 small onion (about 4 ounces), cut into ½-inch dice
1 medium red bell pepper (about 8 ounces), cut into ½-inch dice
1 medium green bell pepper (about 8 ounces), cut into ½-inch dice
2 teaspoons dried oregano
¼ cup all-purpose flour
1½ cups whole or reduced-fat milk
½ cup heavy cream
12 ounces cheddar cheese, coarsely grated (3½ cups)
2 teaspoons Frank's RedHot Sauce (or use your favorite brand), plus more for serving (use less or more depending on how spicy you want it)
½ teaspoon dry mustard powder
Ketchup, for serving (optional)

AUTHOR'S NOTE

Do not use a glass pan or a ceramic dish for this recipe. It can break when set under the broiler.

EDITOR'S WINE CHOICE

Juicy, concentrated Argentinean Malbec: 2011 The Show

To me, the ultimate diner breakfast isn't the eggs you find there, but instead it's the potatoes, especially when they're in the form of home fries. In this mac & cheese, those home-fried potatoes get their just due by acting as the crowning glory on the creamy, cheesy pasta underneath. I don't have to wonder what Dr. Atkins would have said about a potato-on-pasta dish, but this is one splurge worth its weight in carbs.

Position an oven rack about 6 inches below the broiler and preheat to broil. Butter an 8-inch square (1½-quart) metal pan or six 8-ounce ramekins. Set aside.

Fill a 4- to 5-quart pot about three-quarters full with water and add 1 tablespoon of the salt. Bring to a boil and add the pasta. Cook, stirring once or twice, until tender but firm, 4 to 6 minutes for small shells, 8 to 10 minutes for medium shells, and drain. Reserve the pot.

In a large skillet, heat ¼ cup of the oil over medium heat. Add the potatoes and cook, stirring occasionally, until the edges are darkened and the potatoes are crisp, 10 to 12 minutes. Add salt and black pepper to taste. Using a slotted spatula or spoon, transfer the potatoes to a plate.

Using the same skillet, cook the onion and bell peppers, stirring occasionally, until the vegetables are soft and beginning to caramelize (darken) around the edges, 8 to 10 minutes. Add the oregano and salt and black pepper to taste. Turn off the heat and set aside.

Using the same pot you used to cook the pasta, heat the remaining 2 tablespoons oil over medium heat. Slowly whisk in the flour and the remaining ½ teaspoon salt and stir constantly until a paste forms, 30 to 45 seconds. Continue stirring for 1 to 2 minutes more, until the mixture starts to darken slightly and smell a bit nutty. Slowly whisk in the milk and cream and stir until the mixture starts to thicken and is just beginning to bubble around the edges, 5 to 7 minutes. It should be thick enough to coat the back of a wooden spoon. Add 3 cups of the cheese, the hot sauce, and mustard powder and stir until the cheese has melted and the sauce is smooth but not too runny. It should be similar in texture to cake batter. If it's soupy, continue cooking until it thickens.

continued on page 266

SPICY "HOME FRIES" MAC & CHEESE
continued

Turn off the heat and add the pasta and peppers. Stir to combine. Transfer the mixture to the prepared dish. Pile the potatoes on top of the casserole and sprinkle the remaining cheese over the potatoes.

Put the pan on a rimmed baking sheet and place under the broiler. Cook until the cheese is bubbly and golden brown and the potatoes that are peeking out begin to darken, 2 to 3 minutes. Watch carefully, because the cheese and potatoes can burn easily. Let cool for 10 to 15 minutes before serving. Pass extra hot sauce and/or ketchup, if desired, alongside.

ADD-INS

➤ **BACON** Cook 8 slices bacon, crumble them, and add along with the pasta and peppers, or

➤ **BREAKFAST SAUSAGE LINKS OR PATTIES** Brown 8 ounces of sausage, then cut into ½-inch pieces. Add along with the pasta and peppers, and/or

➤ **SPINACH** Add 6 cups, a handful at a time, along with the pasta and peppers.

NACHO MAC & CHEESE

SERVES 12 TO 16

12 ounces tortilla chips

2 tablespoons plus 2 teaspoons kosher salt

1 pound small shell pasta

¼ cup canola or vegetable oil

1 large red onion (about 12 ounces), coarsely chopped (about 2 cups)

¼ cup all-purpose flour

4 cups whole or reduced-fat milk

2 cups heavy cream

1 pound sharp cheddar cheese, coarsely grated (about 5¼ cups)

8 ounces pepper Jack cheese, coarsely grated (about 2½ cups)

1½ cups sour cream

1 cup sliced black olives

1 cup coarsely chopped fresh cilantro leaves, plus sprigs for garnish

¼ cup canned or jarred jalapeño chiles, finely chopped

½ teaspoon cayenne pepper

4 ounces queso fresco, crumbled (or use feta)

Guacamole (recipe follows)

1 cup salsa, homemade (recipe follows) or store-bought

EDITOR'S WINE CHOICE

Fruity, full-bodied Australian Shiraz: 2011 Torbreck Woodcutter's

---

You guessed it. For this recipe, the tried-and-true football-watching snack is transformed into a tasty mac & cheese. The main difference (besides the inclusion of pasta, of course) is that instead of the chips serving as the foundation for the nachos, they create a super-crunchy topping. But don't worry—as you'll see, they still have the requisite melted cheese on top. The rest of the ingredients remain loyal to the dish's inspiration. Feel free to add your own favorite nacho flavor twist, though.

Preheat the oven to 375°F. Butter a 9-by-13-inch (3-quart) baking dish or pan. Set aside.

Place the tortilla chips in the bowl of a food processor and pulse just until the chips are coarse, not sand-like. (Alternatively, put the tortilla chips in a large resealable plastic bag and use a rolling pin or other heavy object to crush the chips.) Set aside.

Fill a 6- to 8-quart pot about three-quarters full with water and add 2 tablespoons of the salt. Bring to a boil and add the pasta. Cook, stirring once or twice, until tender but firm, about 4 minutes, and drain.

Using the same pot you used to cook the pasta, heat the oil over medium heat. Add the onion and cook for 5 minutes, or until soft. Slowly whisk in the flour and stir constantly until the onion is coated with the flour, 30 to 45 seconds. Continue stirring for 1 to 2 minutes more, until the mixture starts to darken slightly and smell a bit nutty. Slowly whisk in the milk, cream, and the remaining 2 teaspoons salt and cook until the mixture starts to thicken and is just beginning to bubble around the edges, 5 to 7 minutes. It should be thick enough to coat the back of a wooden spoon. Add 3 cups of the cheddar and the pepper Jack and stir until the sauce is smooth but not too runny. It should be similar in texture to cake batter. If it's soupy, continue cooking until it thickens.

Add the pasta, ½ cup of the sour cream, the olives, chopped cilantro, jalapeños, and cayenne. Pour into the prepared baking dish. Top with the crushed tortillas, and sprinkle with the remaining cheddar. Put the dish on a rimmed baking sheet and bake until bubbling and golden brown, about 30 minutes.

continued on page 270

NACHO MAC & CHEESE
continued

Remove from the oven and sprinkle with the queso fresco. Let cool for 15 to 20 minutes. To serve, garnish each serving with a cilantro sprig. Pass the guacamole, salsa, and the remaining 1 cup sour cream alongside.

GUACAMOLE

MAKES ABOUT 1 CUP

- 1 ripe avocado (preferably Hass)
- 1 tablespoon fresh lime juice
- ½ teaspoon kosher salt, plus more as needed
- 2 tablespoons coarsely chopped onion
- 2 tablespoons coarsely chopped fresh cilantro
- 1 teaspoon canned or jarred jalapeño chile, finely chopped

Split and pit the avocado, scoop out the flesh, and mash it in a medium bowl with the lime juice and salt, using a potato masher or fork. Do not use a blender or food processor. You want to keep the avocado slightly chunky, not make it soupy. Stir in the onion, cilantro, and chile. Let sit for about 15 minutes to allow the flavors to meld. Taste, and add more salt if necessary.

NOTE You can make this a couple of hours ahead. Just drizzle the surface generously with lime juice to prevent it from browning and refrigerate until ready to use.

SALSA

- 8 ounces tomatillos, husks removed and quartered
- 1 medium white or yellow onion (about 8 ounces), peeled and cut lengthwise into 6 pieces
- 1 serrano chile, halved lengthwise and seeded
- 2 tablespoons canola or vegetable oil
- ½ teaspoon kosher salt, plus more as needed
- Freshly ground black pepper to taste
- ¼ cup coarsely chopped fresh cilantro leaves
- 2 tablespoons water

Preheat the oven to 375°F. Put the tomatillos, onion, and chile on a large rimmed baking sheet. Drizzle with the oil. Sprinkle with the salt and a little black pepper. Roast the vegetables, stirring occasionally, until the tomatillos have collapsed, about 20 minutes. Let cool slightly. Put in a food processor or blender with the cilantro and water and process until smooth. Taste and add more salt if necessary. Set aside.

NOTE This can be made up to 2 days ahead, covered, and refrigerated.

ADD-INS

> **ROTISSERIE CHICKEN** Cut 1½ pounds cooked rotisserie chicken into bite-size pieces. Add along with the pasta. Alternatively, shred the chicken and use to top each serving.

"BLT" MAC & CHEESE

10 TO 12 SERVINGS
ACTIVE: 25 MIN; TOTAL: 2 HR

- 2 pints cherry tomatoes
- ¼ cup olive oil, plus more for drizzling
- Kosher salt and freshly ground black pepper
- ½ pound sliced bacon
- 1 pound small shells or elbow macaroni
- 1 pound medium-sharp cheddar cheese, coarsely shredded
- ½ pound havarti cheese, coarsely shredded
- 3 large eggs
- 3 cups heavy cream
- 2½ cups whole milk
- 1 cup crème fraîche
- ½ teaspoon cayenne pepper
- 6 large curly kale leaves, stems and ribs removed

EDITOR'S WINE CHOICE

Smoky, spicy California Syrah: 2010 Holus Bolus

Werlin combines two classic comfort foods here, mac and cheese and a BLT, but in a fun twist she switches out the lettuce for kale. The result is a crispy kale blanket over cheesy, creamy, bacon-y pasta with roasted tomatoes.

1. Preheat the oven to 400°F. Spread the tomatoes on a rimmed baking sheet and drizzle with the ¼ cup of olive oil; season with salt and black pepper. Lay the bacon strips on a rack set over a baking sheet. Put both baking sheets in the oven. Roast the bacon for about 10 minutes, until golden and crispy. Remove the bacon from the oven and continue roasting the tomatoes for about 10 minutes longer, until the skins are golden in spots and beginning to burst; remove the tomatoes from the oven. Let the bacon and tomatoes cool. Lower the oven temperature to 375°F.

2. Meanwhile, in a large pot of boiling salted water, cook the pasta until almost al dente, 5 to 6 minutes. Drain.

3. Butter a 9-by-13-inch baking dish. In a medium bowl, combine the cheeses. In a large bowl, beat the eggs. Whisk in the heavy cream, milk, crème fraîche, cayenne and 2 teaspoons of salt. Add the tomatoes, pasta and 3 cups of the cheese. Crumble in the bacon and mix well. Pour the pasta into the prepared baking dish and top with the remaining cheese. Cover with the kale leaves and drizzle with a little olive oil. Bake for about 45 minutes, until the pasta is bubbling and golden brown on top. Let the mac and cheese stand for 30 minutes before serving.

MAKE AHEAD The assembled mac and cheese can be refrigerated overnight, without the kale. Bring to room temperature before proceeding.

LAURA WERLIN ONLINE

laurawerlin.com

f *Laura Werlin*

t *@cheezelady*

INDEX

A

INDEX

INDEX

CREDITS

THE GREAT MEAT COOKBOOK

Recipes from *The Great Meat Cookbook* by Bruce Aidells. Copyright © 2012 by Bruce Aidells. Reprinted by permission of Houghton Mifflin Harcourt Publishing Company. All rights reserved. Photographs copyright © 2012 by Luca Trovato.

IN MY KITCHEN

Recipes from *In My Kitchen* by Ted Allen with Barry Rice, copyright © 2012 by Ted Allen. Jacket cover copyright © 2012 by Clarkson Potter. Used by permission of Clarkson Potter/Publishers, an imprint of the Crown Publishing Group, a division of Random House, Inc. Any third party use of this material, outside of this publication, is prohibited. Interested parties must apply directly to Random House, Inc. for permission. Photographs copyright © 2012 by Ben Fink.

THE MILE END COOKBOOK

Recipes from *The Mile End Cookbook: Redefining Jewish Comfort Food from Hash to Hamantaschen* by Noah Bernamoff and Rae Bernamoff, Michael Stokes and Richard Maggi, copyright © 2012 by Mile End Delicatessen. Jacket cover copyright © 2012 by Clarkson Potter. Used by permission of Clarkson Potter/Publishers, an imprint of the Crown Publishing Group, a division of Random House, Inc. Any third party use of this material, outside of this publication, is prohibited. Interested parties must apply directly to Random House, Inc. for permission. Principal photography by Quentin Bacon.

A GIRL & HER PIG

Four recipes with sub-recipes/recipe ingredients, four interior photos, book cover from *A Girl and Her Pig* by April Bloomfield with JJ Goode. Copyright © 2012 by April Bloomfield. Reprinted by permission of HarperCollins Publishers. Photographs by David Loftus.

THE BACK IN THE DAY BAKERY COOKBOOK

Excerpted from *The Back in the Day Bakery Cookbook*. Copyright © 2012 by Cheryl Day and Griffith Day. Used by permission of Artisan, a division of Workman Publishing Co., Inc., New York. All rights reserved. Photographs copyright © 2012 by Squire Fox.

BURMA: RIVERS OF FLAVOR

Excerpted from *Burma: Rivers of Flavor*. Copyright © 2012 by Naomi Duguid. Used by permission of Artisan, a division of Workman Publishing Co., Inc., New York. All rights reserved. Studio photographs copyright © 2012 by Richard Jung.

THE RIVER COTTAGE FISH BOOK

Recipes from *The River Cottage Fish Book: The Definitive Guide to Sourcing and Cooking Sustainable Fish and Shellfish* by Hugh Fearnley-Whittingstall and Nick Fisher, copyright © 2007 by Hugh Fearnley-Whittingstall and Nick Fisher. Jacket cover copyright © 2007 by Ten Speed Press. Used by permission of Ten Speed Press, an imprint of the Crown Publishing Group, a division of Random House, Inc. Any third party use of this material, outside of this publication, is prohibited. Interested parties must apply directly to Random House, Inc. for permission. Photographs copyright © 2007 by Simon Wheeler.

SALTIE

From *Saltie* © 2012 by Caroline Fidanza; photographs by Gentl & Hyers. Used with permission of Chronicle Books LLC, San Francisco. Visit *ChronicleBooks.com*.

BAKING OUT LOUD

Recipes from *Baking Out Loud: Fun Desserts with Big Flavors* by Hedy Goldsmith with Abigail Johnson Dodge, copyright © 2012 by Hedy Goldsmith. Jacket cover copyright © 2012 by Clarkson Potter. Used by permission of Clarkson Potter/Publishers, an imprint of the Crown Publishing Group, a division of Random House, Inc. Any third party use of this material, outside of this publication, is prohibited. Interested parties must apply directly to Random House, Inc. for permission. Photographs copyright © 2012 by Ben Fink.

JAPANESE FARM FOOD

From *Japanese Farm Food* by Nancy Singleton Hachisu. Text copyright © 2012 by Nancy Singleton Hachisu. Photography copyright © 2012 by Kenji Miura. Used by permission of Andrews McMeel Publishing, LLC.

MIKE ISABELLA'S CRAZY GOOD ITALIAN

From *Mike Isabella's Crazy Good Italian* by Mike Isabella with Carol Blymire. Copyright © 2012 by Mike Isabella. Used by permission of Da Capo Press. Photographs © Greg Powers.

BOUCHON BAKERY

Excerpted from *Bouchon Bakery*. Copyright © 2012 by Thomas Keller. Used by permission of Artisan, a division of Workman Publishing Co., Inc., New York. All rights reserved. Photographs copyright © 2012 by Deborah Jones.

EMERIL'S KICKED-UP SANDWICHES

Three recipes with interior photos, sub-recipes, book cover from *Emeril's Kicked-Up Sandwiches* by Emeril Lagasse. Copyright © 2012 by Emeril/ MSLO Acquisitions Sub, LLC. Reprinted by permission of HarperCollins Publishers. Photographs by Steven Freeman.

POLPO: A VENETIAN COOKBOOK (OF SORTS)

From *Polpo: A Venetian Cookbook (of Sorts)*. Copyright © 2012 by Russell Norman. Photography © 2012 by Jenny Zarins. Used by permission of Bloomsbury Publishing Plc.

JERUSALEM

Recipes from *Jerusalem: A Cookbook* by Yotam Ottolenghi and Sami Tamimi, copyright © 2012 by Yotam Ottolenghi and Sami Tamimi. Jacket cover copyright © 2012 by Ten Speed Press. Used by permission of Ten Speed Press, an imprint of the Crown Publishing Group, a division of Random House, Inc. Any third party use of this material, outside of this publication, is prohibited. Interested parties must apply directly to Random House, Inc. for permission. Food photographs copyright © 2012 by Jonathan Lovekin. Location photographs copyright © 2012 by Adam Hinton.

THE SMITTEN KITCHEN COOKBOOK

From *The Smitten Kitchen Cookbook* by Deb Perelman, copyright © 2012 by Deborah Perelman. Used by permission of Alfred A. Knopf, a division of Random House, Inc. Any third party use of this material, outside of this publication, is prohibited. Interested parties must apply directly to Random House, Inc. for permission. Photographs by Deb Perelman.

VIETNAMESE HOME COOKING

Recipes from *Vietnamese Home Cooking* by Charles Phan with Jessica Battilana, copyright © 2012 by Charles Phan. Jacket cover copyright © 2012 by Ten Speed Press. Used by permission of Ten Speed Press, an imprint of the Crown Publishing Group, a division of Random House, Inc. Any third party use of this material, outside of this publication, is prohibited. Interested parties must apply to Random House, Inc. for permission. Photographs copyright © 2012 by Eric Wolfinger.

STANDARD BAKING CO. PASTRIES

From *Standard Baking Co. Pastries*. Copyright © 2012 by Alison Pray and Tara Smith. Photographs by Sean Alonzo Harris. Used by permission of Down East Books.

GRAN COCINA LATINA

From *Gran Cocina Latina: The Food of Latin America* by Maricel E. Presilla. Copyright © 2012 by Maricel E. Presilla. Photographs by Gentl & Hyers. Copyright © 2012 by Gentl & Hyers. Used by permission of W. W. Norton & Company, Inc.

VINTAGE CAKES

Recipes from *Vintage Cakes: Timeless Recipes for Cupcakes, Flips, Rolls, Layer, Angel, Bundt, Chiffon, and Icebox Cakes for Today's Sweet Tooth* by Julie Richardson, copyright © 2012 by Julie Richardson. Photographs by Erin Kunkel, copyright © 2012 by Erin Kunkel. Jacket cover copyright © 2012 by Ten Speed Press. Used by permission of Ten Speed Press, an imprint of the Crown Publishing Group, a division of Random House, Inc. Any third party use of this material, outside of this publication, is prohibited. Interested parties must apply directly to Random House, Inc. for permission.

TACOS, TORTAS & TAMALES

Recipes and photographs from *Tacos, Tortas, and Tamales: Flavors from the Griddles, Pots, and Streetside Kitchens of Mexico* by Roberto Santibañez. Copyright © 2012 by Roberto Santibañez. Reprinted by permission of Houghton Mifflin Harcourt Publishing Company. All rights reserved. Photographs by Todd Coleman.

THIS IS A COOKBOOK

From *This Is a Cookbook: Recipes for Real Life* by Max Sussman and Eli Sussman. Recipes and text © copyright 2012 Eli Sussman and Max Sussman. Used by permission of Weldon Owen, Inc. Photographs by Alex Farnum.

MICHAEL SYMON'S CARNIVORE

Recipes from *Michael Symon's Carnivore: 120 Recipes for Meat Lovers* by Michael Symon with Douglas Trattner, copyright © 2012 by Michael Symon. Jacket cover copyright © 2012 by Clarkson Potter. Used by permission of Clarkson Potter/Publishers, an imprint of the Crown Publishing Group, a division of Random House, Inc. Any use of this material, outside of this publication, is prohibited. Interested parties must apply directly to Random House, Inc. for permission. Photographs copyright © 2012 by Jennifer May.

SIMPLY MING IN YOUR KITCHEN

From *Simply Ming in Your Kitchen* by Ming Tsai and Arthur Boehm. Text copyright © 2012 by Ming Tsai. Photographs copyright © 2012 by Bill Bettencourt. Used by permission of Kyle Books.

MAC & CHEESE, PLEASE!

From *Mac & Cheese, Please!* by Laura Werlin. Copyright © 2012 Laura Werlin. Photographs copyright © 2012 Maren Caruso. Used by permission of Andrews McMeel Publishing, LLC.

BEST OF THE BEST COVER

"French Kitchen Island" by Crate & Barrel, *crateandbarrel.com*.

FOOD&**WINE**
BOOKS

More books from
FOOD&WINE

Annual Cookbook
More than 600 recipes from the world's best cooks,
including celebrity chefs like Alice Waters, Nobu Matsuhisa,
Lidia Bastianich, Mario Batali and René Redzepi.

Cocktails
Over 120 incredible cocktail recipes and dozens of fantastic
dishes from America's most acclaimed mixologists and
chefs, plus an indispensable guide to cocktail basics and the
top new bars and lounges around the country.

Wine Guide
An essential, pocket-size guide focusing on the world's most
reliable producers, with an easy-to-use food pairing primer.

TO ORDER, CALL 800-284-4145
OR LOG ON TO FOODANDWINE.COM/BOOKS